D1213077

Surgery and Life

THE EXTRAORDINARY CAREER
OF ALEXIS CARREL

Theodore I. Malinin

SURGERY AND LIFE

The Extraordinary Career of Alexis Carrel

NEW YORK AND LONDON

HARCOURT BRACE JOVANOVICH

Requests for permission to make copies
of any part of the work should be mailed to:
Permissions, Harcourt Brace Jovanovich, Inc.
757 Third Avenue, New York, N.Y. 10017

Excerpts from MAN, THE UNKNOWN by Alexis Carrel, copyright 1935,
1939 by Harper & Row, Publishers, Inc. Renewed 1967 by Anne De La
Motte Carrel. Reprinted by permission of the publisher.

Printed in the United States of America

Library of Congress Cataloging in Publication Data
Malinin, Theodore I   1933–
Surgery and life.

Bibliography: p.
Includes index.
1. Carrel, Alexis, 1873–1944.   2. Surgeons—France—Biography.
3. Blood vessels—Surgery—History.
I. Title.
[DNLM: 1. Surgery—Biography.   WZ100   c3133MA]
RD27.35.c37M34   617'.41'0924 [B]   78-22265
ISBN 0-15-186882-4

First edition

B C D E

To my friends
JAMES D. NEWTON
and
ELEANOR FORDE NEWTON
this book is dedicated
with affection.

Contents

Contents

Photographs between pages 114 and 115.

Preface

The astonishing enlargement in biological knowledge that has taken place during the last quarter of the nineteenth and the first half of this century can be related, in major portion, to individual scientists for whose work appropriate conditions were created. In 1880, the Imperial Health Office in Berlin made provisions for the establishment of an infectious disease laboratory for Robert Koch, discoverer of the tubercle bacillus. No biological laboratory has since produced so many discoveries in a given period of time. Soon after, in recognition of Louis Pasteur's success in the treatment of rabies, the Pasteur Institute was opened. It was financed by an international subscription. Under the direction of M. Duclaux, Pierre Paul Emile Roux, and Elie Metchnikoff it soon became a most productive center for medical discoveries. These examples led to the establishment of similar institutions in many countries. The Imperial Institute for Experimental Medicine was founded in St. Petersburg; the Lister Institute of Preventive Medicine in London; and the Institute for Infectious Diseases in Berlin.

In 1906, the Rockefeller Institute for Medical Research opened its doors in New York to several outstanding investigators. These included Alexis Carrel, Florence R. Sabin, Karl Landsteiner, P. A. Theodore Levene, Leonor Michaelis, and Peyton Rous. The Institute was directed by a pathologist, Simon Flexner. As long as Flexner was the head of the Institute it remained one of the leading institutions of medical science in the world.

The present book deals with Alexis Carrel, one of the scientists attracted to the Rockefeller Institute by Flexner. The writing of the book was, in part, precipitated by a letter from Dr. Abel L. Robertson, Jr., of the Cleveland Clinic Foundation. The letter, published in *Science*, an official publication of the American Association for the Advancement of Science, reminded its readers that, at the turn of the century, two surgeons were awarded the Nobel Prize, a fact overlooked by the editors of *Science* and largely forgotten by contemporary physicians. The prizes were awarded to Emil Theodor Kocher in 1909 and to Alexis Carrel in 1912. Although in subsequent years Carrel made several contributions to experimental medicine and surgery, the acclaim accorded him by the Nobel Prize Committee came for his demonstration of the feasibility of the suturing together of blood vessels, a procedure now so common that it is taken for granted. The development of this technique laid the foundation for vascular surgery, heart surgery, and transplantation of organs. Curiously, Carrel's work with suturing blood vessels led to one of the early successful blood transfusions. This he performed by connecting an artery from the arm of a father to the leg of an infant suffering from intestinal bleeding. The account of this treatment, with excellent results, was published in the *Journal of the American Medical Association* in 1910.

The fact that the scientific community had to be reminded of the fundamental contributions to human welfare made by an experimental surgeon suggested that a review of his work may be in order. Such a review may shed light, in some small measure, on fundamental surgical research performed in the U.S. in the early part of the century, and on some individuals who were involved in this work. It was, after all, a success story.

In examining Carrel's scientific accomplishments, particular attention must be paid to the methods employed by him, and to the environment which allowed him to perform his work. This includes the interaction with his immediate associates, the most famous of whom was Charles A. Lindbergh.

Carrel's early surgical experiments were conducted at a time which saw a turning point in science. They also came at a time when public attention was captivated by the practical developments in the physical sciences and engineering, and the emergence of new concepts in physics such as those brought forth by Rutherford and Soddy, rather than by the developments in biological sciences. The explanation for this may lie in the fact that the public could visualize translation of advances in physical sciences into changes of everyday living. What better example was needed than the demonstration of this principle by Thomas A. Edison, the Wright brothers, Guglielmo Marconi, Henry Ford, and scores of others.

Among biologists, in this respect Carrel proved to be an exception. He became one of the first medical scientists in America who attracted wide public attention. He was a frequent topic of commentaries in the press, and he gradually entered the realm of public life. This led him to write a book, *Man, the Unknown,* which became a best seller. He was criticized for this by some of his colleagues, and accused of using his success as a medical scientist as a springboard for forming a philosophical platform. In essence, Carrel stood accused by the myopic technicians of becoming concerned with man, rather than with isolated biological facts.

The writing of *Man, the Unknown* was undertaken late in his career as a laboratory scientist. He was possibly in need of diversion to occupy his time. Had he chosen bird watching or golf, the end of his life would not be surrounded by controversy. Examination of Carrel's views on philosophical and sociological questions and their relation to science may add to the understanding of this unique man. However, the main purpose of the present book is to elaborate on his contributions to surgery and biology, and on his attempts to bring scientific concepts to the practice of surgery.

Before the subject is presented to the reader, one rather important detail must be clarified. No proven method or formula exists for making scientific discoveries, particularly for biologists; and medical scientists are, in a broad sense, biologists. The physical and mathematical sciences call for different qualities in their disciples, as compared to biological scientists. The physicists and chemists are more dependent on reasoning and calculations, the biologists on experience and observation. What, then, are the qualities that are most likely to produce the desirable results in a medical researcher? They seem to be a perceptive mind, intuition, and chance. To Paul Ehrlich, discoverer of the first drug effective against syphilis, they were diligence, luck, and money. In surgical research, an additional quality, manual dexterity, is absolutely necessary. Carrel was in possession of a perceptive mind, intuition, and technical skill. He was also lucky. We shall see how he applied his natural talents and acquired skills to produce notable results, and what the circumstances were which allowed him to do so.

The material on which this account is based has been collected from several sources. First, Carrel's scientific publications were examined, as were the commentaries in the press. An additional source of documented information came from the Alexis Carrel Collection of Georgetown University. These Archives contain Carrel's personal notes, laboratory notebooks, manuscripts, and correspondence. The second source of documents was the Lindbergh Collection at the Yale University Library, and copies of personal letters obtained from several sources. Finally, I had the good fortune to be acquainted with several of Carrel's associates, friends, and colleagues with whom I have talked about him. These included Charles A. Lindbergh, James D. Newton, Raymond Parker, Richard J. Bing, Irene E. McFaul, and Katherine G. Crutcher.

I am deeply grateful and indebted to the following persons for their inestimable help in preparing this book:

To my wife, Dorothy R. Malinin, for her help with the manuscript and for her indulgence during the long hours I spent with the Carrel papers.

To Mr. and Mrs. James D. Newton for their continuous help during the preparation of the book and for reading the manuscript.

To Rev. Joseph T. Durkin, S.J., for encouraging me to study diligently the papers of Alexis Carrel and to write this book.

To Mrs. Anne Morrow Lindbergh and Miss Katherine G. Crutcher for their comments on the manuscript.

To Frank Gollan, M.D., for the discussion of the manuscript.

To Robert Zeppa, M.D., for continuous support of my efforts and for reminding his associates that advances in surgery can be made only through scientific investigation.

To Mrs. Katherine M. Vale, who provided invaluable assistance in translating the French papers, and to Mrs. Emily Wilkes for typing the manuscript.

Surgery and Life

THE EXTRAORDINARY CAREER
OF ALEXIS CARREL

1 ❦ The Beginning of Vascular Surgery

Surgery is the oldest branch of therapy; it began in pre-historic times. Primitive man incised and cauterized wounds, trephined the skull, and attempted to stop hemorrhage. Modern surgery started with the antiseptic era; its chief proponent was Joseph Lister. Helped by the development of anesthesia, antiseptic surgery made unprecedented progress. It allowed such noted individuals as Christian A. T. Billroth and Theodor Kocher to work out meticulous techniques of wound repair. A little-appreciated technical advance in surgery was the introduction of silk sutures. These gained general acceptance through the efforts of William S. Halsted, the first Professor of Surgery at the School of Medicine of Johns Hopkins University, who also introduced rubber gloves into the operating room.

One significant milestone in surgery was the development of blood-vessel suturing, which took place mostly in America. The person responsible for it was a Frenchman, Alexis Carrel. Intelligent and outspoken, Carrel was either liked or disliked from the start. His uninhibited manner of expressing himself left little room for less extreme reactions.

The eldest of three children (two boys and a girl), Carrel was born in Sainte-Foy-lès-Lyon near Lyons, France, on June 28, 1873. His father, Alexis Carrel-Billiard, was a well-to-do textile manufacturer. Carrel was baptized Marie-Joseph-Auguste, but he dropped these names and in the family became known as Alexis Carrel. His father died when Alexis was five years old, and the children were raised by their mother in a strong Roman Catholic tradition. He was educated at St. Joseph's College and the University of Lyons, receiving an L.B. degree from the latter in 1890 and an M.D. degree in 1900. Carrel's practical surgical experience was gained during 1896–1900 in the hospitals of Lyons, though he also served one year as a medical officer in the Chasseurs Alpins. In 1898 he secured an appointment as Prosecteur à la Faculté de Médecine, Université de Lyon, in which capacity he taught anatomy and experimental surgery.

Carrel published his first scientific paper on blood-vessel suturing and the transplantation of organs in French in 1902. This was rapidly followed by three more papers on the subject. Carrel's interest in the surgery of blood vessels had apparently been precipitated by the death of President Sadi Carnot in 1894. The President of the French Republic had died of hemorrhage from a portal vein severed by an assassin's knife. At that time surgeons had no means of repairing thin-walled blood vessels, although a few pioneers had attempted to do so. Yet work with blood vessels was not Carrel's first academic endeavor: between 1896 and 1902 he published no fewer than twenty-four papers, ranging in subject from the aneurysms of the arteries to techniques of stomach surgery. Thus when, in 1904, he appeared in Montreal before the Second Congress of Medicine in the French Language of North America, he was already an established medical scientist.

Carrel's trip to Montreal resulted from a considerable professional and psychological setback. He applied for, but did not secure, an appointment as surgeon in a Lyons hospital. This led to bitter feelings toward his French colleagues. He remained in Lyons but a brief while longer, then in 1904 went to Montreal, and in the same year obtained a position at the University of Chicago.

Carrel's first scientific paper in English, "Anastomosis and Transplantation of Blood Vessels," was published in 1905 in *American Medicine*. His second paper, "Transplantation of Organs," appeared in the *Journal of the American Medical Association*. Of nine remaining papers published during the same year, one was written with Carl Beck and eight with C. C. Guthrie. Half the papers were in French, and were published in French journals, which leads one to believe that Carrel was contemplating a return to France and wished to maintain his scientific position in French publications.

During his brief stay in Chicago, Carrel pioneered a reproducible technique for bringing severed blood vessels together, thus allowing them to continue their natural function. But, one may ask, what was so unique in Carrel's contribution? What is so difficult in sewing two pieces of pliable tube together end to end, side to side, or however? Surely somebody must have tried to do this long before Carrel. In fact, many had. In 1779 Eck had sutured two dog veins together, forming a direct communication between the vena cava and the portal vein. However, he did not describe in detail the suturing method he used, and many attempts to repeat his experiments failed. In 1899 a German surgeon, J. Doerfler, described a method for the direct suture of small blood vessels in animals. Yet by 1900 there was only a handful of cases where human arteries had been sutured and remained unobstructed. The failure in vascular surgery arose mainly from the formation of blood clots in vessels operated upon. The chief cause of thrombosis (blood-clot formation) was injury to the inner lining of the blood-vessel wall. Carrel recognized these errors and set out to correct them. (The only alternative to the suturing together of blood vessels is to tie them off;

unless there is another blood vessel supplying the part, the end result is an infarction or gangrene.)

Carrel could address himself to the correction of surgical errors because he possessed the essential perception and delicate skill required for this work. Carrel's methods were novel and original. To control the bleeding while the vessel was being worked on, he dispensed with forceps, which unduly compressed and crushed the vessel walls, and used narrow linen bands instead. (Surgeons now temporarily occlude blood vessels with specially designed clamps which do not crush the tissue.) For sewing the cut ends of blood vessels, he employed very sharp, small, round but not cutting straight needles and very fine sutures of silk. The use of small silk sutures was in striking contrast to the then prevailing use of large, thick, absorbable sutures.

The use of silk was apparently first proposed by Kocher and then by Halsted. However, the silk sutures they used were not suitable for vascular work. Carrel's sutures differed as much from the previously used silk sutures as Halsted's and Kocher's silk sutures had differed from catgut. Carrel coated both the needles and the sutures with Vaseline. When the vessel wall, stretched by the needle passing through it, contracted, the Vaseline rubbed off and sealed the puncture wound, thus preventing contact of blood with injured tissue.

Carrel's technique of bringing ends of severed blood vessels together became known as "triangulation." The method was based on initially approximating the ends of severed veins or arteries by three sutures placed at equal distances from one another along the circumference of the divided vessels. By applying side traction to two of the three sutures, the circumference of the circle was converted to a straight line. The sewing of approximated surfaces in a straight line is relatively easy. By rotating the three original sutures, the entire blood vessel could be united. This method of suturing arteries is still in use today, although some surgeons employ two or four, rather than the original three stay sutures. Simple as it seems, the sewing together of thin membranes such as vein walls requires considerable skill. It is easy to pass even the curved needle used nowadays too deeply, catch the opposite wall, and completely occlude the blood vessel. To practice straight-line suturing, Carrel would sew pieces of paper together. His contemporaries described his ability to sew together two sheets of paper without puncturing either one. Carrel's progress in developing new vascular suturing techniques was remarkable. Although he developed the original concept in France, the bulk of the experimental studies was performed in Chicago, and in a very short span of time. Subsequent work on organ transplantation was no more than an application of this newly developed technique to a practical problem.

Carrel's work attracted the attention of his colleagues and he was visited in Chicago in 1905 by several of America's most prominent surgeons: Harvey Cushing, Rudolph Matas, George Crile, and J. M. T. Finney. For them he demonstrated the techniques of vascular anastomosis on the carotid artery of a dog. Cushing later commented that Carrel's demonstration was the only original experimental work that had been shown in some time. For Carrel, this visit marked a turning point in his career. Some thirty-four years later he wrote to Cushing: "I shall always remember the visit from you and Matas, and the end-to-end anastomosis of a carotid artery in the small laboratory at the University of Chicago." The meeting between Carrel and Cushing resulted in a lifelong friendship. In one of the last letters sent to Carrel by Cushing, on May 6, 1939, Cushing said that the two of them formed a sort of mutual admiration society from the very start.

Carrel's feeling about the facilities at Chicago is implied in the words "small laboratory." The laboratory there was obviously inadequate. He needed a bigger one and better technical assistance, if he were to continue making progress. By 1905 he had proved himself to his American colleagues. At thirty-three years of age, the list of his publications was impressive and did not go unnoticed. At the time, however, finding a place with an adequate environment and facilities for an experimental surgeon was not an easy matter. In the United States the only full-fledged laboratory of experimental surgery then in existence was the Hunterian Laboratory at Johns Hopkins University. It was headed by Cushing, and, had it not been for some unusual circumstances, that is probably where Carrel would have transferred his activities.

As it happened, instead of going to Baltimore, Carrel went to New York. Simon Flexner, Director of Laboratories at the Rockefeller Institute, had read Carrel's paper in *Science* and wanted to interview him. Cushing arranged for the two men to meet, with the aid of William H. Welch, an eminent pathologist, a former chief of Flexner's and the President of the Rockefeller Institute for Medical Research. Welch wrote to Cushing on March 28, 1906, "I shall be interested in doing what I can to aid," but he noted a current tendency to eliminate outside grants in favor of investigations to be conducted in the Rockefeller Institute's own laboratory in New York. Carrel applied for the fellowship, went to New York for an interview, and was offered a position at the Institute.

On May 8, 1906, in response to Carrel's letter describing his meeting with Flexner, Cushing wrote: "I quite agree with all that you say in regard to Flexner. He is a very unusual type of man, and the only person in the country, I believe, who would undertake the work that he is doing at the Rockefeller Institute with any probability of making a success of it. We have not in this country a great many men of the type of those who have, with such self-sacrifice, spent their years at work in the Pasteur Institute in Paris. Flexner, however, is of the same stamp."

Before leaving Chicago, Carrel completed a series of experimental operations on animals. By far the best account of his thoughts at that time on vascular surgery is found in a lecture delivered at the Johns Hopkins Hospital on April 23, 1906.

Vascular surgery may be considered from the standpoint of general therapeutics of tissues and organs. Treatment of lesions of blood vessels, such as wounds, aneurysms, varices, etc., constitutes classical vascular surgery. . . . Application of the vascular operations to general surgery is an almost unexplored field. I shall discuss tonight a few experiments of this character that Doctor Guthrie and I have performed since last August. I began these researches in 1901–1902 at the University of Lyons and continued them last year with Doctor Guthrie at the University of Chicago, through the kindness of Doctor Stewart, who granted us the facilities of his laboratory.

Carrel described in detail his operative methods, their experimental applications, and finally their possible applications to human surgery. He stressed that in performing vascular operations, certain general rules must be observed. If these are adhered to, the success of the operation is virtually assured. Rigid asepsis was absolutely essential. Carrel believed that the degree of asepsis adequate for many surgical operations was insufficient for vascular operations. The dissection of the blood vessels was not dangerous if the wall of the vessel was not crushed. He emphasized the importance of removing the external sheath from the edges of the transected blood vessel.

In discussing clinical applications, Carrel cautioned that it would be improper to draw definite conclusions from the present experiments, because they were incomplete. He could not predict whether operations on vessels of humans would produce results as good as those on dogs or cats. Nevertheless, he thought the improved techniques might be successfully applied to patients. Either Carrel was being unduly modest or he was getting last-minute stage fright;

when eventually applied to humans, his vascular surgery techniques worked just as well as on animals.

Halsted heard Carrel's Johns Hopkins lecture, but did not meet him then. On May 31 he wrote him a note saying he enjoyed Carrel's address exceedingly and apologized for having to leave the meeting without the pleasure of an introduction to Carrel. But Halsted made up for this shortly thereafter, taking a strong interest in Carrel and continuously supporting and encouraging him. How different this was from France, where no one took Carrel's studies seriously, and few prominent surgeons would give him the time of day. In America he talked to the most prominent surgeons and they not only listened but understood him. How could his career in medical research fail, if he could count people such as Halsted and Cushing among his supporters?

After he moved to New York, Carrel continued to practice and to improve the technique of vascular surgery. In 1908, summarizing the development of vascular anastomosis before the American Philosophical Society, he said:

The sewing of blood vessels is today a very easy operation. The vessels heal very quickly and no coagulation of the blood occurs when the operation is aseptic and the union of vascular ends accurate. The scar of the severed vessel is, in many cases, so small that after a few months it is hardly discernible.

. . . Two and three years after the operation, the circulation through the anastomosis remains normal. It must be known also that, if the method is not correctly applied and a fault in technique, even very slight, is made, thrombosis may occur. Success depends much less on the way of handling the needles or passing the threads, than on the knowledge of the causes which are able to produce thrombosis and their removal.

Carrel's pioneering efforts in vascular surgery paid off; he showed that it could be done. Today operations on blood vessels are so common that no one gives them much thought. Numerous special vascular instruments, needles, and sutures have been developed by the scores of surgeons who succeeded Carrel. The original sutures of fine silk, carefully coated with Vaseline and attached to small handmade needles, have receded into surgical history; but for the thousands of patients who leave hospitals the world over, following successful operations on blood vessels, Carrel's sutures of silk have in effect been the threads of life.

2 🦋 France and Canada

The reasons which compelled Carrel to leave France may have been several, but they were all interrelated. Having acquired a bad taste for the French medical and scientific establishment early in life, Carrel let it be known he could not tolerate what was, in his opinion, the reactionary attitude of French physicians toward scientific research—an attitude that left little room for originality.

Carrel suffered his first disappointment in 1901, when he was eliminated as a candidate for a clinical appointment by a colleague who simply had waited for it longer than he had. This forced Carrel to remain in a state of expectation for two years, in anticipation of another vacancy, and made him question the rigid system of seniority and patronage. At approximately the same time, Carrel's attention was drawn to Canada. Several French missionaries working in the north of Canada came to Lyons to get some practical lessons in surgery. These were assigned to Carrel. The missionaries were impressed by Carrel's surgical ability and by his contempt for regimentation. They suggested that he go to Canada with them to practice his art unimpeded. He developed an interest in Canada, read a great deal about it, and compiled voluminous notes. The seed was planted in his mind.

Carrel was finally admitted as a candidate for examination in surgery at the hospitals of Lyons, but he did not hold much hope of passing. Only one vacancy was open and he lacked a sponsor on the examining board. As expected, he did not qualify for the position.

His first major public encounter with the men of the French medical establishment involved religion. As a young intellectual, Carrel had scrutinized and discarded some of the beliefs of his Church, but he was not particularly vociferous on the matter and kept his views to himself. However, an unusual event put him in the public light. In May 1902 a colleague of Carrel's, who was to accompany the sick making an annual pilgrimage from Lyons to the famous shrine of Lourdes in southern France, asked Carrel to go in his place. In need of a diversion, Carrel agreed to do so. Dedicated to the Virgin Mary, Lourdes was widely publicized by the Roman Catholic clergy as a place where miraculous healings had been achieved by prayer to God and the Virgin.

During the journey, Carrel's attention was brought to Marie Bailly, a young girl of seventeen who was presumably suffering from tuberculous peritonitis. Whether or not she had tuberculosis has not been adequately documented, but the fact that she was very ill is undeniable. After an immersion in a pool at Lourdes, undertaken against Carrel's advice, the girl became well. According to R. Soupault in *Alexis Carrel*, when he signed a certificate in the office of the Medical Bureau at Lourdes, Carrel wrote on it: "The nature of that which I have just witnessed? I shall see later. It is, first of all, a cure."

Carrel's feelings about the Marie Bailly case are clear: to the end of his life, he was not sure what had actually happened. In 1936 he received a letter from Dom Francis Izzard, who asked if Carrel had been rightly quoted as saying that "no scientific hypothesis up to the present time accounts for the phenomena of Lourdes." In a reply of December 13, Carrel wrote:

The sentence you quoted in your letter of the tenth of November does not express accurately my opinion about the cures of Lourdes. It should be modified as follows:

Certain facts observed in Lourdes cannot be accounted for by any of the known laws of wound healing and tissue regeneration. In the course of a miraculous cure, the rate of tissue construction greatly exceeds that which has ever been observed in the healing of a wound under optimum conditions. There is also a constant relation between the occurrence of this phenomenon and the state of prayer of the patient or of someone near him. This fact also cannot be accounted for.

Several working hypotheses may be tentatively put forward concerning the mechanism of these important phenomena. As I have been very much interested in this subject for the last twenty years, it is especially gratifying for me to know that a man who is both a physician and a Benedictine monk is making a scientific study of it. From several points of view, it is a fascinating problem.

I hope that you will be able to write the medical history of Marie Bailly from the time of her recovery in 1902 until the present. It was a difficult case, with contradictory opinions from the physicians who attended her. No certain diagnosis could be made. A great deal of light would be thrown on this case, if you could discover what has happened since the cure. I wrote to Doctor Marchand about her two or three years ago, and he told me that she was still living in a convent of St. Vincent de Paul, but that she was about to undergo a serious operation. Some time after that, Doctor Marchand died. This year I have written to Doctor Vallet, the Chief of the Medical Service at Lourdes, and he replied that he did not find any additions made by Marchand to the history of Marie Bailly. It is very probable that today you could find out, far more easily than twenty years ago, the nature of the disease from which she was so suddenly cured at Lourdes.

Carrel's statements regarding Lourdes in 1902 satisfied no one, but they produced some curious results. On the one hand, his lack of belief in the miracle annoyed the clergy. On the other hand, he evoked the criticism of the head of the Medical Bureau at Lourdes for making statements regarding the use of a rosary instead of medical tools, for not examining patients properly, and for not keeping adequate medical histories. Furthermore, some of his medical colleagues who did not subscribe to miracles referred to him acidly as a "credulous priest." In short, Carrel's conclusion that supernatural phenomena may occur satisfied neither believers nor nonbelievers. His acceptance of such phenomena as an extension, rather than a contradiction, of natural science put him squarely into a cross-fire.

In France, where many intellectuals nursed strong anticlerical feelings, the camps were sharply divided. Passions ran so high that no one stopped to take note of what Carrel was actually saying. In essence, he was saying that in nature many things which we do not understand are possible. He was convinced that the well-being of an individual depended in large measure on his inner self. He was raising the question whether this could be intensified by the state of prayer. Carrel wanted to study and document phenomena allegedly occurring at Lourdes. His rational mind suggested that this was the only way to solve the riddle. His views on Lourdes did not change substantially in later years: he thought "miraculous cures" did indeed occur, but very seldom. Despite their small number, they proved the existence of organic and mental processes which were not understood. Science had to explore the entire field of reality and deal with psychic phenomena as it had dealt with others.

The *Voyage to Lourdes* was published some eight years after Carrel's death. The manuscript, dated before World War I, was found among his papers, and later edited by his wife. Under these circumstances, it is possible that things may have been presented out of context. A more complete and impartial analysis of Carrel's experience with Lourdes may be found in Joseph T. Durkin's book *Hope for Our Time*. Be that as it may, Carrel had indeed examined Marie Bailly, attested to her cure without vouching for a miracle, and in so doing antagonized both the clergy and many of his medical colleagues. He was advised by one of his superiors: "My friend, with your ideas you would do well to give up the examinations; from now on you will never pass." Carrel packed his bags and went off to Paris, remained there several months, and in June 1904 departed for Canada. He told friends he was going to Canada to raise cattle and encourage French immigration.

The crossing of the Atlantic was unusually stormy for June and took fourteen days. On his arrival in Montreal Carrel received a letter from Dr. R. Chevrier, the President of the Immigration Society of the Ottawa Valley, outlining in detail the prospects of settling in the fertile regions of New Ontario and Temiscaminique, Quebec. Nothing came of the scheme, and Carrel soon lost interest in farming.

Carrel was introduced to Montreal by Adelstan and François de Martigny, two brothers who were surgeons. There are several somewhat romantic and imaginative accounts as to how Carrel met the de Martignys. One of them tells of Carrel strolling through the streets deep in thought, and finding himself in front of the Hôtel-Dieu on the Avenue des Pins; on impulse he walked into the hospital and proceeded to the surgical wards, where he ran into François de Martigny. The latter, knowing Carrel's name from the surgical literature, invited Carrel to see the hospital, and thus started a friendship.

François de Martigny himself recalled their first meeting in a somewhat different way. He said that he had indeed received Carrel at the Hôtel-Dieu of Montreal one day after Carrel's arrival aboard the *Malou*, but that Carrel was accompanied by two young doctors, Boutin and Chartier, the latter of whom had made an enviable reputation for himself in surgical circles in France. After meeting François, Carrel remained in Montreal for several months and maintained frequent contact with the de Martignys.

François de Martigny did not remember if any overtures

were made by the Faculty of Medicine at Laval University regarding Carrel's joining the institution, but he did not think so. No openings for the faculty existed at the time and, not having any need, the University did not have to accept or refuse him. It was the same at McGill University. However, François de Martigny thought it a good thing that Carrel did not remain in Montreal. Years later he said he believed that if Carrel had offered his services to the University and been given a faculty appointment, it would have been to his own detriment and for the misfortune of surgical science. Canada had no philanthropists like Rockefeller who allow young scientists to work in universities or institutions. Nor was anyone ready to spend millions to aid scientists and to enable them to work in peace and tranquillity for years, in order to make scientific discoveries like those of Carrel, which have allowed thousands of human lives to be saved.

Carrel's first meeting with François's brother Adelstan took place in a restaurant. François invited the two of them to lunch, during which the conversation became animated. When Carrel and Adelstan discussed politics, science, and religion, they banged carafes and glasses of wine on the table. When the conversation turned to Freemasonry, they nearly came to blows. But with François's mediation, the lunch ended peacefully and Adelstan and Carrel became lifelong friends.

On the urging of the de Martignys, Carrel delivered a paper on the techniques of blood-vessel surgery, and gave a surgical demonstration at a French Medical Congress held in Montreal. This was well received, and his paper was published in Canada the same year. However, successful as the lecture and demonstrations had been, Carrel was not able to settle in Montreal. Visits to some highly placed clergymen with letters of introduction from friends of the family yielded no results. On July 25, 1904, his mother, annoyed by the cool reception given her son, wrote to him:

"I understand that in Canada the bishops are presumptuous, and want to keep the people in their present infantile state; they are making a mistake with regard to the future."

Adelstan de Martigny and Carrel together published a paper on a type of bandage invented by de Martigny, but no prospects of employment opened up for Carrel. In an attempt to find Carrel a place to work Adelstan wrote an acquaintance at the University of Chicago:

I have here with me a colleague and a friend from Lyons who is a very accomplished surgeon for bones, joints and arteries.

In addition, he has done some truly extraordinary things which have not been done before or since, such as the suture of arteries and veins, and organ transplants. He made a kidney from one dog live in another, and urinary secretions took place as a consequence. You see what marvelous results might ensue if these experiments were allowed to proceed further. This may permit the replacement of a kidney with Bright's disease, and other analogous operations.

Unfortunately, my friend Doctor Carrel had to interrupt his work, as much due to lack of suitable conditions as to illness. He is traveling right now and would be happy to stay in America if he were named Professor of Surgery in a university and given the means to continue his experiments. He is counting on the surgical audacity of the Americans to provide him with subjects for experimentation. Besides, he would reflect a certain glory upon the university whose professor had performed such marvelous, almost impossible operations. He does have some income and would not seek a practice.

De Martigny's letter was transmitted to George N. Stewart, head of the University of Chicago's Department of Physiology, who offered Carrel a position in the Hull Physiology Laboratory. The transition had finally been made. Carrel had left not only France, but also the French community of the New World. He thought there was no future for him in Montreal because the French Canadian milieu was rather jealous of outsiders, but he departed without bitterness. In fact, he retained warm feelings toward his friends in Canada and visited them from time to time.

In Chicago, Carrel soon became familiar with the American academic scene, and adapted extremely well to it. Thereafter in all his professional endeavors he acted as an American, for he was firmly convinced that he owed his success to the United States. He also acquired some outward American characteristics, though in many ways he remained a Frenchman, especially in his manner of expressing himself.

Formally Carrel remained a French national, although to become an American citizen would have been to his advantage. He suffered painfully the inadequacies of the Third Republic. His critical attitude toward French scientists and governmental administration of science did not mellow with time; on the contrary, reinforced by frequent contacts with representatives of the French medical and scientific community, it became more firmly entrenched in his mind. In 1929 he remarked to René Leriche:

There is certainly a striking difference between the conditions of medicine in this country [the United States] and France. Although things are still very imperfect in this country, the people are at least thoroughly alive. There is a great attempt to improve conditions all the time, and it is this spirit which we should try to cultivate in Europe.

As critical as Carrel was of the French system, he was not blind to the deficiencies of the American academic environment, nor to those of other European countries. On November 3, 1913, he wrote to Doctor Ernst Jeger of Breslau, Germany, a pioneer vascular surgeon who wished to come to the United States:

I fully understand how difficult and unsatisfactory is your position, for when I was living in Europe I myself experienced the unpleasantness of trying to work under unfavorable conditions. I have thought a great deal about your letter, but it is very difficult—almost impossible—to give you any advice. This country is different from Germany in that it does not offer any regular positions which any man who is qualified can obtain, and which will assure his future success in life. The latter depends entirely on his individual initiative and personality, and it is often difficult to know how to account for the failure of a really competent man who appears to merit success as much as anybody. Therefore anyone coming over to America . . . must be prepared to take large risks and reckon with chance.

Carrel himself had reckoned with chance in coming to America, though perhaps he had no other choice. In Montreal his French Canadian colleagues were interested in his work, but in a somewhat abstract sense. Because their resources were limited, they could offer no practical help. In France his colleagues were neither interested nor helpful. Chicago unexpectedly provided him with a breath of fresh air, for he met people there who were interested in and understood his work.

Carrel had gotten a new start in Canada, however, and Montreal served as a bridge between the Old and New Worlds. He crossed that bridge often in both directions, for although he lived and worked in America and, with time, began to prefer it to France, to the end of his days he remained a Frenchman.

3 ✿ Chicago

Carrel arrived in Chicago late in 1904 and began work as soon as the laboratory became operational. While in Chicago he had a chance to acquaint himself with surgery in America. He did not like what he saw, for he realized that surgeons had to make a living through private practice, and could pursue their academic interests only in their spare time. He was not sure he could do this. Besides, at the University of Chicago Carrel was not exactly greeted with open arms by the Surgeon-in-Chief. Privately, Carrel thought the man to be a vain individual who demanded money everywhere. Consequently Carrel had little to do with clinical surgery at the University. George N. Stewart, the head of the Department of Physiology, arranged for Carrel to do all his work in the Hull Physiological Laboratory.

Symptomatically, the Department of Surgery of the University had little to offer in the way of experimental surgery. Carrel's practical knowledge of surgery in Chicago came through a newly acquired friend, Carl Beck, Professor of Surgery and Surgical Pathology at the College of Physicians and Surgeons.

While the laboratory was being organized and the experiments started, Carrel had plenty of time to brood. His biggest concern was that he could not work as much as he wanted to. At one time he became discouraged and thought seriously of going to Central America. However, upon learning what life there was like, he dropped the matter.

Once things got under way his gloom was dissipated. On Stewart's suggestion, Carrel began to work with C. C. Guthrie, a member of the Physiology Department. Prior to his exposure to Carrel, Guthrie was concerned with gastrointestinal problems. He had no experience with blood vessels, but proved an able assistant, quick to learn the new techniques. Carrel's research interests began to be shared by Guthrie, who continually encouraged him to do additional experiments and to publish the results quickly. Carrel's clinical interests were shared by Beck, who was also an immigrant. Beck had studied medicine in Prague, where he had served as an assistant in the Pathological Institute under Hans Chiari, a noted pathologist. Later Beck had become an assistant in the surgical clinic of Billroth, an outstanding Viennese surgeon. He struck up friendships with many of Billroth's students, and especially with Anton F. von Eiselberg, now best remembered for his demonstration of tetany in animals whose parathyroid glands he had removed, and for his contributions to neurologic surgery. Beck had also won a traveling fellowship, under which he visited many European surgical clinics and pathologic institutes, and had then become a ship's surgeon. After several trips to the United States, he had settled in Chicago in 1889, where he joined the Postgraduate Medical College, which became the College of Physicians and Surgeons. This institution formed the nucleus of what is now the University of Illinois.

In Chicago, Beck taught surgery and surgical pathology. This was the first time that surgical pathology was formally taught in Chicago. He introduced the use of experimental animals into the medical school. He was one of the first to attempt implantation of the ureters into the bowel, and was the first to use the cystoscope in the United States. He was first to transplant a toe onto a hand. He published two textbooks: *Surgical Pathology* and *The Crippled Hand*

and Arm. He also wrote a section on plastic surgery in Ochsner's *Textbook of Surgery.* In short, he was a surgeon of great ability, and with a very strong sense of direction. Long after having left Chicago, Carrel wrote to Beck: "How clearly I remember our conversations of thirty years ago in Chicago. You had brought to America the great tradition of German surgery. You had simultaneous knowledge of pathological lesions and clinical symptoms. You had the power to marvel at physiological phenomena that make surgery possible. I still recall how deeply interested you were in the astounding process of the repair of wounds."

C. C. Guthrie was made of a different fiber and had different interests. First of all, he was a "laboratory man." Second, he had definite inclinations toward philosophy and eventually published a long treatise on "Science and Religion." Third, he had no compunction about converting people to his way of thinking. Thus, since he loved the countryside, he persisted in taking his wife to the farm until she had a much better opinion of the country.

Carrel and Guthrie worked together but a brief time, not starting in earnest until June 1905. In September of the same year Guthrie went to the University of Missouri at Columbia to teach for a semester. He did not return to Chicago until January 1906 and then worked with Carrel only until March. By that time both men were dissatisfied with the environment at the University of Chicago and were ready to leave. Carrel departed for New York and Guthrie for St. Louis, where he became the head of the Department of Physiology and Pharmacology at the Washington University Medical School.

On September 11, 1905, Guthrie wrote to Carrel from Columbia, Missouri:

I am glad that the dogs are getting along nicely and that the permanent results of our operations are good. I hope your fear that someone else will steal our ideas will not materialize, but I think you are quite right in that we should publish at once in order to show the scope of our experiments. I suppose the draft of the kidney article will reach me in a few days. It is certain that it will be impossible to get it published in the October number of the *American Journal of Physiology,* as Doctor Porter requires a manuscript six weeks in advance of publication from our laboratory. I think *Science* would insure the earliest publication of any American journal and, if you desire to send it there, the write-up should be as short as possible. I regret that the work is so widely known at this time. . . . If such men as Cushing take it up now, it means that we will be "beat out" in making human applications, as their facilities for such work are at present vastly superior to ours. You understand I mean the opportunities to get and operate on suitable patients. Still, I cannot believe that anyone, or any set of surgeons, can equal our results before they have worked much longer on the technique than you and I have together. I think it might be a good plan to keep the important details of the actual technique to ourselves for a time—not many of them will take the trouble to look up your first paper and, besides, I believe certain details are improvised since then, are they not? A few blood clots would serve to cool their ardor.

I am sorry that I cannot continue with you this autumn, but will return as soon as I can—possibly during the early part of December if necessary, though of course I do not like to leave here just before the Christmas holidays.

Carrel's and Guthrie's experiments began to attract the attention of the press. The *New York Herald* carried a special dispatch regarding their work, which stated that the experiments they had conducted for nearly a year in the Hull Physiological Laboratory promised to revolutionize surgery. The article continued:

While all the experiments have been performed on dogs, the object was to ascertain methods of surgery that could be used on human beings to transform veins into arteries, transplant organs and even to substitute the arteries and veins of an animal for the diseased arteries and veins of a man. . . . Among the facts discovered by the surgeons are these:

The transplantation of veins in arteries produces, from a functional point of view, the transformation of veins into arteries. Transplanted veins adapt themselves to the new functions imposed.

The new arteries transmit the blood indefinitely. After ten months the circulation through the arteries is apparently as active as on the day of the operation.

The ascertained facts are insignificant compared with what the experimenters hope to accomplish by applying their method to human beings. In a scientific treatise they have indulged in speculation to only a moderate extent, but their hypotheses are decidedly startling to the lay mind.

They hope by the transplantation of a vein on another vein to produce a deviation of the blood from one part of the venous system to another. The significance of such deviation is that healthy red blood could be introduced into areas where the blood has become stagnant or unhealthy. They hope to be able by this deviation to cure diseases of the liver, kidneys and even of the brain. Softening of the brain is now incurable, but Drs. Carrel and Guthrie expect to see the time when, by sending red blood surging through the brain, they will be able to revivify the brain cells and restore the patient to a normal mental condition.

If the discoveries are carried to their logical conclusion, various affectations of the heart now considered incurable will be quickly remedied. If your heart is not in the right place it will be transplanted. If your kidney or liver is not hitched to the proper kind of machinery, your veins and arteries will be dissected and grafted together in odd ways that will give new, healthy life to the diseased organ.

Professional commentary solicited by the press came from erudite surgeons. W. T. Bull of New York said he had not given the matter close attention, because he had not seen reports of the experiments in medical journals. George F. Shredy said that Carrel and Guthrie were known as very careful men, and that anything they might say deserved attention. However, to Carrel and Guthrie it was disturbing to find the results of their work published in the newspapers before they could be published in scientific journals.

Guthrie wrote to Carrel:

The newspaper notoriety is deplorable, but it cannot be helped. We should, I suppose, show our animals to absolutely no one in the future. In fact, if we can maintain secrecy for, say, one year, and write all our results in book form, it would be the ideal way, I think, but I suppose that it is not possible now. I am sorry we cannot work entirely by ourselves, as suggestions from other persons must of course be given due credit, but they are really of no value as problems are sure to occur to us as fast, and faster than we can possibly work them out. Besides, and I say this without egotism, we are more competent to discover new problems for the application of our methods than anyone else. Do you not think this is so? I think any seriously thinking scientist would also agree with us. . . . I myself do not care to go on acknowledging *assistance* from any third party, for it is not fair to ourselves. Still, our circumstances place us in a rather dependent attitude as regards this point.

On October 8, 1905, Carrel wrote to Guthrie:

It is not possible to find a proper place to keep the dogs. I fear it will be possible to operate on only a small number. Therefore, it would be interesting to know if, in your university, our experiments can be made in better conditions than here. Harvey Cushing, Crile, and Matas told me these experiments are very interesting. It is too bad to be handicapped by such material conditions.

The problem with housing dogs in Chicago prompted Guthrie to suggest carrying out further experiments in Columbia rather than Chicago, but he was afraid Stewart would oppose this plan. He did.

In this connection, Guthrie suggested to Carrel that they record every problem they thought of in writing, in order to protect themselves from friends with suggestions. Also, he thought it would be worthwhile to publish preliminary papers at the earliest possible moment.

Cushing, Matas, Finney, and Crile visited Carrel's laboratory while Guthrie was in Missouri. Carrel provided Guthrie with a firsthand account of the event:

Last Thursday, Matas introduced me to Crile, who was in Chicago. He is a nice fellow and he has been sorry not to see you.

Harvey Cushing was also in Chicago. He is a splendid fellow, very intelligent and broad-minded. He told me we must do the research very accurately, for it has an important future. On Saturday Matas, Harvey Cushing, and Crile came to the laboratory, but unfortunately, about twenty other people—Monroe, Lecont, Murphy, etc.—came also. It was overcrowded and it was impossible to see anything. Everything must be cleaned before it is possible to operate again. We operated on a dog. Crile was giving the anesthesia.

Now everybody knows our experiments. It is necessary to publish very quickly and to make new experiments as soon as possible. I have been very glad of this occasion to know these three men, Cushing, Matas, and Crile, for they are very good and interesting.

When Guthrie left Carrel to work alone for four months, Carrel obtained a surgical assistant. Guthrie did not care much for the idea. He wrote: "As to the assistant, I do not care to say very much. I would like to know on what basis you have taken him into the work. I hope he is doing it only for the personal benefit to himself in the way of training, otherwise, I think there will be a good chance of friction later on. I say this from knowledge gained from having worked in the laboratory for some time. Personally, he is a very fine fellow and I hope everything will go smoothly. On my return, if we resume the work, I prefer it to be exactly on the same basis as it was before—that is, no third party."

Guthrie's interest in the affairs of other people must have been well known among his peers. For that reason, it seems his colleagues at the University of Chicago were rather reluctant to communicate with him. On one occasion, being in need of some news from the home base, he asked Carrel: "Does Dr. Stewart still take interest in the work? I would be glad to have a 'gossipy' letter about the laboratory—I hear but rarely from anyone but you."

After Carrel had left Chicago and Guthrie had moved to St. Louis, Guthrie still "kept tabs" on the old laboratory. When Carrel's old surgical assistant ran into trouble, Guthrie took note of the fact and wrote Carrel: "Doctor C. and your surgical assistant had a serious clash, the latter telling the former that he was a 'Swede' and an ape and that he could knock him down, etc., etc. Doctor S. had to consider the matter and finally decided that your former assistant would have to apologize before the class, which he did. Don't you wish you were there?"

Guthrie did not do much experimental work at the University of Missouri. On October 31, 1905, he wrote Carrel:

The Dean spent an afternoon with me not long ago and he tried to persuade me to operate for them. I refused, as I have nothing to operate properly with and it is doubtful that I will get anything. I am taking my job here as a joke, but do not mention it. The Dean wants me to give instructions in operative surgery to the class, but of course I also refused to do that. If they give me something to work with, I will give them one or two demonstrations.

Although Guthrie could not actively pursue experimental work in Columbia, he kept abreast of things and worked on the manuscripts and the specimens Carrel sent him. He asked for "100 reprints for me of all our papers. . . . Also, please send me copies of all articles published this summer, and copies of your former papers if you can spare them."

With the departure of both men from Chicago, their active collaboration ceased. At one point Guthrie suggested they might continue their joint experiments, even though

Carrel was in New York. Carrel remained lukewarm to the idea and the matter was not pursued further.

Carrel's first contact with Americans and American scientists in Chicago left a lasting impression on him. In 1940 he wrote to the Reverend Doctor Ambrose M. Bailey, a Baptist minister whom he knew there: "I was extremely pleased to receive your letter with its news of yourself and the recollections it brought back to me of the old days at the University of Chicago. It is always a pleasure for me to be reminded of that time."

Despite Carrel's relatively short stay in Chicago, he first acquired knowledge of Americans and American life there. In addition to Carl Beck, he had made several friends in that city, a number of them not involved in medicine or science. He dined frequently at the University of Chicago Commons with Milton A. Buchanan, a linguist. Also among his acquaintances were Ruth Perry, a portrait photographer of some renown, and the Llewellyn sisters, daughters of former Governor Llewellyn of Kansas. The elder sister was Mrs. Jessie Llewellyn Call, a widow who was intellectual, interesting, and attractive, and had a varied experience in newspaper writing. Among other things, she was the author of a society column under the pseudonym of "Willie Dearborn." She wrote with a peculiar delicacy and her own brand of wit. Her sister, Louise Llewellyn, also wrote for the newspapers, but abandoned this avocation and went to Paris to study music shortly after Carrel left Chicago.

4 🦋 New York

In September 1906 Carrel went to New York and began an association with the Rockefeller Institute that lasted virtually the rest of his life. Except for World War I, he spent the next thirty-three years actively working in its laboratories. He became an Assistant in 1907, an Associate in 1908, an Associate Member in 1909, and a Member in 1912. At the Institute he developed a keen friendship with Simon Flexner, who encouraged his endeavors and gently guided him through the labyrinths of scientific politics. Samuel J. Meltzer, Hideyo Noguchi, Peyton Rous, and Karl Landsteiner collaborated with him, and in no small measure were responsible for influencing Carrel in his scientific thinking.

Carrel's first task was to organize the laboratory so he could continue essentially the same work as in Chicago, but on a larger scale. He was given quarters on the top floor of the Institute. There the operating room was lighted by skylights. Since intense daylight caused much glare, Carrel had the walls of the laboratory painted dark gray. Furthermore, the gowns and the operating-room linen were black, which effectively cut down the glare. Carrel's laboratory was well organized and orderly.

Unlike most Europeans, Carrel entered New York for the first time through the "back" door. He missed the harbor, the Statue of Liberty, Ellis Island, and the wide expanse of the Hudson River. Since he came from Chicago via Baltimore, what he first saw was downtown Manhattan. He did not like the city at first, but over the years he became accustomed to it, to the point of preferring it to Paris.

In 1906 the large, compact, noisy city provided Carrel with an environment strikingly different from anything he had seen before. Pennsylvania Station was being excavated. At Fifth Avenue and 58th Street stood the slender, unsightly forerunner of a skyscraper. A common joke in those days related a conversation between two travelers: "What do you know of New York?" asked one, whereupon the other answered, "Only what I read in Dante." For Carrel New York may have encompassed both the Inferno and Paradise. Certainly life in the green enclave of the Rockefeller Institute was pleasant, not only because of the physical surroundings, but because of the desirable psychological environment.

Outside the Institute, however, the city provided quite a contrast. Among other things, New York was in the middle of an early automobile craze, and at the beginning of a great surge of advertising: the first annual advertising show was held in Madison Square Garden in 1906, while the annual automobile show was in its eighth year.

Carrel could not help but notice the changes the automobile had brought to the lives of New Yorkers. Medical implications of automobile driving were already under discussion. Drivers were being warned about damage to the nervous system caused by high speed, about eyestrain, and about trauma sustained on impact. Carrel observed this influence of mechanization on the urban population for thirty years. Eventually he voiced his concern of its consequences in *Man, the Unknown*.

In the more than thirty years that Carrel lived in New York, he never permanently settled there. He did not own a house, although at one time he contemplated buying one.

31

Nor did he stay in any one place excessively long. At first he lived in a small apartment on the East Side. He then moved several times, settling for a while at 597 Fifth Avenue, at 57 East 58th Street, in Larchmont, in Garden City, and finally at 56 East 89th Street. In 1913 Carrel married a Frenchwoman; at first she lived in New York with him, but later, particularly after 1926, she visited the city infrequently. During most of his thirty-three years at the Rockefeller Institute, Carrel lived alone, spending the summers at his home in France.

Because of the smallness of his quarters and his semi-bachelor status, he seldom had visitors in his apartment. His social life centered around the Century Club, of which he had become a member in 1912. He did most of his entertaining there. He also had a group of close friends whom he saw regularly at the Club. One of these was an international lawyer, Frederick R. Coudert. Carrel was a frequent visitor at the Coudert home.

Carrel's social calendar included numerous dinners or afternoon teas with friends and colleagues. At times he attended concerts, usually with friends or at their invitation. But Carrel was a bit absent-minded and could forget about social engagements, so that his friends had to remind him. Thus Mrs. Herter wrote him: "Will you dine with us on Tuesday evening at 7:10 and go to the Kneisel Quartet concert? This is the reminder I promised to send." Carrel's taste in music can be deduced from the program of the concert in question: Schumann's Quartet in A Minor, Op. 41; Hugo Wolf's "Italienische Serenade"; and Beethoven's Quartet in F Major, Op. 59, No. 1. He did not particularly care for voice recitals, though he attended these on occasion. Yet when his work demanded it, Carrel would go through periods of isolation, working by day in the laboratory and writing and reading in the evening. During one such period in 1907, Miss Perry sent him a note:

Are you still in the land of the living? I tried to send you a wireless, but no response. I hope this will not unpleasantly arouse you from from your seclusion.

What new and startling things have you been doing? You see I rather expect a new and startling development from you, as you have already established a reputation in that.

In some descriptions of Carrel, particularly in his later years, he was portrayed as leading a life of exemplary sobriety, abstinence, and discipline. While the comment about discipline in work is correct, during his life in New York Carrel was certainly no monklike visionary of science. True, he disliked cocktail parties, which he considered a waste of time, but so do many people. However, he was not opposed to drinking. Raymond Parker recalls a supper with Carrel at the Century Club, when Carrel twirled a long-stemmed martini glass in his hand and, after savoring it for a while, declared that alcohol was the greatest invention of man.

Carrel enjoyed some sports. In New York he fenced and went horseback riding regularly. Before going to work, he walked some two miles in Central Park. On weekends he took longer excursions; he liked hiking.

Nor was Carrel shy in the company of women. In addition to his Chicago friends—Ruth Perry and the Llewellyn sisters—he became acquanted with Lilly Bliss, Geneviève Grandcourt, and Elizabeth C. Marsarian. He was extremely courteous to the wives of his colleagues and friends, sending them holiday greetings, thank-you notes, and flowers.

Carrel could be very charming. He was a good conversationalist and attentive. Miss Perry found his company to be genuinely pleasant. After one of Carrel's summer visits to Paris she wrote: "I can hardly tell you how much I enjoyed the few days you were here in Paris. For some unaccountable reason you fill me with genuine joy and delight whenever I see you, and I have noticed you affect other people the same way. It is an indefinable something about your personality. If you happen to know yourself,

perhaps you will tell me the secret of it sometime." In another letter from Europe she said: "It seems a very long
time since I have heard from you, but of course I realize
that it is my own fault because you are always so good
about answering at once. I have thought of you many times
and wonder if New York were still as distasteful to you as
at first, and also if you still planned to come to Europe this
summer. I sincerely hope you will come. It would seem very
delightful to meet the old Chicago people here. Miss
Llewellyn and perhaps Mrs. Call will be here again this
summer. We could have quite a Chicago reunion."

Carrel showed a remarkable amount of understanding
in dealing with people. At times he acted as if he did not
notice their bad moods and dispositions. In fact, he could
reverse the situation. In one of her letters Miss Perry remarked that she was very uncomfortable after being disagreeable with Carrel, but "owing to his superior disposition" she noticed it had not disturbed him in the least.

Chicago friends visited Carrel in New York, Jessie
Llewellyn Call among them. She remained in New York
for several months at a time, and during her stays invited
Carrel frequently to tea or dinner. Her notes indicate a
degree of friendship that Carrel did not extend to too many
people: "If this note reaches you in time, will you not come
over Sunday at seven o'clock instead of eight and have
dinner. . . . I am cook, so you must be prepared to take
an awful chance. Owing to the stress of work I have not
asked the party of people I had intended to have here Sunday, so there will be four of us." Or again: "Louise and I
will be here until Wednesday when we are sailing. Can you
not have tea with us Tuesday at five o'clock?"

Several years after Carrel left Chicago, Mrs. Call developed a "nervous condition" for which she sought help
in Switzerland. While visiting Paris, Mrs. Call wrote Carrel:
"If you hate New York and long for the country, you must
understand how one might dread Paris." In these lines one

senses the feeling of a person used to the wide plains of the Midwest who felt hopelessly caged in.

After Mrs. Call entered the sanitarium in Switzerland Carrel wrote her faithfully at holidays. She replied: "Your Easter card was very eagerly received—messages from the outside mean so much to the ones shut in." And on another occasion: "Your Christmas note was one of the needed proofs in my period of exile of the power of friendship. I was better and happier all week for receiving it."

On returning to America she wrote:

How I envy your life in the midst of ideas where everyone is doing something. I came home with notebooks full from your beautiful country.

How wonderful French women are. It seems to me they are as nature intended them to be, while American women are in a state of transition leading to something heretofore undefined.

Write to me when you find the time. I have always felt as if we were much better acquainted than the exchange of words would verify.

But there was no time to write. In Chicago Mrs. Call felt she would never be well enough again to concentrate, work, or lead a normal life. She checked into the Newberry Hotel, paid a week's rent in advance, and swallowed a vial of cyanide. Her body was found on the floor by a maid. In her room she left telegrams and letters to be mailed to her family and friends.

Carrel must have been affected by Mrs. Call's death, but how deeply no one knows. His interest in the function of the mind seems to date from this traumatic event. It is difficult for a physician accustomed to dealing with organic disease to realize what serious consequences can result from an easily dismissed affliction of the mind. When such an affliction strikes someone close, the tragic circumstances drive the point home.

Carrel's life in New York continued amid the stream of visitors, daily work in the laboratory, social activities, and the summer trips to France. He reached the peak of professional success. At the Rockefeller Institute he performed experimental operations not just for himself, but for other investigators as well. Thus he operated on dogs for Herter, who was interested in gastrointestinal physiology.

In Chicago Carrel's experimental operations had been described in several newspaper reports. In New York the interest of the press in his work had intensified, and Carrel began to enjoy national publicity. On January 16, 1908, Carl Beck wrote that he was very agreeably surprised to read in the Chicago newspapers of the great success Carrel was having with his experiments and the kind spirit in which they were mentioned in the press. The newspaper reports did not escape Guthrie's attention either. On January 15, 1908, he wrote from St. Louis: "Accept my congratulations on your wide press notice. Your name rivals the President's in the frequency of appearance. It is too bad that you do not share in the newspaper profits derived from the harvest. You should not take the matter so much to heart, as you seem to. Think of what historians will say about you."

In St. Louis Guthrie had continued to operate on animals, but he missed Carrel's technical skill. In November 1907 he wrote to Carrel: "I operate from six to twenty times a week and will continue until all my available quarters are filled. Dr. Bartlett was in last week and is coming in next week to assist with some double operations. I wish you could come and operate with us for a couple of weeks, as the three of us with my other assistants would undoubtedly be able to carry out some very complicated and interesting operations. I think we would be able to prepare some material that would create a sensation among the surgeons at the annual meeting next spring."

However, Carrel was not inclined to travel to St. Louis to perform further experiments with Guthrie. Neither had he invited Guthrie to New York. Carrel was probably still annoyed at Guthrie's reaction to the publication of Carrel's lecture on vascular surgery and transplantation. Although the lecture was printed verbatim and consisted of a review of previous work and the discussion of possible future clinical applications of vascular surgery, Guthrie felt his name should have appeared on the paper. When Guthrie realized Carrel did not want to work with him anymore, he took offense and in 1909 wrote a letter to *Science* entitled "On Misleading Statements." After that, the relationship between the two cooled off, and their collaboration ceased altogether.

Carrel's laboratory became a center for visitors. Most surgeons with academic interests thought it their duty to visit him while in New York. Carrel made visiting colleagues most welcome and demonstrated his surgical techniques to all who cared to see them. When coming to visit him, his friends dispensed with formalities, as is evident from the surgeon Joseph C. Bloodgood's letter of January 28, 1907: "I leave here Tuesday night for Albany where I will be on Wednesday, and shall reach New York about ten o'clock on Thursday morning. I plan to come to the Rockefeller Institute and trust to find that you will be operating on that morning. Do not bother to let me know one way or the other. I shall come anyway." A few days later Bloodgood sent him a note: "I wish to thank you again for my charming day in New York. I am enclosing cards of introduction to some of the New York surgeons." Like his chief, Halsted, Bloodgood was most interested in applying the results of animal experiments to humans. He wrote Carrel: "When you find it convenient to come to Baltimore for a visit, let me know and we will see what we can do to arrange interesting operations. I am glad to hear the dog is doing well."

Carrel was courteous and accommodating, not only to surgeons of Bloodgood's stature, but to younger men as well. Bloodgood wanted a young associate of his to go see

Carrel, and so wrote the latter: "Be good enough to let him know what are the best days to see your operative work on dogs. I ask you to write him instead of myself because I plan to leave town the latter part of this week for a day or two."

The German surgeon Ernst Jeger, after studying with Carrel in New York, went to Berlin, where he did interesting work with renal veins and wrote a book on heart and blood-vessel surgery. In 1912 he said he would never have achieved the results he had without the instruction Carrel gave him in New York, and asked Carrel whether he could dedicate his book to him.

Visitors came from many parts of the country. In 1907 Walter B. Cannon, Professor of Physiology at the Harvard Medical School, asked if F. J. Murphy could visit Carrel. "He has been much interested in your work from the beginning and wishes to meet you. I should like ever so much to have him see the work you now have in hand. Are there special days when you operate? As Doctor Murphy is a surgeon, interested in the scientific aspects of surgery, he is naturally much interested in your technique. If you would let him see your technique, I'm sure he would be much pleased."

Murphy did visit Carrel and on his return to Boston wrote him: "My short stay with you was stimulating. Seeing your work has straightened out an endless number of questions in regard to the technical details. Since my return I have been able to arrange for proper sterilization at the Medical School, and am about to start in on some experimental work along your lines. I realize that your perfected technic [sic] has come after a good deal of practice, so I shall not expect remarkable results at first, or be discouraged by failures."

Many surgeons stopped by the Rockefeller Institute just because they were in New York. Charles L. Scudder of Boston wrote to say he would be in the city for three days and asked Carrel to put on a demonstration for him. Carrel obligingly did so.

Carrel also received notes from colleagues who in turn brought visitors. Clarence A. McWilliams wrote on March 22, 1903: "Dr. Paul Clairmont is in town visiting. He is Professor von Eiselberg's assistant in Vienna. He wants to see some of your work. I told him that I expected to go over there on Wednesday and said that I thought you would not object to having him come also. Doctor Hartwell also asked to come with us. Will three be too much of an audience for you?"

The stream of visitors interfered with the daily routine of the laboratory. As time went on, Carrel began to limit their number by saying he would be out of town, no operations were scheduled for this week, please come next week, etc. This annoyed some prospective visitors. However, Carrel never avoided the colleagues who were genuinely interested in vascular surgery, or those who wanted to discuss seriously experimental or clinical problems. Thus when Roswell Park, an extremely versatile and highly esteemed surgeon, wanted to visit Carrel with his two assistants, Carrel was delighted; he gave up a whole day to put on a demonstration for them.

He also answered all serious inquiries, such as one from Willy Meyer who wrote on December 31, 1909:

I am desirous of probing as deeply as possible into the development of intrathoracic surgery and would herewith ask a personal favor of you.

According to the enclosed quotation from Quenu and Longnet, 1896, they seemed to have been the first to conceive the idea of constant differential pressure. They did a few animal experiments, using a sort of diver's helmet for a positive pressure apparatus. However, after the above date I have been unable to find any further mention of their device in the literature.

With your large acquaintance among the French medical profession, would it be possible for you to ascertain whether Quenu and Longnet abandoned the idea as impracticable, or whether they pursued it further?

Carrel's laboratory attracted not only his medical colleagues, but also people from other spheres of life. Theodore Roosevelt, who was then editing *The Outlook*, sent friends over: "Would you allow me to introduce my friend Mr. Arthur Lee, M.P.? He is here for a few days and sails again for England next week. He is greatly interested in the work that is being done under you. May I ask of your courtesy to detail somebody to give him the information he desires? He is one of the members of Parliament who takes a particular interest in just this kind of thing." Carrel was glad to oblige.

Yet Carrel's life in New York did not consist entirely of work in the laboratory, demonstrations, and small dinner parties. In the summers, he left the city, usually for two to three months. He also traveled, giving lectures and presenting the results of his studies at scientific meetings. However, Carrel was selective as to where he gave his lectures. Pecuniary interest was not a determining factor in making the choice. He declined an invitation to deliver the Isaac Ridgeway Trimble Lecture to the Medical and Chirurgical Faculty of Maryland, which carried a considerable stipend, and did so gracefully. Yet he gave a lecture at a medical club in Boston, when invited by Drs. Cannon and Murphy, and himself defrayed the expense of travel.

Carrel also attended the meetings of the Dinner Club and frequented the Century Club. The Dinner Club was presided over by John D. Rockefeller, Jr., and was a no-nonsense gathering. Several weeks before the meeting Rockefeller would send a note like this one of January 27, 1914:

The subject for discussion at the meeting of the Dinner Club on the third Tuesday of March will be the Social Evil, based upon Mr. Abraham Flexner's book *Prostitution in Europe,* a copy of which I am sending to each member in the hope that all may find the time to read it before the dinner.

Mr. Flexner will be the guest of the club that evening, and will be prepared to lead the discussion, which, if generally participated in, will, I think, be both interesting and valuable.

But what Carrel most enjoyed were evenings with his friends at the Century Club. He liked the Club's atmosphere. For a number of years he dined there regularly with Father Cornelius Clifford. During these dinners they engaged in prolonged discussions on biological and philosophical topics.

A group of friends also gathered there regularly. For over twenty-five years when not dining at the Club they dined at the house of Frederick R. Coudert, the lawyer. The group included Frederick Woodbridge, Dean of Columbia University; Judge Benjamin Cardozo, who subsequently became a Justice of the Supreme Court; Charles Butler; and Walter Price. The French philosophers Henri Bergson and Émile Boutroux joined the group when they were in New York. Judge Cardozo semihumorously termed the group "the philosophers."

Although New York never became a true home to Carrel, his life was closely interwoven with that of the city. Being away from it in the summer allowed him to view in perspective the tremendous changes in New York which took place during his lifetime. His concern with the effects of urbanization on human life was based largely on what he noticed in the city.

In December 1913, at the age of forty, Carrel got married in France. This came as somewhat of a suprise to his friends, although his enchantment with Mrs. de la Mairie had been known to his close associates as early as 1911. In a letter to Carrel dated May 13, 1911, Katherine Lilly, an operating-room technician, asked Carrel to give Mrs. de la Mairie her regards. However, the majority of Carrel's colleagues and friends were pretty much in the dark about Carrel's marriage plans. Carl Beck learned of the marriage from the newspapers. In this connection John D. Rockefeller, Jr., wrote Carrel on January 14, 1914:

The night we dined together at Mr. Blumenthal's house, our host told me that your engagement was about to be announced. Since I had not heard it from you, I hesitated at the time to extend my congratulations. Now, however, it gives me such pleasure to wish for Mrs. Carrel and yourself every happiness in this new and delightful relationship into which you have recently entered. From what I hear of Mrs. Carrel, I am glad to believe that she will be an inspiration to you in your work, always interested in it and proud of your achievements.

Mrs. de la Mairie was born Anne-Marie de la Motte. She became a widow in 1909, having had a son by her first marriage. For Carrel, she provided the strong link with France that he himself lacked. Her family belonged to the French aristocracy, their roots were in Brittany, and it was there that the Carrels eventually made their permanent home.

5 ❧ Transplantation of Organs

Prior to World War I, Carrel's investigative endeavors at the Rockefeller Institute proceeded along several lines. He continued to experiment with vascular surgery. An extension of this interest was the refinement of techniques for the transplantation of organs. He also did some work with hypothermic preservation of tissues, particularly arteries. He substituted artificial conduits for excised portions of blood vessels, began work in tissue culture, and studied wound healing. The latter studies laid the foundation for his work during the war. Carrel wanted his studies of wound healing and tissue regeneration to be of practical value. He reputedly said to his French colleague Pierre Lecomte du Nouy that it was not important to know why wounds heal, since such knowledge would be of interest only from a theoretical point of view. What was important was to learn *how* wounds heal, because this knowledge would have practical value and help one to understand tissue regeneration.

The results of Carrel's experiments with the preservation of arterial grafts were published in 1910 in the *Journal of Experimental Medicine*. In this paper, entitled "Latent Life of Arteries," several methods of preservation were discussed. Arteries wrapped in Vaseline and kept in a refrigerator maintained open lumens on transplanation in 80 percent of all cases. A much lower patency rate was obtained for arteries preserved by heat, drying, or immersion in formalin or glycerol. The grafts used in these experiments were subjected to careful microscopic study. Arteries and pieces of peritoneum used for patching aortas, when they were transplanted from one animal to another, became replaced by fibrous tissues of the host. This did not happen when fresh arteries were reimplanted into the same animal.

Carrel's experiments with surgery of the aorta were paving the way for human application. In 1911 Rudolph Matas wrote to him: "Your contribution on 'Surgery of the Aorta' has deservedly created a great sensation throughout the medical world, and it is quite evident that we will have to hear something further of the wonderful work in this direction. As the President of the American Surgical Association, I feel that I must urge you to present a statement of your latest results."

Carrel's surgical experiments were aided by the development of the endotracheal tube by Samuel J. Meltzer and J. Auer, also of the Rockefeller Institute. Now extensively used, the endotracheal tube allows for administering artificial respiration during deep anesthesia. With the endotracheal tube in place, the subject can breathe with the chest open. Thus this discovery facilitated the development of heart and lung surgery. Carrel was quick to grasp the significance of this advance. Using these tubes, he cut out portions of lungs, and operated on the esophagus and the thoracic aorta of animals. He then proceeded to operate on the heart itself. In these experiments Carrel correctly anticipated the development of cardiac surgery. He thought that valvular disease and disease of the coronary arteries might be amenable to surgical treatment. He described his concepts of cardiac operations as early as 1906. In 1914 the results of experimental operations on the pulmonary valves were reported. Incisions into ventricles of the heart were also made. When the technique worked out for cardiac operations was carefully followed, cardiac surgery presented little danger to the life of the animal.

Meltzer, whose invention of the endotracheal insufflation tube made possible these intricate operations, was a man with strong convictions about what medicine must do for humanity. Born in Russia in a small town, he adhered throughout his life to an irrepressible idealism instilled in him in his youth. In search of knowledge, he had gone to Germany to study under the current masters of medicine and physiology. His exposure to scientific physiology made his ideals assume concrete form. His teachers were so impressed with him that he was offered an academic position in Berlin. However, his desire for wider horizons compelled him to decline the offer and instead he went to New York.

Having studied with Rudolf Virchow, Robert Koch, and H. L. F. von Helmholtz, Meltzer found the medical scene in New York disappointing. New York had medical schools, but most of them were not academic institutions. Laboratories were practically nonexistent. He became involved in an effort to improve medical education. Others were championing the same cause, but among men such as William Welch, T. M. Prudden, T. C. Janeway, and Abraham Jacobi, he occupied a unique position. He was in effect the leader of a progressive minority opposing the conservative forces. For this reason, for many years he was unaffiliated with a school or a major hospital. Despite this, he did not abandon experimental research. He held an advantage over many of his contemporaries in that he knew several languages well, craved reading, and retained what he read.

Meltzer frequently introduced new medical discoveries to the public, and he did this extremely well. His success rested on the fact that he did not popularize a subject until he had proved its value to himself by experiments in the laboratory. Late in his life, after witnessing a marked improvement in the quality of American medicine, Meltzer devoted himself entirely to laboratory research. The opening of the Rockefeller Institute and its Division of Experimental Physiology gave him this opportunity. Since Carrel's initial appointment was in Experimental Physiology, his contacts with Meltzer were numerous and enormously useful.

Carrel's success with vascular surgery naturally led to attempts at organ transplantation. Since the establishment of the Laboratory of Experimental Surgery, Carrel continued to devote a large portion of his time to the subject. Several papers on transplantation were published between 1907 and 1912. However, the information contained in these papers is somewhat fragmentary. It may be useful, therefore, to present an overview of the results obtained by Carrel at the time. Carrel knew he must consider the problem of organ transplantation from two points of view: a surgical one, which was primarily that of technique, and a biological one. At first it was necessary to perfect techniques which would permit the re-establishment of circulation in transplanted organs. The second objective was to transplant organs that would continue to function and to observe how long they would do so. Carrel found that although he could solve the first problem, the second one baffled him. He soon distinguished between three types of transplants: the "autoplastic," when an extirpated organ was replaced in the same animal; the "homoplastic," when organs were exchanged between animals of the same species; and the "heteroplastic," when the donor organ came from an animal of a different species. For technical reasons he limited his studies to transplantation of limbs and kidneys. In a very short time he saw that heteroplastic transplants did not work and therefore abandoned them.

Experiments with limb transplantation started by 1908, and consisted of transplanting a leg from one dog to another. The limbs were severed and reattached, either at the upper forelimbs or mid-thigh. Carrel did not take much care in the choice of animals; later he thought that if he had chosen related animals, the results might have been different. In the light of present knowledge, however, we know they would have been the same. He selected animals of the same height, but with as much difference in fur as possible. He thought the results would be easier to determine, if he grafted a white limb on a black dog, or vice versa.

From a technical standpoint, the most important consideration was the matching of bone sizes; the muscle mass and the blood-vessel size could be compensated for. After aseptic preparation, the skin of the donor animal limb was incised, and the blood vessels were dissected and divided, the ends being left as long as possible. The cut surfaces of the limb were immediately covered with silk dressing impregnated with Vaseline. Major arteries were perfused with Ringer's solution, so that they were washed completely free of blood. The muscles and bone were then cut.

The recipient animal underwent limb amputation at the same level as the donor. Again, the blood vessels were left as long as possible. Carrel felt the sutured blood vessel must not be under tension. The transplanted leg was secured in place by means of aluminum intermedullary tubes (tubes placed in the bone marrow cavity). The periosteum (connective tissue surrounding bone) was then sutured together. Following the reuniting of major muscles, the arteries and veins were also sutured together. The circulation was then re-established, usually accompanied by considerable hemorrhage. After securing hemostasis, the operation was completed. Carrel remarked that the remaining portion of the operation was "extremely simple, but monotonous." In succession, each muscle was sutured with catgut. Aponeurosis (tendinous tissue surrounding muscle) and nerves were sutured individually. The skin was then closed. When everything went well, the entire procedure took about one hour and a half. Postoperative care of animals with limb transplants was critical. The transplanted limb was placed in a plaster cast and the animals were cared for on a twenty-four-hour basis.

From the surgical standpoint, these operations were successful. However, after about eight days most transplanted limbs began to swell. Some twelve to fifteen days after transplantation, the limbs became blue and the skin started to peel. Carrel examined a number of transplanted limbs and found the vascular anastomoses (surgical interconnection) to be intact. In a few animals (transplants from one fox terrier to another), edema disappeared at the end of twenty days, and the limbs became firmly affixed to the recipient. On the basis of these observations, Carrel concluded that there was a reaction by the recipient organisms against the transplanted limb. However, in some rare cases in which the cause was not known, the transplanted limb recovered.

Identical results were obtained with kidneys, but since Carrell performed both "autoplasic" and "homoplastic" renal transplants, the results with these were clear-cut. Carrel said that the technique of renal transplants was relatively simple. The kidneys were removed with their blood vessels, pieces of peritoneum (serous membrane lining the abdominal cavity), fatty capsule, and ureters. The removed kidney was perfused with Ringer's solution, wrapped in Vaseline and silk, and left at room temperature. Kidneys were then reimplanted in their normal anatomic sites. The average time between removal and reimplantation was fifty minutes. The other kidney of the recipient animal was removed either during the same operation or a few days later. The only complication that Carrel encountered initially was hydronephrosis (distention of calices and pelves of kidney) due to faulty suturing of the ureters. Once this was corrected, no further technical complications occurred.

Carrel performed renal autotransplants in some dozen dogs. All animals survived; the longest period of observation was two and a half years. The results obtained with kidneys transplanted from one animal to another were strikingly different. The technique of transplantation was the same as with autotransplants, but transplanted kidneys were "rejected" and the animals died in several weeks. Carrel then repeated the experiments on cats. However, in these animals he transplanted both the kidneys with portions of the aorta, vena cava, and urinary bladder. A total of eighteen transplants was made. Two animals survived initially but died two months later. The others died with diseased kidneys within twenty days. Again Carrel thought the failure of these transplants was due to the reaction of the organism against its new organs.

Carrel noted that he never used animals from the same "family," and suggested that transplants between siblings should be investigated. He further stated that his conclusions should not be extended to animals other than dogs and cats. Perhaps in man there would be more similarity between individuals.

Carrel's experiments showed the differences between animals of the same species to be rather marked. Therefore organs could not be interchanged between them with impunity. He thought it important to find out why this was the case. If this were done, perhaps the organism could be modified to accept an organ from another individual. Carrel's assistant, R. Ingebrigtsen, performed a series of experiments designed to select individuals whose organs could be interchanged. He conducted these experiments on the carotid arteries of a large number of cats, and examined the reaction of their blood by mixing red cells and the serum and then observing for hemolysis (breaking up of red blood cells) and cell agglutination. No correlation could be made between reaction of blood and obliteration of arteries.

Carrel succinctly summarized his experience with transplantation of organs in a letter to Theodor Kocher on May 9, 1914: "Concerning homoplastic transplantation (from one animal into another) of organs such as the kidney, I have never found positive results to continue after a few months, whereas in autoplastic transplantation the result was always positive. The biological side of the question has to be investigated very much more and we must find out by what means to prevent the reaction of the organism against a new organ." This summary of the art of organ transplantation is as appropriate today as it was in 1914. Although most major organs can be transplanted successfully, their rejection by the recipient remains the main obstacle to wide clinical application.

Successful as Carrel was with surgical experiments, his endeavors did not please everybody. They particularly displeased antivivisectionists in both Chicago and New York. This petulant group termed Carrel one of the leading practitioners of vivisection. Describing Carrel's experiments, Walter R. Howden, M.D., wrote in the *Abolitionist*:

The kidneys of one set of cats and dogs had been cut out and transplanted in other cats and dogs; and one dog, apparently by way of diversion, had, according to the report, been supplied with kidneys which had been located in its neck instead of in the loins, the ducts of which were made to open into the gullet instead of into their proper receptacle. The condition of a hapless creature from which the kidneys had been taken does not appear to have been described, but the experimenter informed his audience that one of the dogs with transplanted kidneys had already survived a week, and that he succeeded in keeping dogs alive for seventeen days after the operation, when it is presumed they succumbed, whilst one of the cats had possessed its new set of kidneys for two months. The fact is noted that the animals were able to display all the natural propensities of their kind—the cats to spit and the dogs to growl. This is not surprising.

The Chicago antivivisectionist pamphlet added: "And the doctors who do this sort of thing are not only out of jail, but are boasting of their prowess. What would a civilized parent do to his boy if he caught him in such practices?"

Shortly after the publication of the above article, Carrel received a handwritten note from an "admirer," saying, "Remember, when death is drawing near and your heart sinks in fear, you are going to reap what you have sown, no mercy."

The antivivisectionists' campaign was strong enough to cause the Board of Directors of the Rockefeller Institute to pass a resolution requiring Flexner's approval for all animal experiments carried out at the Institute. Similar problems existed at Baltimore, where another experimental surgery laboratory, the Hunterian Laboratory under Cushing, was in operation. At Johns Hopkins the animals could be used only in accordance with certain rules regarding vivisection. The antivivisection group in Baltimore was strong enough to require the approval of these rules by the trustees of the university.

In New York the antivivisection campaign and its recognition by the press continued strong until 1909, when an incident involving direct blood transfusion in a child turned public opinion in Carrel's favor.

While some people were unhappy with Carrel's work, others were not; notable among the latter group was William S. Halsted. A few months after Carrel began experiments at the Rockefeller Institute, Halsted wrote him that he was exceedingly interested in the work Carrel was doing and would like, if possible, to witness one or more of the operations Carrel was performing, particularly those upon the aorta. After seeing Carrel demonstrate vascular suturing, Halsted noted: "It was not simply the fact that arterial suture can be accomplished in this way that impressed me, but the really exquisite manner in which it was accomplished."

Carrel's surgical experiments received wide recognition in the American medical community. In 1909 Carl Beck wrote him from Chicago: "I take this opportunity to state that while I do not write very often, I have you in mind quite frequently and am enjoying the progress you are making. If you will promise not to tell anybody, I will inform you that I, who have been given one of the votes for the Nobel Prize, have given it to you, and have induced two other gentlemen who have also been selected as judges for this coming year, to do likewise."

Similar feelings were expressed by many members of the surgical community throughout the world. Surgery was being elevated from an empirically derived technique to a scientific level. Carrel received a Nobel Prize in 1912, with the following citation:

The Caroline Institute has awarded you the Nobel Prize in Medicine for your work on vascular suture and the transplantation of organs. Sir, you have accomplished great things! You have invented a new method for suturing blood vessels. Thanks to this method, you obtain the patency of the point sewn, and at the same time you prevent postoperative hemorrhage, thrombosis and secondary contraction. Thanks to this same method, it is possible for you to reconstitute vascular continuity, to substitute a segment free of disease for another segment taken from another region or from another individual. You have succeeded in the most daring and extremely difficult operations. Through all these experiments you have extended the boundaries of intervention of human surgery and proved once again that the development of an applied science of surgery follows the lessons learned from animal experimentation.

The presentation of the Nobel Prize in Stockholm caused some complications. Carrel was adamant about not having the French authorities represent him at the ceremony. He was a citizen of the Republic of France, but the work for which the Prize was awarded was performed in the United States. Carrel felt the French medical establishment had done all it could to prevent him from accomplishing this work, therefore they deserved no part of the credit. Finally, a compromise was found by Henry James, Manager of the Rockefeller Institute. According to the rules, the recipient of the Prize could be identified either by a person of standing or by the recipient's own passport. The American

Minister in Stockholm, being a prominent person, could therefore introduce Carrel. This he did on the strength of a letter from the State Department. But the Committee also did not want to offend the French, so the citation included the following paragraph:

Finally, the pure and luminous intelligence that you have received as an inheritance from your country—from that France to which humanity owes so many benefits—is united to the courageous and determined activity of your adopted country, and these marvelous operations of which I speak are the evident result of this happy collaboration.

Carrel could not have objected to this; it was, after all, true.

With the Nobel Prize came $39,000. Among many congratulatory letters, Carrel received one from a close friend, T. Wood Clarke, who wrote in closing: "I most heartily congratulate you and the Institute, and hope you will not get full trying to blow the whole $39,000 at one sitting."

The award of the Nobel Prize to Carrel encouraged American medicine and the Rockefeller Institute. The *New York Medical Journal* expressed the common sentiment in an editorial of October 19, 1912:

It is the first time the prize has been given for researchers in medicine in this country; it marks a change in attitude of those who are entrusted with the selection of the yearly beneficiary. None would regret selections previously made, yet it is true that in several instances the Nobel Prize has been granted for work done years earlier, *i.e.,* long after the honored investigators had finished their work and taken up other lines of research. This fact has evoked criticism in various parts of the world, the specific purpose of the prize being to reward him who had done most for the good of humanity during the preceding year and to aid him with the munificent sum of $39,000 to pursue his good work. In selecting Doctor Carrel for the honor this year, the Nobel Prize Commission has not only complied strictly with the wishes of the generous benefactor who created it, but has shown admirable discernment.

6 ❧ Tissue Culture

The term "tissue culture" is used collectively to describe maintenance and growth of cells and tissues outside the body for varying periods of time. These procedures are also commonly referred to as *in vitro* procedures. *In vitro* literally means "in (or on) glass," but in a general sense it denotes anything performed outside an intact organism.

Tissue culture is a technique, not a scientific discipline. It has been used to study normal and diseased cells. Cultured cells have been used to support the growth of viruses and other microorganisms. Although it would seem that the study of cells grown in a laboratory ought to yield a sizable dividend in terms of understanding disease processes, such did not turn out to be the case. On the other hand, the discovery that many viruses not only proliferate in cultured cells, but also produce easily recognized degenerative changes in the cultures, furnished a tremendous impetus to virology. A well-recognized, practical end result has been the production of vaccines over the last two decades. Thus tissue culture created a potent tool for disease prevention.

From the start, tissue culture was precisely what the term implies. Pieces of tissue referred to as explants were placed in the culture medium on a sterile cover glass, over which a hollow slide was placed. If cells grew, they migrated from the edges of the explant and spread on the glass. When cells became too numerous for the original vessel, they were transferred to others. After tissue-culture techniques went through several evolutionary changes, another refinement was added: dispersing the cells before placing them in the culture medium. This produced cultures of cells which grew in a single layer. However, to disperse cells from solid tissues, it is necessary to expose the tissues to chemicals, and also to subject the cells to centrifugation. These procedures are undoubtedly injurious to the cells and favor the selection of resistant cell populations.

The possibility of actually growing cells in the laboratory captivated the imagination of many biologists in the latter part of the nineteenth century. It is therefore not surprising that reports of the successful cultivation of amphibian nerve cells by the American researcher Ross G. Harrison in 1907 attracted wide attention among his contemporaries. Carrel thought Harrison's technique might be adapted to *in vitro* maintenance of extirpated organs and tissues, so that these could be used for the replacement of similar structures destroyed by disease or removed by surgery. In 1909 he sent his associate, Montrose T. Burrows, to Harrison's laboratory at Yale University to learn the new technique. Burrows succeeded in adapting it to cells of warmblooded animals. His first report on the growth of the chick embryo tissue outside the animal body, with special reference to the nervous system, appeared in 1911. Upon his return to the Rockefeller Institute, he and Carrel refined the method of tissue culturing.

As with so many new discoveries, the development by Harrison of a method by which explanted amphibian tissue fragments could be grown in a laboratory stemmed from a different interest. Harrison was an embryologist and his early work was performed in the Department of Anatomy of Johns Hopkins University. At the time, a pressing question confronting embryologists was the development of the nerve cells. Specifically, the mode of development of the individual nerve fibers was a subject of debate. Some contended that each nerve fiber, no matter how long, grew out of a single parent cell, while others supported the view that nerve fibers were built near the tissues through which they passed with locally produced individual fibers somehow joined end to end. Direct visualization in tissue culture of the growth of nerve fibers from single parent cells finally settled the controversy.

Harrison devised a rather simple method which allowed him to observe the growth of nerve fibers unobscured by other cells. He cut out a fragment from the spinal cord of a frog embryo and placed it in a drop of clotted lymph. As the cells grew, he observed the sprouting of nerve fibers. However, cultivation for a few days of fragments of embryonic tissues from a coldblooded frog, growing in coagulated lymph at room temperature, was by no means the same as prolonged cultivation of cells from warmblooded animals. Methods for cultivating mammalian and avian tissues were developed by Burrows and Carrel. The early procedure, derived from Harrison's experiments, consisted merely of placing a fragment of tissue in a drop of lymph, plasma, serum, saline, or other medium hanging in a sealed hollow slide. Under these conditions the medium deteriorated within a short time, and the cultured cells had to be transferred into another hanging drop.

Scientific discoveries are often made concomitantly by different individuals. While Harrison was experimenting with frog embryos, Rhoda Erdmann in Berlin was cultivating amoebae on nutrient agar (a standard culture medium used in bacteriology) mixed with physiological salt solution. Margaret Reed (later Margaret Lewis), while visiting Erdmann's laboratory in 1908, placed a small piece of guinea-pig bone marrow in this medium. She put the tube in an incubator, and after a few days noted the growth and multiplication of bone-marrow cells. After a few more days, degeneration began and cell death occurred. Thus in these experiments, published in 1911, the tissues were not cultivated in the present sense of the word.

Carrel was well aware of the contribution made to the study of animal-cell cultures by Rhoda Erdmann. Although accused by some contemporaries of dealing with colleagues in a high-handed manner, and of being pompous and haughty—particularly when tissue culture was involved—Carrel was humble with people whom he respected. His relationship with Erdmann is a case in point. There is little doubt that he had a showman's streak in his character, and perhaps his attitude toward some of the scientists using tissue culture was precipitated by sharp early criticism of his work. (Carrel's work with tissue culture had nothing to do with his winning the Nobel Prize.)

In 1930–1931 Carrel became involved in organizing the Second International Congress of Cell Workers, and later the International Society for Experimental Cell Research. In the course of these activities, he was tardy in answering some of Erdmann's letters. She let her displeasure be known by writing him on January 26, 1931:

Months have slipped away and I have heard nothing from you. I shall not write you again if you do not answer me. You freely assumed the official position to work out in a small commission the statutes of the International Society for Experimental Cell Research. Long ago I sent you the statutes, but have no expression of opinion from you. . . . Therefore I should like to ask you to resign your position. I cannot work with members who cause obstruction.

In the same letter she suggested that Carrel might be thinking of forming a society of his own, either in New York or Paris; if this were the case, she said, he would be engaged in scientific isolationism. Finally she presented Carrel with an ultimatum: "If in four weeks I have no reply, I shall have the statutes finished by two other gentlemen."

Carrel was not unduly perturbed, took no offense, and after waiting just over four weeks, replied: "I have not answered your letter sooner because I could not say anything about the organization of the International Society for Experimental Cell Research without consulting Doctor Chambers. As Doctor Chambers was in Europe, this was not possible. He came back only a few days ago. I hope to have an opportunity of meeting him soon."

Carrel and Chambers finally finished the draft of statutes for the Society, and on November 22, 1931, Carrel wrote Erdmann:

Doctor Chambers remained abroad longer than he at first planned, and when he returned, I had to go to Europe. The result of these complications was that we have only just now had the opportunity of discussing this matter. I understand how unpleasant it has been for you to wait such a long time for our opinion. Unfortunately, the delay has been caused by circumstances independent of our own wills. I beg to be pardoned, and I am sure you will understand the situation.

In the same letter he added, "The only detail I cannot agree with is my nomination as the President of the Society."

These excerpts from Carrel's correspondence shed some light on his character and behavior. First, he maintained his composure and did not allow Erdmann's irritation to precipitate a hasty response that might have ruined their relationship altogether. Second, he declined a prestigious nomination to be the president of an international scientific organization.

The results of the first experiments in tissue culture, performed at the Rockefeller Institute, were published by Carrel and Burrows in 1910 in the *Journal of the American Medical Association*. He gave the following reasons for doing this work: "The solution of many problems of human pathology depends in a large measure on the finding of still unknown physiological laws of generation, growth and evolution of cells. We must, therefore, develop new methods which permit the discovery of those laws. . . . The starting point of our research was the beautiful work of Harrison on the embryonic tissues of the frog."

The initial experiments at the Rockefeller Institute were performed on tissues of dogs, cats, and adult frogs. Carrel and Burrows inoculated what they termed "plasmatic media" with fragments of many tissues and organs. All multiplied and grew, but all the growing cells exhibited common characteristics and looked alike. The time of the beginning of cellular proliferation depended primarily on the age of the donor and the nature of the tissue. In cultivation of glandular organs of adult dogs, the cell growth started after forty-six or forty-eight hours. But, if the animal was only a few days old, new cells appeared in the culture after ten or twelve hours. Arterial sheath, connective tissue, cartilage, peritoneum, bone marrow, skin, thyroid, spleen, and kidney were the subjects of cultivation. The second part of Carrel's initial tissue-culture studies consisted of attempting to transfer the growing tissue into a second flask. This was accomplished with thyroid gland tissue.

The results of these tissue-culture experiments were summarized by Carrel and Burrows in a few words: "Adult tissues and organs of mammals can be cultivated outside of the animal body." Although this conclusion with regard to organs now seems unduly optimistic, it probably did not seem so at the time. After all, cultivation of cells and tissues was a tremendous technical leap forward. It seemed natural that the culture of organs would follow shortly.

Carrel's reports on cultivating cells of animals and humans in a test tube were truly sensational, and were soon taken up by the daily press. Except to a few scientists who were familiar with Harrison's work and understood the subject, such reports sounded surprising and incredible. His colleague Albert Fischer tells of the dramatic scenes evoked by Carrel's showing his tissue cultures in Paris. University professors attacked Carrel in violent terms. A famous French biologist stood up at a demonstration on December 2, 1910, stating emphatically that what he saw in cultures was not the growth of cells, but their decay. He further declared that Carrel was abusing the language by designating the tubes as cultures. One cannot escape a feeling that such tactics by French scientists were precipitated by more than disbelief in the credibility of Carrel's scientific results. The underlying hostility must have reflected a personal dislike. By this time Carrel, having achieved a place of prominence in science, began to criticize systematically the French scientific establishment. Rather than looking into the validity of his arguments, the members of that establishment responded as usual with administrative pressures and abuse.

The initial skepticism toward tissue culture gained momentum when attempts were made to reproduce Carrel's experiments. The results obtained were very poor. It took several years before tissues were cultured successfully in laboratories other than those of the Rockefeller Institute. Since Carrel's laboratory was well organized, to an outsider the tissue-culture work looked very simple. However, those who sought to reproduce Carrel's experiments soon learned that special training and a meticulous adherence to the established methods were prerequisites for success.

The experience gained by growing cells *in vitro* led Carrel to predict that the development of tissue-culture methods might render possible the cultivation of certain microorganisms in living cells. This prediction was accurate regarding future developments in microbiology. Were it not for tissue culture, the propagation of many viruses and the preparation of vaccines, including those for poliomyelitis and measles, would not be possible.

A logical use of cell-culture techniques would be the study of the growth of cancerous tissues. Therefore it is not surprising that Carrel and Burrows proceeded to cultivate tissue from a sarcoma (a highly malignant tumor originating from connective tissue). For this they initially used fowl sarcoma obtained from Peyton Rous, also of the Rockefeller Institute. Rous succeeded in transmitting avian sarcoma from animal to animal with a cell-free fluid filtrate, thus implicating viruses as possible causes of cancer. (For this work, performed in 1911–1912, Rous was belatedly awarded the Nobel Prize in 1970.)

Carrel and Burrows noted that the growth of Rous sarcoma cells in culture was extremely rapid. These experiments were followed by cultivation of a human sarcoma. Fragments of a human tumor were placed in culture vessels thirty minutes after its surgical extirpation. Clotted plasma used for the medium was obtained from the patient's own blood. Sixteen hours later the plasma clot was dissolved by the tumor cells. Cell growth occurred in ten out of twelve cultures. Carrel concluded that it was possible to cultivate *in vitro* fragments of a human sarcoma, in a manner similar to that of animal sarcoma.

The first phase of Carrel's work with tissue culture came during 1910–1914, when it was found that degeneration and death of cultured cells could be prevented by adding embryo extract to the medium. This made it possible to cultivate cells in the modern sense. A long interruption in tissue-culture studies was caused by World War I. A second phase of investigation began with the development, in 1921, of procedures permitting some specific cell types to be obtained in "pure" cultures. Blood and tissue macrophages, iris epithelium, cartilage cells, and several types of cells from malignant tumors were maintained and studied in culture. It became possible to measure with relative accuracy the growth of tissues in culture.

Carrel's interest in tissue culture continued as long as he

had a laboratory at the Rockefeller Institute. However, tissue culture per se never occupied him entirely. During the twenty-seven years that he studied tissue culture, Carrel trained and co-operated with several scientists to whom he turned over most tissue-culture work, and who left a distinct mark on the development and refinement of the technique. These included Albert H. Ebeling, Lillian E. Baker, Raymond C. Parker, and Albert Fischer.

Carrel summarized his feeling on tissue culture in an address delivered at the Congress of Experimental Cytology in 1937. By that time he was personally all but finished with tissue culture and could take a somewhat detached retrospective view. What he said, in effect, was that tissue-culture studies had produced a jungle of new facts, but that the facts were disparate, difficult to interpret, and without relation to one another. This being the case, what then was the result of his and his associates' maintaining a tissue-culture laboratory for almost three decades? The result was the development and refinement of a new laboratory technique, subsequently used by numerous scientists for multitudes of studies.

It should be pointed out that maintaining cells in culture now is much simpler than in Carrel's day. The advantages enjoyed by present-day investigators include the availability of antibiotics, freeze-preservation of cells, disposable sterile plastic culture vessels, commercially prepared media and sera, etc. However, despite an intensive effort, no breakthrough in the understanding of cancer or other diseases through tissue culture has taken place. Nor was the tissue-culture technique directly applicable to surgery. Therefore it is easy to understand why, throughout the late 1920s and early 1930s, Carrel was searching for a technique which would allow him to culture whole organs. In his opinion, organ cultures would solve the problem which tissue cultures had failed to solve. He was plagued by methodological difficulties which he could not overcome until the arrival of Charles A. Lindbergh in his laboratory.

Tissue culture in its early phases was used extensively in morphological studies, but its application to physiological problems was delayed because the technique was not adapted to the requirements of such investigations. The research in tissue culture carried out in Carrel's laboratory followed a general plan of studying cells, tissues, and organs in relation to their environment. These studies showed that cultured cells could be characterized not only by their appearance, but also by their behavior. Carrel and Baker determined many of the nutritional requirements of cells. Results of their investigations formed the basis of more recent work in cell nutrition. According to Raymond C. Parker, tissue-culture work in the Experimental Surgery Division of the Rockefeller Institute yielded fundamental information that has been, and will continue to be, built upon by other investigators.

One cannot conclude the description of Carrel's tissue-culture studies without mentioning the "old strain" of chick heart cells. On January 17, 1912, a minute piece of heart muscle was removed from an unhatched chick embryo. This tiny heart fragment, during repeated transfer from medium to medium, pulsated for some hundred days. By that time, connective tissue cells (fibroblasts) had gradually outgrown the muscle cells. The result was the formation of the "old strain" of fibroblasts, which no longer pulsated. These cultures were maintained by Carrel and his associates for thirty-four years. This strain of cells was developed not as a stunt, nor as a means of showing that the cells were "immortal," but rather to provide a continuous source of biological test material for making a quantitative assay of substances that might inhibit or stimulate cell multiplication.

The history of the "old strain" was closely related to the development of tissue-culture technique in Carrel's laboratory. Although the achievement of maintaining a cell line for over thirty years, and not losing it to bacterial contamination, is impressive enough, some fantastic accounts of this experiment have been rendered in the lay press. According to these tales, the original pieces of embryonic heart had grown into a full-sized organ, and pieces had to be snipped off to keep it within bounds. Another popular misconception was that of a chicken heart beating in a glass jar on a marble table, with a group of scientists sitting close by and watching the heart around the clock.

The medium in which the cells of the "old strain" proliferated was composed of chicken plasma, chick embryo extract, and Tyrode's solution. Each fluid change was preceded by washing the plasma clot with the Tyrode's solution. The embryo extract was prepared from nine- to ten-day-old embryos removed aseptically from the egg. The embryos were ground into a fine pulp. The pulp was placed in a graduated cylinder and diluted with Tyrode's solution. The mixture was then shaken in an Erlenmeyer flask and allowed to stand for about an hour. Then it was centrifuged and the supernatant fluid aspirated.

The strain of chicken heart cells was maintained for over thirty years, first at the Rockefeller Institute and then by Ebeling at Lederle Laboratories. Hence the cells outlived the chicken into which the embryo would have developed. The average lifetime of a barnyard chicken, if it can escape the kitchen, is about ten years. In a few instances chickens have lived over twenty years. The maintenance of the chicken-heart fibroblasts by Carrel and his associates has been questioned by some recent investigators, who suggested the cultures were continuously replenished with fresh cells from the embryo extract. Although this does not appear likely, such a possibility exists. However, this speculation arose from the fact that present-day investigators cannot maintain most cells in culture beyond a certain number of generations. These investigators inevitably work with cells exposed to enzymes, either for the original dispersion of tissues or for detaching cells from glass or plastic surfaces. The medium now commonly used differs radically from that used by Carrel. Cell cultures in Carrel's laboratory were transferred mechanically without exposure to enzymes or chelating agents (chemical compounds in which metallic ions are sequestered and bound to the chelating molecule). Therefore the results of experiments with the "old strain" should be questioned only after they are reproduced in an identical fashion. To the best of the author's knowledge, this has not been done.

Although Carrel had very high hopes for tissue culture in solving medical problems, these hopes did not materialize in his lifetime. He therefore redirected his efforts toward developing organ-culture techniques. However, his and his associates' efforts firmly established tissue culture as a technique to be employed by all physiologists, virologists, cytologists, and cytogeneticists. From the practical standpoint, the most important offshoot of tissue-culture studies was their use for the cultivation of viruses. Without these, neither poliomyelitis nor measles vaccines would have been available.

7 🕮 World War I

By 1917, when the United States entered World War I, Carrel's method of treating infected wounds by meticulous intermittent irrigation with Dakin's solution had already proved its value. In the two years since its perfection, it had established itself as a routine form of treatment in many Allied war hospitals. However, the acceptance of the Carrel-Dakin method of treatment was slow and painful. Sir Almroth Wright, a noted British pathologist who introduced the hypertonic salt-solution irrigation for infected wounds, had observed, upon hearing of Carrel's proposal to employ antiseptics in wound sterilization, that the treatment of suppurating wounds with antiseptics is illusory, and that belief in its efficacy is based on false reasoning. He had maintained his position until 1916, but, being a fair-minded man, he changed his opinion after examining the scientific evidence. Sir Almroth wrote in *Lancet* in 1917:

I now come to Carrel's procedure of intercalating between the complete dressings a frequent flushing and refreshing of the wound surface and for carrying out this flushing unlaboriously. Allow me to say that we have here, I think, far the most important contribution made to surgical techniques since the beginning of the war. But to that let me add that, while Carrel's procedure gives us a new and improved technique for the application of antiseptics, much more does it give us a new and improved technique of physiological treatment. For that treatment the assiduous removal of corrupt and corruptible discharges is, as you know, the primary desideratum.

The controversy associated with the Carrel-Dakin treatment of infected wounds went largely unnoticed because, among the stupidities and blunders of World War I, it represented a minor event. After all, if each army of the major belligerents counted some four million men wounded and over a million dead, what difference did it make if several hundred thousand could have been listed as "wounded" instead of "killed in action"? Soldiers were expected to die in the war, and an acceptable level of casualties was largely agreed upon. Men who strove to deviate from the "normal" loss of war were oddities, often viewed with suspicion, particularly when they proposed improvements and by implication criticized the established order of things. The medical departments of major armies were not glamorous enough to be in the limelight, but many of their leaders shared the undesirable qualities so common among the general officers of the period, being narrow-minded, behind the times, and bound by tradition. Medical departments dealt with unpleasant things which most military leaders would have liked to forget. As Walt Whitman observed, the tragedy of war is most evident in the hospitals.

The hospital view of the war was amply illuminated by Harvey Cushing in his book, *From a Surgeon's Journal.* Cushing went to France in 1915 to serve in the American Ambulance Hospital, and with short interruptions remained there until the Armistice. The operation of the American Ambulance Hospital was financed by William Lindsey of Boston; an additional one thousand dollars was donated by the trustees of the Peter Bent Brigham Hospital. Before embarking for France, on March 8, 1915, Cushing wrote to Carrel, who was already in service there:

I have long wanted to write you but have only just heard from

Flexner where you are to be reached. Crile may possibly have told you that I am coming over with a contingent from Harvard to be at the American Ambulance Hospital for the three months after April first. I shall probably be able to stay only a part of the time, but I am planning to go over to help get the group established. Of just how much use we shall be, I cannot tell; I fear not very much. I have some little apprehension in regard to the way in which the American Ambulance Hospital may be looked upon by the French surgeons.

Cushing was obviously worried as to how the surgeons of the Harvard unit would be received by their French colleagues. If they went to France but the French army surgeons did not send them casualties, the entire effort would be wasted. This, of course, could well have happened. Since Carrel himself was hardly popular among French surgeons, Cushing was somewhat naive if he thought Carrel could smooth things out with his French compatriots.

As it worked out, the Harvard unit was welcomed in France, and Cushing gained an invaluable opportunity to view the war from an operating room, over an endless procession of dirty, mangled soldiers laid out on canvas stretchers. The numbers of these cases stagger the imagination. In 1915, within a few months, 43,000 casualties passed through Cushing's hospital.

Busy as he was, Cushing had several opportunities to visit and talk with Carrel at the latter's hospital in Compiègne. Both men understood the problem of the wounded, and each in his own way rendered what help he could. Cushing spent his energies in the operating rooms, working frequently sixteen hours at a stretch. Carrel took a broader view; he set out to demonstrate that, with a logical and scientific approach, new modes of effective treatment of the wounded could be devised.

When one views in retrospect the medical and surgical history of World War I, the episode of the Carrel-Dakin treatment presents a strange chapter. This can be attributed not so much to the method's simplicity, obviousness, and effectiveness, as to the bitter and inexplicable opposition that it created, particularly among the French surgeons. The members of the French Academy of Medicine dismissed the method without attempting to test it. On first hearing of Carrel's proposal to employ chemical sterilization of infected wounds, a prominent member of the Surgical Society of France was quoted as saying, "And you bring that from America? Pardon me if I laugh."

Throughout the war Carrel refused to enter into public controversy with his adversaries. He chose to let the facts speak for themselves, on the premise that once the evidence was examined, those who ignored it would look rather foolish. Had he had the inclination, he could have laughed quite heartily at their expense. But he remained serious; man's suffering and untimely loss of life did not produce merriment in him. In 1918 he wrote to Flexner in connection with his investigations: "The practical results would be most important because a great many men are dying on account of our ignorance."

As he was being taken to task to the point of ridicule by Sir Almroth Wright, Carrel made no disparaging remarks about him in public, although Wright's hypertonic saline treatment of wounds proved a complete failure. Carrel was content merely to say in a private letter to Henry Dakin that Wright's strong opinions were based on illusions.

At one point, Carrel was asked by an editor of a medical journal to comment on a paper published by Wright. He replied:

I do not feel like giving my views in the form of a letter in your correspondence columns, or in any other way; I do not want to start any controversy on this subject, because Sir Almroth Wright is a man whom I very much admire, and because today we have to deal with concrete facts and not indulge in academic discussions. Therefore, the following remarks are offered as a mere suggestion for possible editorial comment, but without myself being quoted.

First: The very ingenious experiments described by Sir Almroth Wright in his article are *in vitro* experiments. They are most artificial. A test tube standing on spiked legs, for instance, cannot in any way represent a war wound with diverticula. Experiments must be made under the real clinical conditions of the treatment, if sound conclusions are to be reached. Throughout the article, Sir Almroth Wright uses the most brilliant but dangerous form of reasoning, that is, reasoning by analogy.

Second: Experience gained during the last two years has shown that the practical outcome of Sir Almroth Wright's experiments with hypertonic solution is not successful in sterilizing a wound. In his last article he still speaks of pus, and does not appear to know that at this stage of war surgery we can easily banish suppuration from our hospitals by chemical sterilization. Theories are of no importance; facts alone count. Today no surgeon must be allowed to have a suppurating wound in a hospital.

Third: What is described in Sir Almroth Wright's article as the "Carrel method" is not accurate. . . .

Was Carrel's work so strange and unusual as to merit a strong negative reaction? Hardly: his approach to the treatment of wounds was suggested by common sense. But what Carrel preached contradicted experience with antiseptics accumulated to date. The initial adverse reaction to the new method of wound sterilization becomes understandable from even a cursory look at the history of antisepsis in surgery. New antiseptic techniques have tended to appear either amid great controversy or by accident. Frequently the advocacy of an effective regimen has proven harmful to its proponents, as was the case with the Hungarian physician Ignaz P. Semmelweis. At the Vienna General Hospital Semmelweis showed that childbirth fever, which at the time accounted for the death of about twelve mothers for every hundred deliveries, was spread by the obstetricians themselves. If doctors washed and disinfected their hands, the incidence of childbirth fever could be reduced to virtually nothing. Opponents of Semmelweis's idea attacked him fiercely, caused his complete professional downfall, and brought on his premature death at the age of forty-seven. The English surgeon Lister performed the first aseptic operation in 1865, the very year of Semmelweis's death.

The growth of a unified concept of surgical asepsis resulted from Lister's adaptation of Pasteur's laboratory findings to surgery. Lister's antiseptic—carbolic acid or phenol—was suggested to him by a pharmacist who had seen it used to purify sewage. Lister's idea of preventing postoperative infections, correct as it was, initially also met with much resistance. However, after it was tried and further developed by several Continental (not English) surgeons, Lister's technique finally gained acceptance. But while the principle of applying antiseptics to surgical wounds was agreed upon, there continued to exist a divergence of opinion as to which antiseptic solution to use under what circumstances. Ernst von Behrman abandoned carbolic acid and substituted mercuric bichloride, which he used to irrigate wounds at the close of an operation. Mercuric bichloride was indirectly responsible for the introduction of rubber gloves into surgery. In 1889 the American surgeon William S. Halsted made his scrub nurse wear rubber gloves to protect her hands from contact with the solutions of bichloride of mercury, to which she was sensitive. The gloves were used for this purpose for five years, until Joseph C. Bloodgood recognized their advantage in preventing direct contact of the surgeon's hands with the tissues.

Rigid control of surgical asepsis had been exercised for only about twenty-five years before World War I broke out. In this relatively short span of time various antiseptics and techniques had been tried, discarded, and tried again. The final result of this trial-and-error procedure was the convincing demonstration by Halsted that asepsis and surgical technique must be blended to achieve adequate healing of wounds. But this success in preventing wound infections had been achieved on clean surgical wounds. No major military conflict producing large numbers of casualties with infected wounds took place during the golden era of surgical antisepsis preceding World War I. Thus during World War I the high incidence of wound infections, particularly gas gangrene, caught most surgeons unprepared.

Wounds sustained by soldiers in World War I presented some unique problems. A large portion of the fighting took place on ground heavily contaminated by animal and human excrement. Within a month after the start of the war, fighting in the open was replaced by siege warfare alternating with attacks, counterattacks, and slow advances and retreats. The amount of artillery employed by both sides was unprecedented. Coupled with trench mortars and hand and rifle grenades, these projectiles inflicted lacerations by ragged fragments of metal. This tissue mutilation and destruction produced highly favorable conditions for the proliferation of bacteria, particularly the gas gangrene–producing organisms. Furthermore, in addition to the unfavorable external environment, many wounded soldiers suffered from general physical deterioration due to fatigue, extremely poor living conditions, and dietary deficiencies. Surgeons treating casualties noted an almost universal presence of wound infections in soldiers who had spent time in the trenches, as compared to fresh replacement troops.

In view of these circumstances, the question of antiseptics assumed great importance from the outset. Those available—carbolic acid, bichloride of mercury, tincture of iodine, etc.—proved of little use. When applied to large wounds they either produced a general toxic effect, or so irritated the tissues as to prevent healing. In the presence of serum and wound discharge, they rapidly lost their bactericidal properties. In brief, they seemed to aid rather than inhibit infection and consequently fell into disuse.

However, in view of the ever increasing number of infected wounds and high mortality resulting, the need for new nonirritating antiseptics became apparent to military surgeons. The first step in this direction was taken by Sir Almroth Wright, who suggested irrigating wounds with concentrated salt solutions. This produced little benefit, because many bacteria survive exposure to even highly concentrated salt solutions. This form of treatment was tried without adequate preliminary laboratory work; had such work been done, the outcome would have become readily apparent.

Carrel was quick to formulate the desirable properties of a suitable antiseptic solution. He also knew where to turn in the search for the needed substance. He asked Flexner to find a chemist to work with him. Flexner suggested Henry D. Dakin, who soon produced what Carrel needed. Carrel never thought that an antiseptic, no matter how bactericidal and nonirritating, could by itself decontaminate and heal wounds. Therefore, in addition to securing what he thought the best antiseptic solution available, he designed a special method of applying it.

For the most part, Carrel's work during World War I was performed in Compiègne, a picturesque and historic city located on the river Oise some forty miles northeast of Paris. The city is surrounded by the Forest of Compiègne, where Joan of Arc was captured by the Burgundians. The city was taken by the Germans at the beginning of the war, but retaken by the French and British after the German drive was stopped on the Marne. The Allied counterattack was stopped in turn some dozen miles beyond Compiègne, where the front line remained almost stationary throughout the rest of the war. Consequently, the city remained in the Army Zone, which meant that access to and from it was controlled by the Army. Compiègne later served as Allied Headquarters, and the Armistice was signed in a railroad coach a few miles from the city.

Carrel's road to Compiègne was not a straight one. When the war started he was spending the summer in France. Being a French citizen with previous military service, Carrel was called to active duty with the rank of major and posted to the railroad marshaling yards in Lyons. His job was to sort out the arriving casualties and to channel them to the appropriate military hospitals for treatment. Carrel soon noticed a large number of infected wounds and cases of gas gangrene among the wounded. As the war progressed, the casualties mounted, and it became apparent that it would be a long-drawn-out conflict. Carrel gave up hope of an early return to New York and settled down to the task at hand.

Feeling his talents were not fully utilized in a semi-administrative job, Carrel asked to be transferred to a surgical service in a hospital in Lyons, and he was assigned to work with Professor Léon Bérard at the old Hôtel-Dieu. Carrel would probably have spent the entire war in Lyons, had it not been for James H. Hyde, an influential American acquaintance who lived in France. Hyde arranged for Carrel to see the Foreign Minister, who in turn arranged for Carrel's transfer to the hospital at Compiègne.

The French Army hospital at Compiègne was designated Temporary Hospital No. 21. It was installed in a new hotel, the Rond-Royal, at the end of an avenue leading from the château to the forest and had a capacity of some eighty beds, many in single rooms. The hospital remained in Compiègne until 1918, when it was evacuated because of the final German offensive and the damage sustained by night air attacks.

Although Carrel was a French Army surgeon, and the hospital was maintained by the French Health Service, he could not obtain funds from the French government for even a primitive laboratory. Apparently surgical research laboratories were considered superfluous by the administrators who ran the Health Service. Carrel turned to the Rockefeller Foundation, which agreed to support the laboratory at a cost of some 50,000 francs a year.

At first, Carrel's principal surgical colleague was Georges Dehelly of Le Havre. Dehelly was later succeeded by Doctor M. Guillot. Drs. H. Woimant, Audiganne, and J. Dumas joined the staff subsequently to assist with surgery. The chemical work was done by Maurice Daufresne, who modified the method for producing Dakin's solution. Bacteriology was done by Doctor J. Vincent; calculations of the rates of wound healing were made by Drs. Pierre Lecompte Du Nouy and Jaubert Beaujeu. Toward the end of the war, studies on shock were initiated by Carrel with a physiologist on loan from the French Navy. Major H. Bernaud of the Colonial Army was in charge of the administration and actual operation of the hospital and laboratories. A contingent of experienced volunteer Swiss nurses came to work at the hospital at Theodor Kocher's suggestion. In order to help researchers study abdominal wounds and wounds of the head, in 1916 a first-line field ambulance was assigned to the hospital. Doctor Woimant was appointed surgeon-in-chief of the ambulance.

Before Carrel could start work in earnest, he had to select an antiseptic solution which would be both germicidal and nonirritating. Dakin performed laboratory experiments at the Rockefeller Institute and recommended sodium hypochlorite solution. The first solution prepared by Dakin was made from bleaching powder. Subsequently, Daufresne prepared stable hypochlorite solution by an electrolytic method. The solution retained Dakin's name because it possessed the chief characteristics of the product made from bleaching powder. However, at Compiègne only the electrolytically prepared solution was used.

The principles of treatment of infected wounds set forth by Carrel were simple and sound. They were: mechanical cleansing, surgical debridement (removal of foreign material and excision of devitalized tissue), and adequate chemical sterilization, followed by the secondary closure of the wound.

The initial management of wounds depended entirely on good surgical technique. Carrel felt the surgeon's scalpel was the most effective tool in the treatment of infected wounds. In superficial wounds, scrubbing with neutral soap and water was all that was required. In deep wounds, mechanical cleansing and extensive surgical debridement were carried out. Carrel insisted on the meticulous removal of all foreign bodies, fragments of clothing, bone, etc. Chemical sterilization by the use of Dakin's solution followed wound preparation. In the employment of this antiseptic, the active ingredient of which was hypochlorous acid, emphasis was placed on the time of exposure, contact with microorganisms, and effective concentration. Carrel felt that an ideal antiseptic for the sterilization of wounds should be a short-acting one. It would be neither absorbed nor retained by the injured tissue, thus avoiding local and systemic toxic effects. Hypochlorous acid fulfilled this requirement. Upon contact with tissues, it became inactivated after about an hour. This was why the wounds were sprayed hourly through perforated tubes placed in the wound.

Carrel's reasons for selecting an unstable antiseptic substance can be found in a letter to Halsted. Carrel noted that in some experiments he had conducted about 1909, the curve of healing had become horizontal after application of carbolic acid.

This action of carbolic acid on cicatrization is one of the reasons which determined me to select, among substances studied by Dakin, an unstable substance. A stable chemical substance like mercuric bichloride kills the bacteria but remains on the surface of the wound and decreases the rate of healing. On the contrary, an unstable substance like sodium, magnesium or calcium hypochlorite, or chloramine-T, kills the bacteria and is destroyed a very short time afterwards by the tissues. This explains why such substances interfere very little with the process of healing.

Perhaps the most important contribution made by Carrel in the care of the wounded was his conviction of the impossibility of assessing wound contamination by observation alone until it was too late. As may be expected, this did not make a favorable impression on his colleagues, some of whom felt he was casting aspersions on their professional skill. Carrel instituted "bacteriological control" of the wound, which depended entirely on laboratory studies. The bacterial content of the wound was studied by culturing microorganisms and by daily smears, which provided rough quantitative information on the bacterial population. An easy way to estimate the number of organisms was to make a smear of a wound discharge and to count stained bacteria under a microscope. As the treatment progressed, the bacterial count decreased. Carrel and his co-workers determined that the wound would be closed only when the bacterial count fell to not more than two organisms visible in five oil immersion microscope fields. Thus they showed that rational wound treatment was impossible without bacteriological help, and that a surgeon and bacteriologist must work together. This notion has withstood the test of time; a large portion of surgical progress has been due to bacteriological research. On this subject Carrel wrote to Major W. E. Driver of the Walter Reed Army Hospital: "It is my opinion that in every surgical hospital there should be a bacteriologist to work for the surgeons. We found that, for examination of wounds, trained technicians are sufficient, but they should be trained in a very precise way. An organization might be started, the aim of which should be to supply this type of bacteriologist."

One of the early reports on the progress of Carrel's work in France was given to American surgeons by Charles L. Gibson of the New York Hospital. Gibson came to Belgium and France in 1916 to study conditions at the military hospitals and the methods of treating the wounded. He first visited H. H. M. Lyle, a surgeon of St. Luke's Hospital in New York, who was in charge of the Franco-British Hospital maintained by contributions from Mrs. Chauncey Depew. The hospital was located four miles from Compiègne, nearer the front. With his close proximity to Carrel, Lyle had had ample opportunity to become familiar with the work at Compiègne and to test independently the method of wound treatment Carrel was proposing. Carrel told Gibson that Lyle was one of the two individuals outside Compiègne who understood the principles involved and employed his method correctly from the start. The other was a Belgian, Professor Antoine Depage, who was in charge of a military hospital at La Panne.

In Paris, Gibson found a sharp division of opinion regarding the value of Carrel's method. A small and enthusiastic group which, by his own admission, Gibson himself subsequently joined, was much impressed by the results. This party was composed exclusively of surgeons who took the trouble to go to Compiègne or La Panne to see things for themselves. Gibson admitted that until his own trip to Compiègne he himself had understood neither the principles nor the application of Carrel's treatment.

When hypochlorite was first introduced, its potential was highly exaggerated. Contrary to repeated statements by Carrel, false hopes were raised that it could sterilize tissues so efficiently as to eliminate the necessity for surgical debridement. To add to the difficulties, the solution was applied in a conventional manner by pouring it on the wound or dressing. Finally, it was realized that neither this antiseptic solution nor any other could replace sound surgical treatment. In some quarters, this realization produced a reaction against the Carrel-Dakin method. This reaction was mixed with personal prejudices which even the proven success of the method had failed to dispel.

In his account of the trip to France, Gibson stated:

At one of the meetings [of the Paris Surgical Society] I heard some discussion of the Carrel method, precipitated by a report of Depage, and it was interesting for me to note that one of the prominent opponents of the method had to confirm that he was not personally familiar with its details. The fact was noteworthy, as I found it so frequently repeated. It was astonishing to find that the method should be so little considered by men living only a few miles away from where it was demonstrated. *Per contrare,* all Americans I saw over there had one fixed purpose—to get to Compiègne (not always an easy matter, as it is in the Army Zone) and see things for themselves. Those who did came back most thoroughly convinced of the value of the discovery and the necessity to get it right in order to get good results.

An authoritative commentary on the Carrel-Dakin treatment can be found in the book *War Surgery,* written by the British surgeons Basil Hughes and H. Stanley Banks. These authors formed an opinion on the matter on the basis of three and a half years' experience in treating the wounded during World War I, both in the Western and Eastern theaters of war. They found that the "Carrel-Dakin treatment, when properly and systematically applied to war wounds, gives results superior to those that can be obtained by any other system of treatment." They further observed: "We have witnessed the evolution of the management of wounds from the beginning of the war, and we have seen the undeniably ghastly results of the earlier methods of treatment. Since the advent of this system of treatment the whole outlook has changed and today, on this front and elsewhere, we are witnessing the successful results of a universal and continuous treatment of wounds which has surpassed anything previously tried." Hughes and Banks recorded an average hospital stay of seventeen days for two thousand severely wounded patients included in their study. In preantibiotic days this was not an insignificant achievement.

By the end of 1916, following the publication of Carrel and Georges Dehelly's book *Treatment of Infected Wounds,* the method finally gained acceptance, but not by a majority of French military surgeons. On November 29, 1916, Theodore Roosevelt wrote Carrel:

Through the courtesy of Doctor William O'Neill Sherman I had the pleasure of seeing a number of photographs of the French wounded which were treated by your method. I was literally astounded at the wonderful results secured by this new treatment. I extend to you heartiest congratulations. Even a layman like myself can see the immense value your discovery will have, not only in military but in civil, especially industrial, surgery. If accepted in the army, your new method of treatment will not only conserve life and limb—which from the economic and military standpoint is of vital importance, but it will also alleviate most of the pain and suffering of the wounded. I wish it were possible to standardize this method of treatment so as to give the wounded the best that science affords.

In 1915, while Carrel's method of treating wounds was still in its pioneer stage, some unexpected help in gaining recognition of the work arrived from an American friend. Frederic Coudert was in London with Arthur Balfour, who had succeeded Churchill as First Lord of the Admiralty. Balfour told Coudert of his great chagrin in finding large numbers of the wounded returning on ships from Gallipoli dying of gangrene.

Gallipoli was one of the worst Allied fiascos in World War I. Conceived and presided over by Churchill, this operation precipitated his resignation as First Lord of the Admiralty, and considerably embarrassed the British government. The embarrassment was well justified. British and Australian forces had landed at Gallipoli on April 25, 1915, but failed to break through the Turkish defenses. Lord Kitchener said that he had been misled by the Admiralty as to the number of men required for the operation and that, at the rate things were going, it was impossible for him to provide the needed troops. When Lloyd George asked Churchill at the beginning of the campaign whether it would develop into a long operation, he had replied, "Oh, no! Nothing of the kind. We shall go through in quite a short time." The operation lasted until January 1916, though the decision to evacuate Gallipoli had been reached on November 15. The British casualties exceeded 214,000.

Having a large number of wounded at Gallipoli as an aftermath of a blunder which had caught the public eye was bad enough; having them die of gangrene on the way home was worse. When Coudert told Balfour of the success Carrel had had in eliminating gangrene from wounds, Balfour asked for the address of Carrel's hospital, telegraphed Carrel, and asked him for help. Henry Dakin was sent to the Admiralty, and as a result the transports bringing the wounded from Gallipoli were equipped for treating the wounded with the Carrel-Dakin method.

Carrel encountered difficulties with the French Army Health Service from the very start of the war. After all, his appointment to direct the hospital at Compiègne was engendered through political pressure by an American, and supported by the Rockefeller Foundation. French Army Health Service officers naturally resented interference from above and from abroad; after all, it emphasized their own inadequacies. It is therefore not surprising to find that what Carrel recommended was either simply ignored or resisted. One such recommendation dealt with the common practice of immediately closing wounds, even if they might be contaminated. On December 16, 1916, the Chief of the Surgical Section of Chartres, Major Schwartz, sent a report to the Chief of Health Service which dealt with the subject.

The report, made "on the advice of the Chief Doctor of the Hospital of Compiègne," stated that the immediate suturing of contaminated wounds, even after a thorough debridement, was a dangerous one and should be abandoned, since these wounds almost inevitably became infected and had to be reopened. This report suggested that the problem of initial wound management was serious enough to warrant a special study. To the best of the author's knowledge, this suggestion did not go further than the official files. It is of interest to note that the practice of not immediately suturing potentially contaminated wounds met with wide acceptance after the experience gained during the Vietnam War.

The attitude of the French medical establishment toward Carrel and his American friends was reflected by Flexner's nomination for election as a Free Associate of the French Academy of Medicine. The sponsor of the nomination, Dr. Netter, wrote Carrel on November 21, 1916, that he had "just left a secret meeting of the Academy where a report was read placing Flexner in the lead for the election of Free Associates. The Commission last Tuesday pronounced very categorically in his favor, and I made great use of the letter which you addressed to me." However, Flexner's election did not materialize.

A very energetic campaign ensued, tinged with chauvinism, which ended in the Commission's resignation. Flexner was blamed for being a brother of Abraham Flexner, a well-known educator, who had German university teaching connections, and for not having signed the manifesto condemning German activities. Netter remarked that it was undignified for the Academy to accept or reject a candidate because he failed to sign a political document when a candidate had long been designated by the appropriate commission and was judged worthy. These arguments were supported by many, but failed to convince the majority. Therefore he asked Carrel to intervene again, and to repeat what had already been said regarding the value of impartiality and the sympathy that Flexner had for France. The election of Flexner now became a matter of principle. It would add nothing to his merit, but a boycott of Flexner would be an unwarranted affront to him, and a grave error for the Academy.

Carrel replied on November 23, 1916:

I thank you very sincerely for having wanted to write me about the election of a Free Associate to the Academy of Medicine. The attitude of the Academy is absurd and did him [Flexner] a great wrong. But the Academy of Paris does not have the power either to raise or to lower a man such as Flexner. I think, therefore, that it would be useless to write about this subject to the President of the Commission.

Problems with French military authorities manifested themselves in several areas. Requests for personnel were denied whenever possible. The simple matter of referring patients for special surgery was complicated. Carrel wanted to send a soldier with a leg shortened because of a wound to a special military hospital in Paris for corrective surgery. The surgeon at the hospital, though willing to perform the operation, advised Carrel informally that a certain Doctor Cotte was opposed to issuing a transfer order, and was of the opinion that the wounded man had been cured and did not require further treatment. The surgeon in Paris felt that if he were to insist on having the patient transferred, this would provoke a "disagreeable incident." He then explained to Carrel how the red tape could be circumvented and the patient transferred anyway.

Théodore Tuffier was made the Ministry of War's Special Inspector of the Health Service. During the war he inspected different hospitals and organized courses to teach war surgery. Tuffier's sympathy for Carrel reputedly earned him the "cold-shoulder treatment" from many French Army surgeons. Even a man of Tuffier's stature could not break through the defenses of the French medical military establishment.

Carrel's associates also did not escape the weight of the Establishment. On July 28, 1916, Dehelly received an official reprimand for writing a letter to the father of a deceased officer concerning the reason for the officer's death. A month later he was sent to Romania for "the large-scale study of the treatment of wounded by the sterilizing method." Dehelly remained a lieutenant until 1918, when he was promoted to captain. At the time, he was in charge of the surgical services and teaching at the War Demonstration Hospital in New York. Since most of his students were captains and majors, Dehelly's rank of lieutenant must have seemed rather odd.

For his service in World War I, Carrel received several decorations: Officier de l'Ordre de Léopold (Belgium); Ordre de Commandeur de l'Étoile Polaire (Sweden); Cross of a Knight Commander of St. Michael and St. George (Great Britain); and the Distinguished Service Medal (U.S.A.). Significant French decorations were conspicuously absent, nor was he promoted in rank. He had received the Legion of Honor (Commander Class) in 1913, following the Nobel Prize award. When Carrel and Dehelly's book on the treatment of infected wounds was published in English, the introduction was written by Sir Anthony H. Boulby, the Surgeon General of the British Army Medical Service.

Carrel remained aloof during the war and refrained from publicly criticizing his French colleagues. However, privately he maintained a low opinion of the French surgical establishment. In a letter to Tuffier concerning Tuffier's appearance before the American Surgical Association, written him in New York, Carrel said: "You are just exactly the man to represent France at the meetings of the Scientific Societies, and it is very important that you should come to make people here forget the very bad representatives who have been sent by the French Government during the War."

However, Carrel's distaste for the mediocrity of French government officialdom should not be confused with his feeling for France and his countrymen. He was deeply concerned about the wounded Allied soldiers and the outcome of the war. Whatever criticisms can be leveled against Carrel, lack of contribution to the war effort could not be one of them. Not only was he laboring to improve the care of the wounded, but he also lent his support to various organizations with casualties. Among these was the American Fund for French Wounded. When Carrel agreed to participate in its organization, Mrs. B. J. Lathrop, Chairman of the Fund, wrote: "You must know the people of the United States have such profound respect and admiration for you and your work, that your approval of what we are doing in France will mean a great deal to your many admirers who are so eager to help in the small work that we are able to do."

The success achieved with the treatment of infected wounds did not go unnoticed in the enemy camp. The *Deutsche Medizinische Wochenschrift* of November 16, 1916, carried the following note signed by A. Bier:

I have your letter regarding the method of treating infected wounds with Dakin's solution, developed by Doctor Carrel and his co-workers and now so widely used in France. You ask (1) whether this method has justified its reports, (2) whether the procedure is something entirely new, and (3) whether it constitutes a great discovery.

(1) I cannot personally judge whether this procedure is all that the French claim, or is of greater value than antiseptic methods which have been brought into prominence by the war, for I have had no experience with it. To my knowledge, there have been only a few experiments made with this method in the German Army.

(2) The procedure is not a radically new one. As long as antiseptics have been in existence, the problem has been to find an antiseptic which is bactericidal, but which will not

injure the tissues. Countless physicians have studied this problem without solving it. It is largely due to the fact that no solution of the problem could be found, that asepsis took the place of antiseptics. Even before Lister's time, chlorine was largely used as an antiseptic either as chlorine water, calcium chloride, or as sodium hypochlorite in from 5% to 6% solutions. I cannot say whether Dakin's hypochlorite of soda substantially excels these substances. In former days, infected wounds were also permanently irrigated with antiseptic solutions.

(3) But if the procedure in question has proved itself to be really as valuable as is reported, I believe it to be a great discovery. If the reports are true, then the long-needed and long-sought antiseptic (which is either directly or indirectly bactericidal and can be used without injuring the tissues) has been found.

That the idea is an old one and that similar means have been used before does not belittle the service to science of those men who have now elaborated a working method.

If the Germans were not enthusiastic about an Allied discovery, they at least maintained scientific objectivity. One could only wish Carrel's French colleagues had done the same.

The entry of the United States into the war in 1917 brought a surge of activity in the U.S. Army Medical Department. To aid the government in the war effort, the Rockefeller Institute organized a hospital on its grounds for the purpose of transmitting the experience gained in France to the Army medical personnel. On July 16, 1917, the opening of the New Rockefeller Demonstration Hospital for War Training at Avenue A and 64th Street, New York, was announced in the *New York Herald*:

Unusual interest is centered around the project, as it will be in the charge of Doctor Alexis Carrel, who has received a leave of absence from the French government for that purpose. Since the beginning of the war he has been the Director of the Research Hospital at Compiègne, France, operated by the French War Department in conjunction with the Institute. It was there that Doctor Carrel successfully applied his new method for treating wounds.

Carrel was to be assisted by Adrian V. S. Lambert of the College of Physicians and Surgeons, and Dehelly, who by then had returned from Romania.

The sixty-six-bed hospital at the Rockefeller Institute did not look imposing. There were fifteen long, narrow, unpainted wooden buildings on the lower terrace of the grounds in front of the Institute. Designed by Charles Butler as a completely self-sufficient facility, the hospital could be taken down and reassembled in two weeks. A special feature of the field hospital was the walls: five-foot wall sections were hinged from the bottom, so that in an emergency they could be lowered and the patients moved out instantly. The purpose of the Demonstration Hospital was manifold. American military surgeons were to be instructed there in the treatment of infected wounds, while civilian surgeons would be offered training in the care of trauma patients.

On the occasion of the hospital's opening, the *New York Telegram* described Carrel as "one of the most modest of men." This was evidenced by his insistence at all times that credit be given generously to those who had worked with him. He did not claim to have developed anything new in surgical procedure. His colleagues had known of hypochlorite of soda for decades, and irrigation in itself was not a novelty.

After three years' absence, Carrel had returned to New York. However, his work had tired him out. He did not even go to Chicago to attend a surgical meeting. He wrote to Alton Ochsner that he could not go because he was overtired and did not feel he should take part in the discussion of as important a subject in his present physical condition. He said the pressure he was under, first for three years in France and then throughout the entire summer at the War

Demonstration Hospital, had rendered him temporarily unfit.

The first class reported at the War Demonstration Hospital on August 2, 1917, and the last class completed its work on March 29, 1919. Instruction was given to the medical officers of the Army and Navy, to enlisted men in both services, to civilian surgeons, and to female nurses of the Red Cross and civilian hospitals.

The War Demonstration Hospital attracted much attention in professional, military, and governmental circles. Winston Churchill visited the hospital and Carrel's laboratory at the Rockefeller Institute on April 25, 1918. He was much interested in tissue cultures, and spent a great deal of time looking at them through a microscope. Yet despite the well-recognized success of Carrel's method of wound treatment, Arthur Dean Bevan, a Professor of Surgery from Chicago, published a highly critical letter on the War Demonstration Hospital in the *Journal of the American Medical Association* (November 17, 1917). But America was not France. Among American surgeons, the academic position alone did not qualify one for unconditional respect, and Carrel did not have to come to his own defense. Edward Wallace Lee, a New York surgeon, took Bevan to task in his letter of December 10, 1917: "You spent two hours at the Carrel Clinic, upon which you base your judgment of a complete method which took years to develop. It takes from at least two to four weeks to get proper knowledge of the technique and of the results obtained. I am glad to tell you that the case you saw operated upon on October 11th, an acute infection of parapatellar bursa, left the hospital on November 15th cured." Lee pointed out that Bevan completely misunderstood the method, which was based on a combination of clinical, pathological, bacteriological and chemical knowledge combined with minute observation of clinical detail so often overlooked by even the most skilled surgeons. It was obviously the most up-to-date way of treating infected wounds—and all wounds in the war were infected. The value of the method was not dependent on the literature, but was based on the statistics.

In the same connection Lee, who was by then on active duty in the U.S. Army, sent a report to the Surgeon General, General W. C. Gorgas, officially evaluating the work of the War Demonstration Hospital. In the covering memorandum he said:

My object in this report is to emphasize the value of the Carrel Technique when carried out according to the principles Carrel and Dakin have established. . . . I have been in the practice of surgery 30 years and feel qualified to pass judgement, and I do emphatically state that if the technique is carried out as set forth by Major Carrel it is far superior and more efficient than any procedure now before the surgical profession. But surgeons must be trained in this technique in order to accomplish the desired results, and strict observation of minute details is absolutely essential.

Two letters of reply to Bevan were published in the *Journal of the American Medical Association,* December 15, 1917. One was from Joseph C. Bloodgood, the other from A. T. McCormick of Bowling Green, Kentucky. Bloodgood said he could not agree with Bevan's observations, and that he did not claim Carrel's method to be the ultimate solution to the problem. However, he did claim Carrel's method to be a great contribution to wound treatment and was sure the ultimate treatment would be due to, and based on, Carrel's clinical and scientific research. McCormick stated that no man, however distinguished himself, can be a final judge on scientific matters. If he be in a position of great responsibility conferred on him by the profession, he has no right to give publicity to a personal feeling. This lends the weight of his authority to a destructive criticism without a semblance of investigation or knowledge of a conscientious scientific investigator and his associates. He further said Bevan's misconception of Carrel's technique and purposes was the only thing made plain in his letter.

Halsted carefully followed Carrel's work in France and came to see things for himself at the War Demonstration Hospital. He became convinced of the practicality of Carrel's method of wound sterilization, and was instrumental in popularizing its application to civilian practice.

In March 1917 Halsted visited Carrel in New York. On returning to Baltimore, he wrote: "My visit to you was very stimulating and I only regret that I cannot return to France with you to keep in closer touch with your problems, which should be mine also. Your method of wound treatment will surely be universally and promptly adopted in this country. Those of us who are convinced apostles must see to it that it must be considered a misdemeanor not to employ it."

As the year 1917 drew to a close, the work at the War Demonstration Hospital was well under way. The time came for Carrel to return to France to resume his duties and studies at Compiègne. Carrel's last months in New York were saddened by news from Canada: Adelstan de Martigny had died on November 15. Meanwhile Dehelly remained in New York, where he had done extremely well at the War Demonstration Hospital, both as surgeon and as teacher.

In France, Carrel's mind became occupied with two pressing problems: abdominal surgery and shock. He devised an apparatus for warming the patient, and felt it mandatory to discover a better fluid to give intravenously, instead of saline or Ringer's solution. Numerous experiments were also performed with intra-abdominal instillation of Dakin's solution. It was found that hypochlorite could be infused into the peritoneal cavity, provided its concentration did not exceed 3 percent.

Compiègne hospital was evacuated because of the German spring offensive of 1918, and bomb damage inflicted on March 23. Carrel was not in Compiègne when the hospital was bombed, but at the front with his ambulance. On returning, he remarked: "As nobody was killed, we could not wish for a finer end of the Compiègne hospital."

Since Carrel's interest in shock required work on animals and suitable housing was in short supply, the hospital was moved to Noisiel and the laboratory to Saint-Cloud. Thus the laboratory of the Rockefeller Institute became a separate entity. In this laboratory Carrel's last involvement with war surgery took place. The Rockefeller Institute asked William T. Porter, a physiologist from Harvard, to go to France to study shock in war casualties, determine its cause, and find a remedy. Porter visited Carrel at Compiègne, then proceeded to La Panne and the front-line aid stations, where he took serial blood pressure measurements and recorded respirations and pulse on soldiers a few minutes after they were wounded. He noticed severe respiratory impairment in casualties with open fractures and concluded that all shock was caused by fat emboli. To combat respiratory distress, he made a respiratory assistance device. Although he was correct with respect to fat emboli, he overlooked the so-called "hemorrhagic shock," a condition resulting from blood loss.

Carrel, on the other hand, was convinced that in the majority of cases a drop in blood pressure was the direct result of blood loss, and set out to prove this in his laboratory. He first experimented with replacing blood by serum and gum solutions in experimental animals, and worked on isolated hearts perfused through a Langendorf column (simple gravity perfusion). A large number of experiments were made to determine whether there was a constant relationship between the volume of a hemorrhage and the fall in blood pressure. The relation between the volume of hemorrhage and fluctuations in blood pressure depended not only on the quantity of shed blood, but on other factors as well. As for the treatment of hemorrhage, whole blood or washed red blood cells provided best results. Saline or lactated Ringer's solution could be used prior to blood transfusions to re-establish quickly, though temporarily, the volume of lost blood. This treatment is exactly the same as used now.

In the United States, the effort that Carrel made on behalf of the General Medical Board of the Council of National Defense's Advisory Commission did not go unnoticed. Upon dissolution of the Board after the termination of hostilities, Newton D. Baker, Secretary of War, wrote Carrel:

I cannot permit the occasion to pass without expressing my grateful appreciation of the work you have done and the singleness of spirit with which your associates and yourself have devoted themselves to the great work which was placed in the hands of the General Medical Board of the Council of National Defense. While it would be invidious to make any appraisal of the work of your Board in comparison with any other agency organized in the emergency, I need not, I know, assure you that the government appreciates deeply and genuinely the great and essential contribution which has been made by the Medical Board in the mobilization of the civilian profession, its classification as to the specialties and fitness and in the preparation and organization of information which would enable the Department to secure from the manufacturers of the country the vitally necessary instruments and supplies for the medical care and attention of our men in the field.

Reflecting on his surgical experience during the war, Carrel wrote General Finney on the need for special training in bone surgery: "Last spring I had an opportunity to investigate about 500 cases of osteomyelitis in France. It was very interesting to observe that some of the wounded had been in a condition of suppuration since August and September of 1914, in spite of the many operations performed, although the surgeons were often men of national or even international reputation." Carrel at first thought these failures were due to the nature of the lesions, but then he ran into two surgeons whose results with bone surgery were far superior to those of the best in France. Their astounding results were due to the fact that they were trained in bone surgery. Therefore Carrel recommended that the U.S. Army institute a special training program in this field. Time proved Carrel correct; orthopedic surgery indeed became a separate specialty.

Immediately after the Armistice Carrel stopped in London to rest alone for a few days. He took time to reflect on the past four years, and summarized his feelings about his part in World War I in a letter to a nephew:

I have just spent the most terrible years of my life, not because of the War, but because I had to live in an atmosphere of incompetence, vanity, and jealousy which made all efforts useless. It is also very painful to think every day of the same thing. I did what I wanted to do, but the success gave me no pleasure, because its practical results were minimal. I would have been able to save a great number of men. Thanks to French medicine, that was not possible.

8 ♞ The New Laboratory

The war had affected Carrel in several ways. First of all, it left him physically tired, if not exhausted. Second, it reinforced his feelings bordering on contempt toward the way things were done in France. Third, the knowledge of German behavior in occupied parts of France and Belgium left a deep impression on him. The Pasteur Institute of Lille had not only been damaged by the Germans, but emptied of most of its scientific instruments and materials. The horses conditioned and used for the production of antisera had been confiscated. The wife of Doctor A. Calmette, an acquaintance of Carrel's, had been deported and held hostage in Germany. Hostages had also been taken in Belgium. For people brought up in a civilized environment, such reversions to barbarism were difficult to understand. The war, with all its ramifications, ended the era of external gentlemanly behavior, and for Carrel dispelled any illusions about possible changes for the better in Europe.

The service Carrel rendered to France during the war made him no more acceptable in his native land than before the war. Return to New York provided him with a much-needed change from a crude and chaotic environment to normal life. Instead of having to deal with the mediocre gentlemen of the French Health Service, he could once again rely on the sound judgment of Flexner. But return to America was not without its problems. Carrel had to move into new laboratories, and much of the work had to be started over again. This required stamina which he found difficult to regain.

During the war Flexner served in the Army, but he had remained at the Institute so as to supervise the War Demonstration Hospital. The Institute continued its work, despite considerable loss of staff. Flexner succeeded in keeping the nucleus of scientists together so that organization was not permanently lost nor even seriously damaged. Therefore the full-scale operations of the Institute were quickly re-established once the war was over.

As for Carrel, he was seeking a new orientation in his work. He had already done much to advance new surgical techniques. The application of these to humans would come with time. Nearing fifty, he would give up surgical experiments, which required exactness, good vision, and physical endurance. In so doing, he must have had in mind the example of Paul Ehrlich, who after discovering 606 and Salvarsan, tried to keep his hands in the clinical applications of these drugs and by so doing made a nuisance of himself.

Carrel had demonstrated how, by using small round needles and delicate sutures of silk, vascular surgery could be performed with relative ease. In France he proved Lister's broad concepts of antisepsis to be correct, but close contact with the majority of his French colleagues left a bad taste in his mouth. He simply did not want to waste more time on these people. His method of vascular anastomosis, his needles and the fine Vaseline-coated silk sutures, as well as his technique for treating infected wounds, were not used on patients. Only the future would show whether these would find a broad application in clinical surgery.

In the last year of the war and in the immediate postwar period Carrel developed a desire to extend his studies in the area of broad biological significance. He was personally divorced from tissue culture work for over five years. He could not devote a major portion of time to it entirely. By studying cells in culture and by beginning to work on organ culture, he hoped to uncover the principles of their growth and function. To devote himself to this type of work he had to exchange the suturing of vessels with silk sutures to growing cells and organs in specially designed containers of glass. The tissue-culture glassware, including the "Carrel Flask," proved as important to tissue culture as the atraumatic needles and silk sutures were to vascular surgery.

No matter how hard Carrel tried, things were just not the same after the war. In 1924 he wrote to a German colleague, Professor O. Wenzel:

How little we realized what would happen to the world and that our lives would be profoundly modified by a war. I wish to express to you my deep sympathy for the sorrow which the war brought to you.

When I came back from the war, I reorganized my laboratories at the Rockefeller Institute entirely. I realized that surgical problems should be investigated from a broader point of view, and I transformed the laboratories so that I can study any subject with different methods, physiological, chemical, and physical.

Modernized after the war, Carrel's new laboratory attracted many visitors. A commentary by one of them, the English surgeon Robert Dalbey, is interesting. His account of visits to some leading medical centers in the United States, entitled "An English Surgeon in America," was published in 1926 in the *Japan Advertiser.* Not originally intended for publication, the text was written as a private letter to a friend in Tokyo, who thought an evaluation of American medical institutions by a leading British surgeon would have general interest.

I had a wonderful three weeks at the Rockefeller Institute in New York. The surgery in general in that city did not particularly impress me. The one outstanding experience was a wonderful blood transfusion done by Unger. I find that New York surgeons have no great reputation in America. But it was all so different at the Rockefeller. I lunched with Alexis Carrel and spent a morning with him. He has now given up blood-vessel surgery . . . and spends all his time with tissue culture. He showed me his famous piece of fibroblastic tissue that has been growing for 14 years. It says a lot for the organization of his department that the medium has been changed every 24 hours for that period and never once been forgotten.

Carrel's operative theatre is all black; so are the gowns of his assistants and himself. In fact, all is black, with the exception of his operation area. He can get his fine needles made only in England. It takes a month of effort before his theatre sister can thread these needles; the filament of silk is pushed through the eye of the needle obliquely along the shank. The operating theatre for animals is as perfectly equipped as any I've seen for human beings.

The simple quality of all at luncheon impressed me very much. The most junior laboratory assistant sits alongside the most senior and distinguished chief. I saw Noguchi and Rous wandering in the luncheon room, unable to get a seat. All have the same food, which was bad, and badly cooked. But there was no fault to find with the mental food. I almost used the much abused word "democratic" when I saw the absolute equality of all.

World War I left a gap in Carrel's life. He had to make not only professional postwar adjustments, but personal ones as well. Anne, Carrel's wife of less than a year, had worked with him at Compiègne and remained in France while Carrel came to New York to help set up the War Demonstration Hospital. In Compiègne the Carrels had lived as in a glass house, with little privacy and no time for personal affairs. After the destruction of Compiègne hospital in 1918, the Carrels had been separated; Mrs.

Carrel followed the hospital while Carrel spent most of his time at the laboratory in Saint-Cloud. They met in Paris whenever they could.

Upon returning to New York, Carrel made a genuine effort to settle in the United States. He started looking for a house and found several to his liking. However, his wife did not share his enthusiasm for America. Instead of buying a house near New York, in 1922 the Carrels bought the island of Saint-Gildas off the coast of Normandy, with an old stone house, and this became their home. Mrs. Carrel spent most of her time there. Her visits to New York became infrequent. Carrel used her poor health as an excuse for her staying away from New York. Paragraphs such as one found in a letter written to a colleague in 1942 were typical: "My wife has been in poor health these last few years on account of the hardships she suffered during the War. For this reason, she has not been able to come to America." This leaves something unsaid. Had Carrel been seriously concerned about his wife's health, he would probably have brought her to America, rather than leaving her alone in France. He knew most of the leading medical men in the United States, and all indications suggest that, with rare exceptions, he trusted them much more than their French counterparts. Furthermore, it is difficult to envision what hardships Mrs. Carrel suffered during the war; for the most part, she lived in Compiègne in a luxury hotel converted into a hospital, surrounded by orderlies, and with plenty of food available.

Carrel would travel to Saint-Gildas each summer to spend some three months on his island, while he lived the remainder of the year in New York pretty much as he had done before his marriage and before the war. His trips to Saint-Gildas were often pictured as sojourns into creativity, which was not altogether true. While the summers on the island provided him with much-needed rest and tranquillity, he did not do much work there. Most of his writing was done in New York, as is evident from a letter to his nephew written on Saint-Gildas on July 18, 1938: "I can write only very slowly. Saint-Gildas, strangely, is not a favorable place for intellectual work, at least not for me."

In the early and mid-1920s Carrel made several attempts to bring his wife into the midstream of American life, but apparently he did not succeed. Years later she admitted that she liked neither the United States nor most of the Americans with whom Carrel associated. Mrs. Carrel's reluctance to spend much time in America manifested itself in several ways. Sometimes she refused to cross the Atlantic because of poor health, which in retrospect appears a bit exaggerated, since she outlived her husband by some thirty years. On occasions when she was in America, and Carrel had made arrangements to spend the holidays there, at the last moment she would find a reason for having to return to France. One of the last episodes of this kind took place in 1938. Carrel had made arrangements to spend two weeks at the Skytop Lodge in Pennsylvania, but on March 23, 1938, he suddenly wrote the manager that Mrs. Carrel had been called back to France very suddenly, so that their plans were changed entirely.

While Carrel was in New York, his preoccupation with laboratory research was intense. Several major studies were carried out by him and his colleagues in the 1920s and early 1930s. These included experiments with animal and human tumors, radiation, propagation of viruses, and multiple studies on a large colony of mice. Except for those with mice, these studies depended heavily on tissue-culture techniques.

The description of these studies by George W. Corner, the author of *A History of the Rockefeller Institute, 1901–1953: Origin and Growth* (1964), is noteworthy. This presumably official publication of the Institute states:

Few people, even within The Rockefeller Institute, knew of Alexis Carrel's most elaborate venture into the field of cancer research. Both as a surgeon and as a speculative thinker, Carrel was fascinated by the problem of malignancy. His laboratory's command of tissue culture methods enabled him and his associates to conduct or to cooperate in a number of investigations of the behavior of cancer cells *in vitro* and of environmental factors in the culture media which affect their growth and multiplication. Finally, he developed ideas of his own about the cause of cancer and obtained from Flexner ample financial support with which to try them out. The story of this venture is almost wholly undocumented.

Corner makes it sound as if no one had ever heard of Carrel's cancer studies. But someone must have—he received the Nordhoff-Jung Prize for Cancer Research in 1931. Indeed, between 1923 and 1931 Carrel and his associates published no fewer than fourteen papers dealing with experimental sarcomas of fowl (Rous sarcoma) and rats (Jensen sarcoma). In addition, numerous papers by them on tissue culture which had a bearing on malignancy appeared in scientific journals.

In a biographical sketch of Carrel written for the American Philosophical Society, the same author, when describing Carrel's studies with cancer, says: "The study, concealed from fellow-scientists, conducted without adequate controls, and disregarding other possible causes of cancer, came to naught. This episode is sufficient evidence that Carrel was not a profound analyst, but rather a superb applied scientist advancing the progress of biology and surgery, much as Thomas A. Edison advanced the practical use of electricity."

With regard to studies on cancer, this is a rather harsh statement. Not only did Carrel and his co-workers publish on the subject, but Carrel frequently spoke at scientific meetings about his work with malignant cells. True, Carrel's studies of malignant tumors in animals, and of cancer cells in tissue culture, failed to reveal the cause or causes of the disease. However, scores of respected scientists have traveled, and are still traveling, the same road. To imply that their efforts went for naught, and to cite this as evidence that these people were not profound analysts, is presumptuous, unless of course Corner knew of a "profound" analyst who had discovered the cause of cancer but kept it a secret.

Among the many things that Carrel did during the period of his "secret endeavors" was to make motion pictures of living cells in culture. The construction of microflasks for growing tissue cultures permitted the use of the oil immersion objective of the microscope without special preparation of the cultures. Cinematographic recordings of tissue-culture experiments are now a routine procedure, but in Carrel's day the technique was still in its infancy.

Carrel made detailed studies of the modes of locomotion of certain cells (macrophages and fibroblasts) and the effect on them of the chemical composition of the medium. The cinematographic apparatus Carrel used was made for him by an optical engineer, Heinz Rosenberger, who had emigrated to America from Germany after the war. Rosenberger installed a new timing device on the photographic apparatus which made time-lapse photography possible. Thus the cultures could be photographed for periods of from twenty-four to forty-eight hours.

The movies of the living cells made by Carrel and Rosenberger were of good quality. In April 1924 Flexner showed some of them at the meeting of the National Academy of Sciences in Washington. On April 29 he wrote to Carrel from the Hotel Lafayette: "I was at the New Academy building. . . . I saw a good many of the men who had seen the moving picture of your growing cells—among them, leaders of the Academy, and they were very enthusiastic about it."

Carrel's interest in the propagation of viruses was shared by Flexner, who said in a letter written in the summer of 1933:

I am so much impressed with the great significance of your observations on the increase of certain viruses in egg yolk that I am inclined to suggest that you delay publication until you can run through a new series of tests in the autumn. The importance of observation is so great, the results are so out of harmony with present-day belief and theory, that I should like to add to them the additional weight of confirmation a year hence. I say "a year hence" because I note that the best results in the experiments were obtained in the autumn and earlier winter months.

The experiments with mice were conducted on a large scale, and reports of the progress in the "mousery" were made in detail. A 1930 report on the Division of Experimental Surgery devoted five pages to the studies conducted on mice. A description of the work done with mouse tumors was given in the 1931 annual report.

The "mousery" project was extremely ambitious. Initially, it was to continue for three years, its purpose being to study 12,000 mice of many strains for several generations under different environmental conditions and with varied diets. Much time and care were given to planning the building that would house so many mice. The mousery was built directly upon the low tile roof of the power house. It contained three main units: the greenhouse, the house and sterilizing rooms, and the office laboratory and a kitchen. The greenhouse was carefully constructed and screened, so that neither insects nor wild mice could find their way inside.

The mousery experiments showed that variation of diet sufficed to bring about marked changes in developing animals. In one of the populations of inbred mice, the average weight of the young at the age of one month was 6 grams, while in another population of the same inbred mice it was 11 grams. The duration of life was also easily modified. In a large group of animals subjected to the best regimen available, 9 percent of the mice lived over 20 months. In another group receiving exactly the same food and care, but starved for two days a week, the number living more than 20 months rose to 60 percent.

A summary of the results of the mice studies was presented by Carrel in the Hitchcock Lecture at the University of California, Berkeley, in 1936. In view of later developments, the studies may be of limited significance today, but they represented quite an accomplishment and were innovative at the time. They demonstrated that, up to a certain point, environmental factors may override genetic potential. But by far the most intriguing concept derived by Carrel from these experiments was the notion that such studies might someday help improve humans without resorting to eugenics.

In the mid-1930s Carrel began working with Karl Landsteiner and Raymond C. Parker on the immune properties of serum proteins. Landsteiner had discovered the A, B, O groupings of human blood and later, with S. Wiener, the Rh factor. He was also the first to demonstrate the experimental transmission of poliomyelitis from man to monkeys.

Around 1930 Carrel became somewhat disillusioned with the applicability of cell and tissue-culture techniques to surgery, and became seriously concerned with the problem of cultivating organs. He explained his plans to Rosenberger and asked him to construct the needed apparatus. The apparatus was to have circulating fluid regulated by an automatic mechanism. None of the pumps that had been built to date had fulfilled Carrel's requirements. Rosenberger made a new magnetic perfusion pump. The apparatus was constructed primarily of glass, but it also contained several metal parts which came in contact with perfusion fluid. The piston into which an iron core was fused was set in motion by two electromagnets which created a magnetic field. Two solenoids surrounded the pump cylinder. They were magnetized intermittently by an electric current which was closed and opened by a four-pole mercury switch. The efficiency of the pump was one milliliter of fluid per stroke and ninety strokes per minute. The Rosenberger pump was highly efficient and was mechanically perfect, but it had one drawback: it could not be sterilized readily. Thus organs placed in the pump became contaminated with bacteria. The machine could not be used for the purpose for which it was intended.

In the years between the wars, in addition to the laboratory studies Carrel developed an interest in the broad implication of scientific research. Carrel's concern for France was also ever present. Despite his disappointment in the way things were done in his native country, he held out hope for future improvement, and maintained faith in the French people. Since his livelihood did not depend on French institutions, he could afford to criticize them. This he did freely, both in private and in public. In many instances, when he criticized the democratic form of government, he was really speaking of democracy as practiced in France. He had little firsthand knowledge of the governments in other countries, including the United States. Since he had never taken out American citizenship or owned any property, his dealings with various governmental agencies were through the Rockefeller Institute. Except for a brief period after his retirement, in the United States he spent little leisure time outside New York, returning instead to France three months each year. The time of his American trips was occupied with professional matters. He would almost always return to New York immediately on completion of the lecture he was giving or the meeting he was attending.

In Carrel's opinion, shortly after the war France had returned to the usual political bickering, manipulating, and high-style living. The development of science and medicine was neglected. Carrel made it clear that he thought priorities in France were mixed up. He felt the French people, talented as they were, to be fully capable of closing the gap in scientific development. The country had adequate resources to attain this end, if only it channeled them in the right direction.

In 1920–1921 the need for radiotherapy for cancer patients and radium for research became apparent. Yet neither the French government nor the private financial and industrial sectors wanted to undertake this absolutely necessary expenditure. French physicians and scientists turned abroad for help. Carrel received a letter from a colleague in Lyons, asking him to help secure money in America for the purchase of radium. Carrel replied he was very sorry to learn that radium could not be secured for the patients in Lyons. Regarding the possibility of getting help from America he regretted that it was absolutely out of the question. Everyone in the United States knew that a good many men in the industrial cities of France made a great deal of money during the war. It was the duty of these Frenchmen to give the hospitals and the poor the radium they needed.

The situation reached ridiculous proportions when, in the whole of France, no money could be found to buy one gram of radium for Madame Curie. Without this she could not continue her world-acclaimed work. To help in the matter, a Marie Curie Radium Fund was started in America. Chaired by Mrs. William Brown Meloney, the Fund's aim was to raise enough money by subscription to buy radium for the noted French scientist. Carrel was appalled. Had his countrymen lost all their dignity and pride? Although personally very accommodating and courteous to Madame Curie, he refused to participate in the drive, citing the same reasons he gave to the Lyons colleague. However, enough money was raised to purchase the radium, and President Harding was to give it to Madame Curie at a White House ceremony. Carrel was invited to attend the ceremony, but he wrote to Mrs. Robert G. Mead, who was arranging the Fund's guest list: "I appreciate very much your courtesy in wishing me to receive an invitation for the ceremony at the White House when President Harding is to give Madame Curie a gram of radium, and I regret exceedingly that it will be impossible for me to leave New York on that day. Unfortunately, none of my associates feel that they can go either, so that I am unable to take advantage of your courteous suggestion to send the name of a friend to you." So as not to give the wrong impression, he added, "We have been greatly interested in the splendid plan to give Madame Curie a gram of radium, which will enable her to continue her important research, and we are delighted that your efforts were so eminently successful." To be critical of his fellow countrymen was one thing; to offend his American friends who were helping French scientists would be an altogether different proposition.

Carrel's severest criticism was leveled at the pillar of French scientific institutions: the Pasteur Institute. Carrel was quoted by the *New York Sun* as saying, "France is atrophying and stifling her great minds by formulas of another age. . . . Independent spirits and ideas find insurmountable barriers before them. The French Faculty of Medicine in the Pasteur Institute opens its doors only to the specially select; scientific audacity is not tolerated; discoveries are restrained to the point where it is becoming sterile." He was never forgiven for this criticism. When the opportunity arose, Pasteur L. Vallery-Radot, Director of the Pasteur Institute, paid Carrel back with interest. At the end of World War II, on the basis of rumors and false allegations, he publicly removed Carrel from a position he then occupied. One may assume Vallery-Radot derived some satisfaction from finally "discrediting" the critic of French scientific ineptitude, for he had to wait some thirty years to do it.

Carrel was relentless in pointing out the faults of the French system. In 1930 in reply to a letter from Carl Beck in which the latter asked about the anticancer drug

Delbiase, developed in France, Carrel said: "I believe that the experimental work of Delbet is all bunk. You can find in the *Presse Médicale* of 1928 or 1929 the so-called experimental work on which his treatment is based. The truth is that magnesium was used long ago as a treatment of warts, especially by Swedish physicians, but I do not know whether it has any effect. Is it not extraordinary that the University of Paris keeps as a Professor of Surgery a man who advises patent medicine?"

Were Carrel's criticisms justified? Probably so, because they were leveled at archaic and bureaucratic institutions. The administrative process which neglected the laboratory as a tool of medical investigation warranted revision. Théodore Tuffier, a noted French surgeon who, among other things, introduced spinal anesthesia into surgery, and for whom Carrel had profound respect, regretted the lack of experimental surgery laboratories. He went so far as to say that this alone held back his surgical progress. In 1924 Tuffier wrote Carrel regarding two scientific developments in France which, on the surface, appeared promising: localization of tumors by injecting patients with radioactive colloidal material, and an antituberculous serum. Tuffier thought these "discoveries" should be investigated in the laboratories of the Rockefeller Institute. But before the arrangements could be made, they were tried on patients in France. A few months later Tuffier wrote that all the "discoveries" ended in vain. The advocate of colloidal radium departed for Constantinople "in search of new victims," while patients treated with the antituberculous serum showed no improvement. Had adequate laboratory facilities existed and the new "discoveries" been subjected to evaluation in animals, they would never have been applied to patients.

Carrel was attracted to and friendly with Tuffier, from whom he received inspiration and practical advice. However, the conditions under which Tuffier worked were less than satisfactory. Carrel summarized his sentiments about Tuffier in an article published in the *Revue de Paris*:

In the modest surgical division of Beujon the hospital rooms are transfigured by the inspiring words that express [Tuffier's] powerful intelligence. This humble assemblage has become a center for teaching for the whole world. Students and doctors from all nations flock to this ancient hospital to learn the essence of medicine, the art of caring for and healing the sick. There are no luxurious operating rooms . . . no large and expensively equipped laboratories. But there is here a man, the great surgeon of Paris. . . . He devotes each morning to operating, then visits the hospital wards and lectures to his students. After completing an operation, he describes it to his students and draws the anatomical diagram on the blackboard. He is a teacher in the true sense of the word. It is impossible not to understand him, for he is so fascinated by his subject that each detail of his lecture is charged with interest for his listeners.

Like all great clinicians, Tuffier understood that diseases are not merely useful abstractions for teaching students, but that the doctor deals with a person who is sick. He realized that in pathological states the laws of normal physiology still apply. To study the relationship between physiology and pathology, Tuffier wanted to experiment on animals, but he had never had the opportunity to do so. During his entire professional life he had not had at his disposal, like Halsted, a laboratory of experimental surgery.

To Carrel, this epitomized the sorry condition of medical science in France. He tried to help, and raised his voice in protest. His voice remained a cry in the wilderness. The only thing it gained Carrel was the enmity of French scientific administrators.

9 ✿ Man, the Unknown

In 1935 Carrel published a nonmedical book, *Man, the Unknown*. He wrote it viewing human events through a prism of his experiences and subjective feelings. The achievements of medicine during the first third of the twentieth century were used as examples of what science can do for mankind. The theme of the book was that many facts about man have been uncovered, but that these have not been added up to give a true estimate of human potential. In *Man, the Unknown* Carrel outlined his views and the conclusons he drew from his endeavors as a scientist and doctor. The book created quite a stir, became a best seller, and was translated into over a dozen languages.

Carrel wrote *Man, the Unknown* at the urging of the "philosophers" of the Century Club. The story goes that upon completing the manuscript he showed it to a French publisher who was duly impressed with its content, but said that "not thirty people in France will read it." Carrel naturally became discouraged, and would have abandoned trying to get the work published, had it not been for the urging of his American friends. Once the book was published in the United States, Carrel again had the satisfaction of seeing himself proven correct and the acknowledged experts wrong.

In the preface to *Man, the Unknown* Carrel asserted he was neither a professional writer nor a philosopher. His view of modern civilization was pessimistic; he had scarcely a good word to say about it. Critical readers could find in the book many unsupported generalizatons and dogmatic statements and might gain the impression that Carrel was far more successful in outlining the ills of modern society than in proposing remedies for their cure. Despite its short-comings, the book became very popular, and perhaps for a simple reason: Carrel verbalized a legitimate public concern that science was not doing enough for humanity, and that the rapid development of technology might be detrimental to mankind. Also, he subscribed to a popular view on crime, maintaining that society is organized for average "normal" individuals, and that criminals who do not fit this pattern must be segregated from it.

Carrel tried to place contemporary knowledge in perspective. He asserted that sciences dealt with human beings in a very mechanistic way: while achieving technical triumphs, they had neglected the individual. He thought this should be corrected by making medicine a "superscience" which could effectively guide civilization in accord with the true nature of man. The review of *Man, the Unknown* in the *British Medical Journal* took Carrel to task for this stand. Its author, Sir Arthur Keith, was critical of Carrel for venturing beyond the limits of medical science. He also noted that *Man, the Unknown* revealed more about Carrel than about man. *Time* Magazine editorialized on Carrel's proposals for solving the problems of modern civilization, observing that it was impossible to tell whether Carrel was making some suggestions seriously or with tongue in cheek.

If *Man, the Unknown* did not please some scientists, it struck the right chord with many others. Chauncey D. Leake wrote to Carrel on March 18, 1936: "During the last few weeks I have been studying your recent book. Most of us here have been doing the same thing, naturally.

All of us have profited by the opportunity to become acquainted with your thoughts as to the present state of man and the future opportunities of medicine. Your conception is a grand one, and I sincerely hope that it may inspire some young men to make the sacrifice you suggest."

Carrel's treatment of philosophical concepts and sociological problems made a lasting impression on some erudite readers. Rabbi Stephen S. Wise of New York wrote Carrel on December 31, 1935:

I said on Sunday morning, preaching to my people about *Man, the Unknown,* it is not merely a great book. It is epochal. I have a definite conviction that your book will live for ages. It deals with the destiny of the human genus as significantly as Darwin dealt with the origin of species. Truly, I have been waiting for years to say the word that you have said, that only a scientist could have said in authentic fashion. I said to the congregation, "It is not a book to be talked about from the pulpit, but to be discussed in seminar fashion for many hours with a class."

I think of your volume as an oasis of beauty in a wilderness of things that are just muck and ruck and truck without beauty and dignity, without spaciousness and nobility. I shall go back to your book again and again.

Man, the Unknown was not a technical book. It was a popularization of general concepts, some of them based on Carrel's scientific experience and others on deductions and observations. It is not difficult to understand why the book had a strong popular appeal. Here was an acclaimed scientist saying that, despite all its accomplishments, science did precious little for the common man, that it may in fact work to his detriment. But this was not all: governments took advantage of people, and unscrupulous politicians and businessmen profited from abuses. Carrel's strongest public appeal lay in the fact that he also said this did not have to be so. Proper direction can make science work for man, and man can indeed determine his own individual and collective history. While many propositions in *Man, the Unknown* were delivered in a very dogmatic fashion, Carrel said this was done to initiate discussion of the issues raised.

Although the book summed up Carrel's thoughts and opinions, it is difficult to summarize. By Carrel's own admission it was composed of mere sketches and a superficial description of many subjects. A complete separate treatise could have been written on each of these. However, the main themes of Carrel's thought regarding the science of man were there. These were subsequently refined and expanded upon in a lecture delivered at the Century Club on May 5, 1936; in a series of lectures at the University of California; in addresses delivered at Dartmouth College and in Muncie, Indiana; and in an interview with Agnes Meyer for the *Washington Post*.

Carrel's main contention was that, despite the intense investigation of various phases of human activity, very little was known about man himself. Enormous amounts of money had been spent to acquire data on certain aspects of physiology, medicine, hygiene, psychology, etc., yet the detailed knowledge of isolated human functions remained astonishingly sterile. The reason for this may be that, in order to study man, man had to be divided into fragments, each of which called for a set of specialists. But when these fragmentary studies were added up, their sum did not seem to represent a whole. During the process of analysis, some things appeared to have been overlooked.

For a long time man had no need to obtain knowledge of himself. At first he developed like a wild animal; natural selection took place in the struggle for food and shelter. But then man somehow developed an organized society no longer governed by the laws of the wild. Science and technology transformed man's physical environment and created conditions for special mental attitudes. All gifts of technology were accepted blindly, while the comfort derived from these was paid for by crowding into cities, by noise, pollution, and new diseases. Carrel maintained that the results of technological advances were indiscriminately applied to man without due consideration of his nature. Thus Western civilization created conditions which rendered life difficult, if not impossible.

To back up his argument, Carrel cited the blending of criminals with the urban environment, the increase in mental disease, and the lack of economic security and spiritual strength. He also pointed out that, although man's technical knowledge had increased, the level of human intelligence had remained stationary. Thus man became incapable of controlling the world he himself had created. The only solution to the problem was to acquire new knowledge, in order to determine exactly what man can and cannot do. An environment adjusted to human needs must be constructed.

If one discards many embellishments of Carrel's arguments, such as his repeated statements regarding the decay of Western civilization, what remains is exactly what people wanted to hear: let's make a better world for everybody! The popularity of Carrel's proposal to establish a science of man was enhanced by his insistence that the knowledge thus obtained must not remain confined to a group of scientists—it should reach every man and woman. Carrel wrote:

There is no hope that politicians, even with the assistance of specialists in economics and sociology, will succeed in patching the present world order. Should we submit to the remote or immediate past, to the principles of democracy, socialism, nazism, communism? Should we not discard those remains of other times, overthrow industrial civilization, build up new concepts of human progress? Cannot man develop better methods for the existence of individuals, nations, and races, and utilize the immense progress of science and technology according to the natural laws of his body and mind? Such a revolution would be possible if each man and woman were ready to take part in it.

Carrel proposed to fight the principles of industrial civilization by means of an intellectual revolution. His call invited every man and woman to share in intellectual pursuits, just as conventional revolutionaries invited the poor to share in the wealth of the rich. Carrel said that industrial civilization can be fought "as the French people at the end of the eighteenth century fought the *ancien régime*." He went on to say that our world obviously cannot be an economic machine, but neither should it be a spiritual system. It has to represent both material and spiritual activities. He acknowledged the slow evolution of new doctrines, but said that once a doctrine becomes accepted it turns into faith, and faith is irresistible.

In developing his concept of the science of man, Carrel said that to be useful, knowledge must be positive. It should be based exclusively on observation and experiment. Needless to say, the results of both observation and experiment are subject to interpretation, and interpretation is frequently subjected to the biases of the interpreter. Carrel chose not to elaborate on this point. Instead, he conveyed the impression that the suggested approach would eliminate all data of dubious nature. Whether this would be the case is, of course, open to question. Carrel placed all his bets on scientific method. According to his plan, it would take about a century for the suggested experiments to run their course.

Carrel called for the liberation of new concepts from scientific, religious, and philosophical doctrines—"from the beliefs and dreams accumulated by humanity during the course of ages." Recognizing the dangers of dogma, he added: "We will discard vitalism and mechanism, materialism and spiritualism, monism and dualism. In the search for truth, scientific systems are as dangerous as philosophical ones."

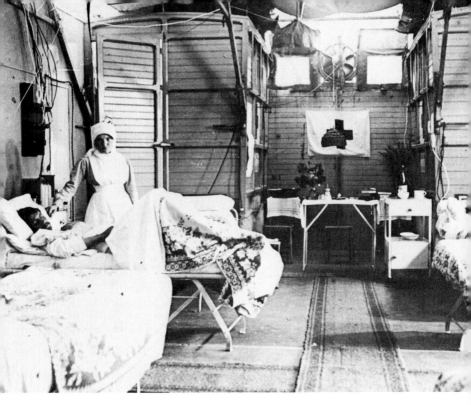

Improvised hospital ward in Compiègne

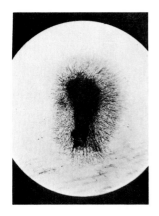

Fragment of tissue
in culture,
showing growing cells

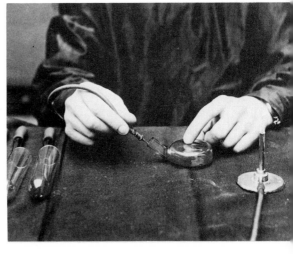

Changing fluid in tissue-culture flask in
Carrel's laboratory at Rockefeller Institute

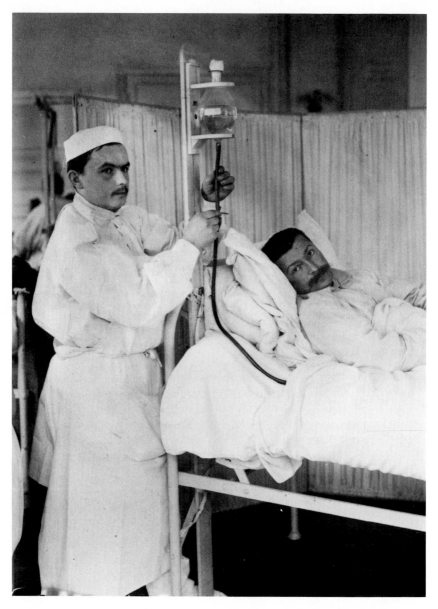

Patient in traction with open wounds irrigated by Dakin's solution

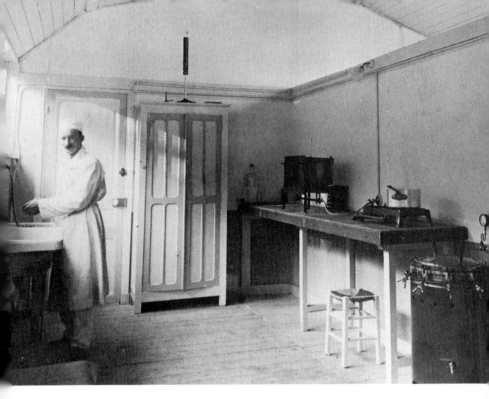

Sterilizing facility at the hospital in Compiègne

Portable X-ray table at the hospital in Compiègne

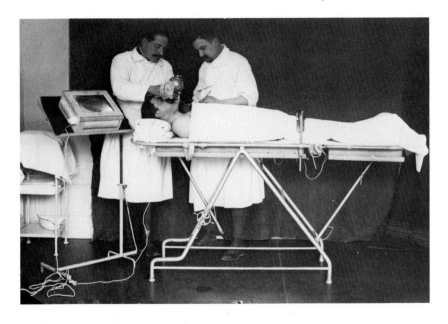

Alexis and Anne Carrel
in 1913

Carrel at his home
on the island
of Saint-Gildas
in the summer
of 1939

Alexis Carrel at Rockefeller Institute after World War I

Carrel, Dr. William S. Halsted, and Dr. William H. Welch
in 1918

Class at Rockefeller Institute's War Demonstration Hospital in 1918;
Carrel in white cap

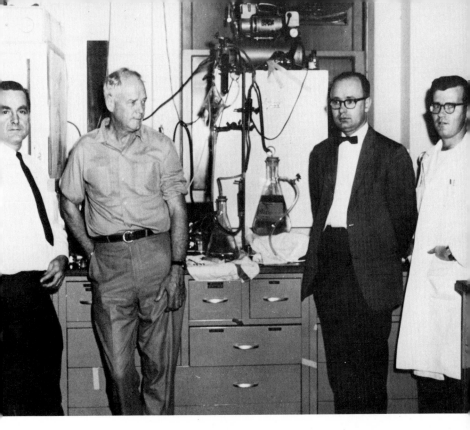

New organ perfusion apparatus
at Naval Medical Research Institute, 1966;
V. P. Perry, Charles A. Lindbergh, Theodore I. Malinin, G. L. Mouer

Lindbergh's
organ perfusion apparatus,
with three pumps
connected to an oil flask

Alexis Carrel in Paris one month before his death

In describing the proposed "science of man" Carrel pointed out that man can be analyzed in many aspects, but that the knowledge thus obtained must be integrated. He did not think this could be accomplished by committees: "a true synthesis has never been obtained in a round-table conference of specialists." Carrel foresaw many difficulties in the proposed endeavors, one of the main ones being that the observers would live and age at the same rate as the observed. Therefore the research should be planned and conducted so as not to be interrupted by the death of individual scientists, so that the lapse of time would be of no consequence.

Carrel raised the question as to whether current scientific methods could yield data which would provide man with complete self-knowledge. Are the existing techniques applicable to the analysis of human activities? Laboratory measurements apply only to entities having dimension and weight. They are incapable of measuring such common human activities as love, hate, perception of beauty, and inspiration. Science by definition does not enter the spiritual world, because the realm of mental activity lies outside known physical limits. However, since physiological reflections of psychological states can be recorded, science may develop the means of dealing with such human activities.

Mind, Carrel said, is often considered a separate entity connected in some manner to the body. Body and soul are views taken of the same object by different methods. The antithesis of matter and mind represents merely the opposition of two techniques. The error of Descartes was to believe in the reality of this abstraction. Cartesian dualism has weighed heavily upon all subsequent attempts to understand man.

It has engendered the false problems of the relations of soul and body. Since neither soul nor body can be investigated separately, no such problem exists. The operational concept of the mind is equivalent to the analysis made of our own self and of the manifestations on the self of our fellow men. We observe only certain activities, which are apprehended by techniques different from physiological techniques. It is convenient to divide mental activities into intellectual, moral, aesthetic, and religious. But such classificaiton is artificial. These activities . . . cannot be measured, but they have been observed to be characteristic of humans throughout history. Man has expressed his inner tendencies by erecting statues, temples, theaters, cathedrals, hospitals, laboratories, universities, factories. . . . There is no reason to assign mental activities a lesser reality than physiologic activities. Soul and body are equally carved out from an indivisible whole. Soul cannot be separated from body, structure from function, the cell from its medium, multiplicity from unity.

In *Man, the Unknown* Carrel flatly stated not only that man is not independent of his environment, but that economic and social environments are as important as the physical ones. From the dawn of history man has manifested the same impulses. These include the need for freedom, justice, adventure, and a certain amount of security. The tendencies to acquire, possess, and create are inherent in human nature.

Anticipating his critics, Carrel himself questioned whether it was utopian to try to develop the science of man. He acknowledged the difficulties of the task, but expressed a belief that if human creativity were directed toward man and his environment, the challenge could be met. He envisioned the science of man as consisting of two parts, the first encompassing the acquisition of data and their analysis, and the second dealing with the organization of the information thus obtained. He emphasized the need for institutions where the "problems concerning our body, our soul, and our relations with our fellow man and the cosmic world can be investigated." He said that no scientific institutions existed where comprehensive research could be conducted on human beings and intelligent animals without interruption. Scientists must be content with short, fragmentary experiments on mice, rats, and rabbits—or sometimes on a few dogs, monkeys, or chimpanzees.

Carrel questioned the wisdom of continuously compiling the information from scientific discoveries, if this mass of knowledge is not used to further human welfare and happines. The data obtained by scientists are scattered among groups of people working separately. Most are scarcely known to the public leaders.

The progress of science has liberated man from some superstitions and diseases. Organized research has become an inexhaustible source of technical discoveries which have brought mankind more goods, less work, and a longer average life. But it has also brought with it something unexpected—the inability of mankind to adapt itself to technological progress. Regrettably, technological progress has not brought mankind the happiness that may have been anticipated. A large toll of life is extracted by automotive and industrial accidents. Instead of dying rapidly of infectious diseases, as in the past, people now die more slowly and painfully of degenerative diseases, tumors, and diseases aggravated or produced by the altered external environment. Medicine has extended life, but it has not prevented human suffering. Carrel pondered the incompatibility of the fragile human organism with potentially violent and harsh technological developments. Exposures to speed, noise, radiation, and chemical pollution were not experienced by man on a large scale prior to the twentieth century.

The conclusions Carrel reached were in keeping with his background: before the problems can be solved, they must be studied. He could not propose logical solutions for existing problems before the necessary studies were done. Nor did he expect these to be completed in his lifetime. Some of his suggestions were preliminary and rather curious. *Time* quoted him as proposing a High Council of Doctors to rule the world for its own good, and as hinting that he himself would make a fitting member. He did not offer any reasons for elevating doctors to such a high status. Most likely the suggestion was made in jest, and *Time* allowed for this possibility. Carrel presented no evidence, historic or otherwise, that doctors would make great or even acceptable governors of men, for such evidence would be hard to find. Carrel knew doctors only too well. Nor is contemporary and past American experience with physicians in high government office reassuring. Having witnessed constant arguments and bickering among physicians, Carrel did not dwell on the subject.

Carrel wanted *Man, the Unknown* to reach a large audience. To enhance the popular appeal of his work, he dealt with some topics sure to be of common interest. One of these was sex, which in those days was not often discussed in popular writing. Carrel showed no hesitation to take a few bold strides in this direction. He said that the sex glands exerted a profound influence on the strength and quality of the mind. "In general, great poets, artists, and saints, as well as conquerors, were strongly sexed." On the premise—not necessarily correct—that almost all great artists were great lovers, he deduced that artistic inspiration seemed to depend on a certain condition of the sex glands. Yet he did not explain why it is that, if all artists are great lovers, all great lovers are certainly not artists.

Having taken this stand, Carrel developed an unexpected theme. Using Dante as an example, Carrel said that love stimulated the mind most actively when it did not attain its object. Therefore, in the face of a strong sexual drive, sexual deprivation may be just what is needed to produce creativity. To support this contention, Carrel argued that, had Beatrice become Dante's mistress, he would most likely have spent his time doing things other than writing the *Divine Comedy*. Yet this is not at all certain, for if Dante's literary creativity depended on frustrations, these could have derived just as easily from physical closeness to the object of his admiration, as from its unattainability. Carrel went even further by suggesting that religious mystics were driven to renunciation and complete sacrifice by their un-assuaged sexual appetites. On the other hand, he said that it was well known that sexual excesses impeded intellectual activity. He did not specify what constituted such excesses, nor did he state whether this applied to both males and females, and in what particular age groups. However, he did draw definite conclusions from his conjectures: "A workman's wife can request the services of her husband every day. But the wife of an artist or of a philosopher has not the right to do so as often."

The idea of sexual deprivation as an intellectual stimulus was persistent in Carrel's mind. He was quoted by *Time* as saying that women must not make excessive demands on men of genius. *Time* did not lose the opportunity to suggest that Carrel applied the principle to himself, stressing the fact he did not marry until he was forty. The quotation about sexual demands was printed below a not-too-compli-mentary photograph of Mrs. Carrel taken in 1935. The implication was that, under the circumstances, it was not too difficult to practice what he preached.

In dealing with sex, Carrel acknowledged a Freudian influence. In mentioning Freud, he again developed his view of the mental activities in a rather mechanistic fashion. He did not subscribe to the concept that placed the soul exclusively in the brain. For Carrel the entire body was a substratum of mental and spiritual energies, thought being an offspring of the endocrine glands as well as of the cerebral cortex.

Naturally such views produced varied reactions. One reviewer of *Man, the Unknown* was struck by what he termed a rather naive enthusiasm regarding the power of science, but another entitled his review, "Can Science Save

Society?" Arnold Klebs said in a letter, "You cannot write like Bergson or Santayana, so you write like Carrel. This is a very great virtue. . . . Harvey Cushing . . . ought to be cheered by what you have to say of surgery, a fine article. You could not say the same of medicine, which has lost the magic touch, the only thing that could save it."

At the Rockefeller Institute Carrel's colleagues read the book with interest. James B. Murphy noted: "I enjoyed and profited from reading [the book], particularly Chapter 8. I wish such phenomena as mental telepathy could be established by scientific methods. While many people are convinced by personal experience, it is hard to be satisfied with the so-called demonstrations. I wish it were possible for younger men with scientific training to undertake a study. I cannot help feeling uncomfortable about Lodge and others of advanced age, with loss of some of their critical faculties. Why not a division for the study of psychic phenomena at the Rockefeller Institute?"

In literary and publishing circles the reaction was generally favorable. George T. Cameron, publisher of the *San Francisco Chronicle*, wrote Carrel: "I seldom enjoyed a book as I did this. It expressed so clearly so many of the things with which I am sympathetic."

Mrs. Eugene Meyer of the *Washington Post* saw no conflict between Carrel's views and her own liberal stance. In fact, she went so far as to say she agreed with Carrel that all educational work should rest on experimentation and observation, and also on a feeling of reality. According to Mrs. Meyer this was precisely what Dewey had done in knocking out all the old theoretical concepts and basing the new education entirely on scientific methods. Everything Carrel said was really in line with Dewey's thinking. She thought when Carrel got to know both Dewey and herself a little better, he would find out they were not far removed from each other in their ideas.

In 1937 Mrs. Meyer interviewed Carrel and published

an article in the *Washington Post* on his philosophy and the Institute of Man, the creation of which Carrel was advocating. She intended this article to be one of a series of interviews with "leading statesmen" of every shade of opinion, in order to have them express what social and political developments they advocated in the United States. In 1937 Mrs. Meyer felt the greatest difficulties in America could be traced to the fact that no one was clear as to what kind of a program the country should pursue.

The main thrust of Carrel's thought as revealed in Mrs. Meyer's article dealt with his desire to further the progress of man. Carrel felt the era now drawing to a close was dedicated to the progress of machines. The new era must be dedicated to the progress of man. In the United States several public men were coming to recognize the difference between science and technology, and the failure of mankind to organize its collective life and adapt to existing conditions.

Mrs. Meyer thought that publishing an interview with Carrel would help emphasize the necessity for co-operative thinking between statesmen and scientists. In a letter inviting Carrel to Washington, she said: "Naturally I realize that you avoid interviews as a rule, but what I propose is of much more serious nature than is usually comprehended under the word 'interview' and its purpose would be twofold, an immediate influence on all of our congressmen and senators who read the paper every morning, as well as a furtherance of your very important conception of a new foundation for the humanities which you arrived at scientifically and I could only arrive at intuitively."

Mrs. Meyer was a professional journalist. Prior to publishing her interview with Carrel, she had written an article on Thomas Mann, to bring his thoughts to the American public. In condensed form she presented the content of *Man, the Unknown*, subject to Carrel's subsequent modifications and without undue reliance on unproven opinions and controversial statements. Pleased with the results, Carrel wrote to Mrs. Meyer:

My short visit in Washington was like a charming dream. How extraordinarily beautiful were the Potomac River and its rocky islands covered with trees. It was an exceptional pleasure to me to listen to the conversation between yourself, Eugene Meyer, Henry Wallace, Senator Clarke, Walter Lippmann, and to hear, at the same time, the quiet music of the rapids at the foot of the hill. I shall not forget the spring sun on the Lincoln Monument, or the peace of the terrace of your house among the flowers, the monastery-like appearance of the basement of the Museum, the treasures of Mr. Lodge, the astounding beauty of the slender leaves. The luncheon with Henry Wallace was extremely interesting for me. I have profound sympathy for his intellectual attitude and for his character. He is a very remarkable man.

Carrel's ideas found their way into the minds of people with diverse backgrounds. Gordon B. Scheibell, an attorney from East Orange, New Jersey, expressed his reaction as follows: "I was given to an overwhelming interest in your thoughts. At that time my background of studies in psychology, my mechanistic concepts of existence, and my understanding of physiology received a vitalizing reorganization at your hands. Thus arriving at such a new concept of the world, as one suddenly emerging from a dark room into a brilliantly sunlit garden through an unexpected door, my enthusiasm was quite appreciable."

Wrote Upton Sinclair: "My wife and I have been reading your new book with great interest, and you may be glad to know of the very favorable comment I heard yesterday from a well-known psychiatrist here. It happens, oddly enough, that I have been writing along the same lines."

Interesting and pertinent comments came from Carrel's friend Henry James, a noted author and philosopher himself:

The politico-social remedies that you propose don't always appeal to me. There seems to be Utopian simplification about some. But it's very helpful to consider Utopias. On the other hand, your diagnoses command my ready sympathy and agreement, and consequently I am sure that you're a very wise man! I'm glad you did not hesitate to publish your interest in telepathy, etc., and the whole treatment of the spatial and temporal extension of personality was very skillful and suggestive. Your antiurbanisms and your discussion of the new relation between man and his artificial environment interested me quite particularly. That is a matter that has been much thrust upon my attention. Indeed I've sometimes thought of trying to write about it.

Sometime when we will meet I'd like to discuss with you your belief that natural selection has ceased to operate as an effective process in modern society. For though I suspect that many people will agree with you, I seem to see the process working very actively.

If I may do so without impertinence, I'd like to compliment you on the style in which the book is written. Knowing you, I should have expected it to be terse, and clear and animated. But to express oneself in a language which was not the language of childhood and to achieve so much flexibility and variety and sometimes eloquence—well, it is to prove your own thesis about maintaining the capacity for adaptation.

Publication of *Man, the Unknown* put Carrel again in the limelight, but not the type of limelight he was used to. Instead of remaining on firm grounds of medical science, he advanced into the sociopolitical sphere with its ever-shifting winds. Carrel became known as a reformer and a successful writer, and was invited to give lectures and public addresses, and to write articles for popular magazines. He also came in contact with various political leaders. At the age of sixty-two he could have abandoned his scientific career and switched to writing, and could have done so successfully; in fact, he started working on a sequel. But scientific investigation was Carrel's first love—for its sake, he even left his native country. He could not picture himself doing anything else.

10 ❧ Perfusion of Organs

To my knowledge, the first recorded attempts at perfusion of an isolated organ were made by Loebel, who published the results of his studies in 1849. A simple organ-perfusion technique still in use was devised by Langendorf in 1895. The Langendorf apparatus consisted of a medium reservoir and a siphon tube connected to the organ. The system was nonpulsatile; the medium was infused by gravity and did not recirculate.

At the turn of the century, considerable interest was shown in perfusion of the isolated heart. Martin, of Johns Hopkins University, devised a method for perfusion of the coronary arteries *in vitro*. Kuliabko and Popelsky of St. Petersburg described resuscitation of the cardiac activity of *in vitro* perfused human hearts. While attempts to maintain renal function by perfusion were not successful, it was demonstrated that kidneys attached to heart-lung preparations and perfused with blood secreted urine.

In the twentieth century, perfusion experiments became rather routine, to the point of being described in standard textbooks of physiology. Thus the stage for experimentation with organ perfusion had been set before Carrel became involved in the problem. However, until the publication of Carrel's results with the culture of thyroid glands, none of the perfusion techniques then in existence could be adapted to the long-term extracorporeal maintenance of organs. The reason for this was a simple one: all perfusion apparatuses were open, resulting inevitably in bacterial contamination of organs perfused for more than a day in these machines. Attempts to keep organs in apparatuses which were difficult to sterilize, and in which the fluid came in contact with the metal, resulted in failure. This continued to be the case until Charles Lindbergh developed an all-glass apparatus which produced sterile pulsating circulation. Even by current standards, the results obtained with this apparatus were spectacular. However, the technique used in the experiments was meticulous and precise. After Carrel's retirement and death, the experiments with the Lindbergh apparatus were not pursued further. Instead, serious doubts were cast on the validity of the work, presumably because other investigators were unable to obtain similar results by the use of dissimilar apparatuses and methods. That the latter was the case is true, but this only attests to the uniqueness of the apparatus and the perfusion methods used by Carrel and Lindbergh.

Carrel's career as a medical scientist may be said to have come to an end with the publication of his and Lindbergh's book, *The Culture of Organs*, in 1938. At the time the book was written, Carrel realized that cultivation of organs had not reached its final form. He anticipated that the phenomena of regeneration, growth, nutrition, and internal secretions could be rendered more comprehensive by studies with prolonged organ perfusion. He based his views on Claude Bernard's notion that "we will acquire a scientific explanation of the phenomenon only when we are capable of determining, within the internal organic medium, the general conditions of nutrition by all histologic elements, together with the nutrient agents specific to each of these elements."

Ever since his student days, Carrel had been concerned with the physiology of tissues and organs from the surgical point of view. His interest in keeping alive isolated functioning organs dates from experiments with organ transplantation. He always entertained an ambitious idea of substituting healthy organs for diseased ones.

His interest in the preservation of tissues for surgical use was concomitant with that of transplantation. He stated in 1912 that his clinical experience, coupled with that of Tuffier and Magitot, demonstrated the feasibility of tissue preservation in cold storage for use in human surgery. This led him to advocate collection and storage of human skin and bone grafts from cadavers. However, he soon learned that hypothermic storage, which allowed for preservation of skin and bone, did not meet with a large measure of success when applied to complex organs. Thus one of his early ambitions was to perfect a perfusion culture system allowing for extracorporeal survival of isolated organs.

Carrel's interest in organ culture was longstanding. He noted that the culture of organs is, from a technical point of view, extremely difficult, and that no one had ever succeeded in protecting a perfused organ from bacterial infection. However, he also noted that if it were possible to culture whole organs, a diseased organ or part thereof could be removed, treated outside the body, and grafted back into the patient. Therefore, when cultivation of an organ was rendered possible by the advent of Lindbergh's apparatus, Carrel's attention was captured. From this point on, Carrel's experiments were centered around the apparatus; his last scientific paper from the Rockefeller Institute dealt with abnormal human thyroid glands cultured in it.

Lindbergh's involvement in a biological problem was neither casual nor spontaneous. His interest stemmed from his childhood, when he had become aware of the phenomena of life and death, and was disturbed by the unsatisfactory answers grownups gave to his inquiries. At one time he considered studying biology and possibly taking up medicine. However, his low school marks and abhorrence of Latin, which he thought required of medical students, discouraged him, and he chose mechanical engineering instead. Yet at the University of Wisconsin he found engineering courses difficult and rather boring. Lindbergh left the University in his sophomore year, but his interest in biology continued. In 1928, a year after the solo transatlantic flight to Paris that made him world-famous overnight, he purchased a number of textbooks on the subject. He reduced his activities in aviation so that he could devote a reasonable amount of time to biological studies. In 1929 he bought a microscope and was planning to set up a small laboratory in the basement of a house he was building in New Jersey. He began visiting biological laboratories at Princeton, Cold Spring Harbor, and elsewhere whenever he could.

At this point his wife's older sister, Elizabeth Morrow, contracted pneumonia and was found also to have rheumatic fever. Her doctor prescribed a full year of bed rest. In the winter of 1929–1930 the seriousness of the situation became obvious, and Lindbergh asked if an operation could be performed to repair the damaged heart valve. Miss Morrow's doctor said an operation could not be performed on the heart, because the heart could not be stopped long enough for surgeons to work on it. Lindbergh asked why a mechanical pump could not be used for circulating the blood while the heart was artificially stopped. No one seemed to know whether or not this was possible.

Lindbergh was astounded by the fact that eminent physicians could not answer such a question. Though he knew nothing of cardiopulmonary physiology or surgical techniques, it seemed to him quite simple to design a mechanical pump capable of circulating blood through the body during the short period required for an operation. Lindbergh did not realize that the problem lay not only in pumping the blood, but also in oxygenating it; technically, because of blood-vessel configuration, the heart could not be bypassed without also bypassing the lungs. But Lindbergh, having an inquisitive mind, continued to pursue the question.

While waiting for the birth of his first son in June 1930, Lindbergh struck up a conversation with his wife's obstetrician and anesthesiologist, Doctor Paluel J. Flagg. Again he inquired of Dr. Flagg about the feasibility of using a mechanical heart during operations. Flagg said he could not answer that question, but knew a man who could—Carrel. Flagg arranged a luncheon with Carrel at the Rockefeller Institute where only Lindbergh, Carrel, and Flagg were present. At the luncheon Carrel listened patiently to Lindbergh's questions, outlined clearly the problems of coagulation and hemolysis (breaking up of RBCs), and after lunch escorted Lindbergh and Flagg through the laboratories. Carrel showed them an apparatus on a cabinet shelf designed for circulating nutrient media over tissue cultures, and others designed for the perfusion of organs, none of which worked satisfactorily.

So crude were these apparatuses that Lindbergh immediately felt he could design better ones. This was particularly true with regard to perfusion pumps. Of course perfusion pumps were not "artificial hearts," but they represented a step in the right direction. Carrel had not been encouraging about the use of artificial hearts in surgical procedures, but Lindbergh thought that if he could build a satisfactory perfusion pump, a mechanical heart might follow.

During the visit to the Rockefeller Institute Lindbergh was tremendously impressed by Carrel himself. Carrel towered over other physicians Lindbergh knew like a mountain over foothills. He was working in the very fields of biology that Lindbergh had become interested in. Lindbergh came to realize that tissue culture and surgery were essential for the experiments he hoped to perform. By the time of the visit to Carrel's laboratories, he had bought and read books on cytology and surgery. He had also visited a tissue-culture laboratory at Princeton, and with Flagg had visited several laboratories in New York where surgical experiments were performed. But here he was in the laboratories of a great surgeon and biologist, a man overflowing with new ideas—in laboratories far more adequate than he could dream of establishing in the basement of his New Jersey home. Lindbergh was eager to try to design a new perfusion pump, but wondered if he could really make a contribution that would justify a diversion of Carrel's time. He asked Carrel if he would let him try designing a better pump. To Lindbergh's surprise, Carrel replied he could use the laboratories and facilities for this purpose to whatever extent he wished. It was typical of Lindbergh that he went to work that very night, making sketches of a rocking-coil type of Pyrex-glass perfusion pump.

The coil pump was simple and presented no unusual problems of construction or sterilization. The initial experiments consisted of perfusing a segment of a cat artery in an organ chamber made from a Petri dish. For the first time prolonged perfusion could be carried out without infection! But the perfusion pressure in the coil pump was low, and there was no pulsation. Although infection could be avoided during perfusion, the attachment of the cannula (a tube for insertion into an artery) in the open organ chamber still resulted in considerable bacterial contamination. An improved design was needed for the type of experiments Carrel wanted to perform.

Lindbergh began the design of a capillary lift–type perfusion pump, i.e., a perfusion apparatus in which perfusate was propelled by a capillary motion of fluid. It exerted greater pressure on the organ, but was fragile and likewise did not produce pulsations. The need for pulsatile perfusion was becoming more and more apparent. The major problem was to introduce a pulsating force into the perfusion pump without bringing microorganisms with it. The second problem was that of transferring the pulsating force into perfusion fluid, so that the final effect would be similar to that produced by the heart.

When not on cross-country flights and airline surveys, Lindbergh spent more and more time in the laboratories, often working long after midnight. He realized he could find no greater opportunity to study the aspects of life that had intrigued him since childhood. He began studying tissue culture and designed a flask for continuous cultivation of large quantities of cells. He spent hours inside a large incubator—an extremely uncomfortable environment—watching the movements of living cells through the microscope.

Carrel left Lindbergh alone. He took no part in the development of the perfusion apparatus. However, he was tremendously interested in the project and was ready to adapt his techniques to the apparatus Lindbergh developed. Carrel would often come into the room where Lindbergh was working and simply stand there briefly and watch. Lindbergh recalled one occasion when he brought Albert Einstein with him. At the time a battery of perfusion pumps was in operation.

One of the findings leading to the pulsatile perfusion pump was the realization that air from a laboratory pipeline could be passed indefinitely through nonabsorbent cotton without carrying microorganisms with it. Additional features of the new apparatus were a slanted, relatively narrow-necked organ chamber, which reduced infection during organ installation to a fraction of that experienced with the Petri-dish chamber. The construction of the pulsatile perfusion pump required careful study and understanding of the details, which usually involved definite limits of dimensions.

The apparatus that Lindbergh produced in 1935, with the aid of Otto Hopf, the Rockefeller Institute's scientific glassblower, could maintain pulsatile circulation under sterile conditions for time periods limited only by the condition of the organ and the nutrient fluid. The maximum and minimum pressures and the rate of pulsation were easily adjusted. The composition of the gas in contact with the circulating fluid, and with the exterior of the organ, could be controlled. The organ, which was enclosed in a glass chamber, was kept moist and could be observed at all times.

The apparatus containing the organ and the perfusion fluid was a single piece of glass, with the exception of two floating ground-glass valves and the stopper at the top of the organ chamber. It had two narrow necks for the introduction of fluid and gas. During the operation the necks were closed with rubber stoppers, through which passed glass tubes that were connected to cotton filter bulbs by rubber tubing. Under pressure, the gas transmitted its pressure to the perfusion fluid.

The apparatus consisted of three chambers: the organ chamber on top, the pressure-equalizing chamber in the middle, and the fluid chamber at the bottom. The fluid chamber was always under a pressure varying from approximately the minimum to the maximum exerted on the organ. The organ chamber was under a practically constant pressure of about 20 millimeters of mercury. The pressure-equalizing chamber was under the same pressure as the fluid chamber at maximum pressure, and under slightly less than the organ chamber at minimum pressure. Consequently, at minimum pressure the fluid in the organ chamber, having passed through the organ, flowed down into the pressure-equalizing chamber, while at maximum pressure it was forced down to the fluid chamber. From the fluid chamber it was driven by pulsating gas pressure to the organ chamber, thus completing the cycle. Backward flow of fluid was prevented by the floating ground-glass valves. Power and pulsations were provided by compressed air passed through rotating brass valves operated by a small motor. The pulsations were transmitted through the oil column in a separate flask to a gaseous mixture of known composition, introduced separately into the oil flask.

Carrel hoped that an organ could be, in effect, "transplanted" into this apparatus. In this manner one could dissect the body into parts without depriving those parts of life. Organ culture was not to be a substitute for tissue culture. Its technique, as well as its purpose, was quite different. Tissue and blood cells could be grown like bacteria in flasks containing appropriate media, making the technique of cell culture somewhat analogous to bacteriological techniques, although far more intricate. But the cultivation of organs involved more complex mechanical and surgical procedures—just the thing that Carrel loved! Carrel envisioned organ culture as a method bridging the fields of anatomy and physiology, so as to allow him to study simultaneously the structure and function of tissues and organs. Study and the manufacture *in vitro* of the secretions of the endocrine glands could be effected by organ culture. Perhaps arteries could be placed in the apparatus, treated for disease, and then put back in patients.

The plans Carrel had for organ culture were indeed ambitious, but the time in which he could do his work was short. He conducted organ perfusion experiments for just four years. Lindbergh's time was diverted by other responsibilities; after 1935 he spent but little time with different versions of the perfusion apparatus, and did not resume these studies until some thirty years later.

Between April 1935 and May 14, 1939, a total of 898 individual experiments were carried out in Carrel's laboratories, using the Lindbergh–Rockefeller Institute perfusion apparatus. Once slight modifications in the pump had been made, it did so well that no experiment had to be interrupted because of its malfunction. Sterility was maintained by observing precise aseptic techniques when fluid was sampled or introduced into the pump, and when an organ was removed from the chamber. However, even with strict adherence to the rigidly controlled aseptic environment, a number of experiments were lost to bacterial contamination. In many perfused organs, small and sizable areas of necrosis (areas of dead tissue) were noted. These were attributed to mechanical disturbances of the circulation such as occlusion of small arteries by emboli, compression of arteries, and twisting and hyperextension of small vessels. The perfusion medium used for organ perfusion was usually Tyrode's or Ringer's solution mixed with 50-percent serum. Neither red blood cells nor hemoglobin were used in the perfusion fluid because the red blood cells agglutinated and were rapidly damaged.

The majority of perfusion experiments performed by Carrel were carried out on thyroid glands. Secretory activity of cultivated glands was estimated by measuring the iodine content of the tissue and the perfusion fluid. The experiments demonstrated that morphologically inactive glands secreted large amounts of iodine under cultivation, whereas histologically active glands secreted little iodine. Thyrotropic hormone (pituitary gland hormone which stimulates the activity of the thyroid gland), when introduced into the pump, caused an increase in iodine secretion, and also brought about a corresponding decrease in the iodine content of the gland.

The longest survival of thyroid glands in the perfusion apparatus was obtained when high pulse rates and pulse pressures were used. However, the response to perfusion depended not only on the mechanics of the pump, but also on the composition of the medium. The applicability of Carrel's perfusion techniques to the study of human thyroid glands was tested by N. Chandler Foot at Cornell University Medical College and by L. Baker at the Institute. This study demonstrated that, like animal thyroid, human thyroid could be maintained in a viable condition for at least three weeks, provided the blood vessels remained patent.

Many technical developments in organ perfusion and preservation techniques have come about since the 1930s.

These account for the advances made in human organ transplantation. Since methods for organ storage by freezing have not yet been perfected, perfusion of isolated organs constitutes the only available method for their preservation. These organs are generally perfused at hypothermic temperatures. A major distinction should be made between perfusion conducted at body or reduced temperatures. The studies conducted at body temperature can be justifiably referred to as organ culture, but perfusion at hypothermia is a different matter. It is usually conducted solely for the purpose of organ preservation. Carrel's and Lindbergh's interest was in the realm of organ culture. They deserve full credit for pioneering the technique and for indicating the direction of further studies.

11 ✦ Charles A. Lindbergh

Charles A. Lindbergh occupied a unique place among Carrel's friends and co-workers. From Lindbergh's first meeting with Carrel in 1930 until Carrel's departure for France in 1942, the Lindberghs were in constant contact with the Carrels. Many philosophical concepts expounded by Lindbergh in later life may be traced to his association with Carrel. The relationship between Lindbergh and Carrel was particularly intense in the middle and late 1930s. When not in personal contact they corresponded frequently, covering a wide range of topics in their letters. Lindbergh was deeply involved in Carrel's attempts to organize an independent research institute. Although this endeavor was not successful, the plans which were drawn up for the institute were detailed and carefully thought out.

After Carrel's death, Lindbergh remained in touch with his wife, and maintained an interest in Carrel's ideas and his work. It is largely through Lindbergh's efforts and encouragements that the organ-perfusion experiments performed by Carrel and his associates in the late 1930s were repeated in the 1960s. This re-established the validity of the method and dispelled unwarranted criticism by investigators who could not reproduce the experiments.

Soon after starting work in Carrel's laboratories, Lindbergh found Carrel himself even more interesting than the experiments he performed. At the Alexis Carrel Centennial conference at Georgetown University, on June 28, 1973, Lindbergh said: "There seemed to be no limit to the breadth and penetration of his thought. One day he might discuss the future of organ perfusion, for which I was building an apparatus. On another, he would be talking to a professional animal trainer about the relative intelligence of dogs and monkeys, and the difficulty of teaching a camel to walk backwards. I once looked up from my work to see him step into the room with Albert Einstein discussing extrasensory perception." Ten years after Carrel's death Lindbergh wrote to Carrel's colleague Raymond Parker: "He was one of the most extraordinary men I have ever known, and I say this being aware of many of his eccentricities. I have never felt more deeply about anyone as a friend, and never found anyone more stimulating to my mind."

Lindbergh acknowledged Carrel's contributions to science, including his pioneer work with blood vessels, the treatment of war wounded, and the development of tissue culture. But his appraisal of Carrel went beyond that. He came to feel Carrel was correct in emphasizing how closely the functions of body, spirit, and mind are intertwined. Carrel was responsible for a concept of which Lindbergh became a firm advocate: the advances of each of these functions depend on the others. This explains Lindbergh's feeling against overspecialization. Lindbergh's summary of scientific philosophy in his book *Autobiography of Values*, and particularly in the chapter "Banana River," intellectually represents a far cry from making an airplane fly for so many hours without a mechanical failure.

At approximately the same time that his interest in biology took concrete form, Lindbergh reached a major decision: he would not write technical papers on aviation and astronautics. Had he started doing so, he would have had little time for anything else. Not long after the flight to Paris in the *Spirit of St. Louis*, his life assumed new dimensions; it was no longer centered around aviation. The life style he chose for himself was not dictated by circumstances; the gradual changes in it were made by his own choice. Much as he appreciated the public honors, he did not like speeches and social activities. At first he thought he could curtail these by carefully selecting the invitations he accepted. But this did not work out too well. Every activity in which he participated seemed to start a chain reaction which led far beyond the apparent requirement of the occasion itself. Finally he realized that the only way he could concentrate on his own interests was to forsake public appearances altogether. What he needed was a refuge where he could pursue his interests unobtrusively. Unexpectedly, this was provided by Carrel and the Rockefeller Institute.

He spent only a few years at the Institute, but his dedication to work and his agility of mind soon gained the respect of Carrel and his co-workers. For the most part, Lindbergh worked alone, without assistants. Whether he was dealing with a centrifuge, a cell-culture flask, or a perfusion apparatus, he would first make a design and then construct a simple prototype of the apparatus. He had a remarkable ability, much admired by Carrel, to concentrate on a given task. When Lindbergh was working, Carrel did not interrupt him with irrelevant conversation; at lunch in the Institute's dining room and at the Century Club, however, their discussions, dealing with a wide range of topics, were very animated.

Lindbergh's initial work at the Rockefeller Institute dealt with devising a method for washing red blood corpuscles in suspension. He bought a standard centrifuge and had it modified so that it would rotate at 4,000 rpm. (The standard model would not rotate faster than 3,000 rpm.) He then designed a conical chamber into which cell suspensions were placed. During centrifugation the replacement fluid was introduced at the narrow outer end of the chamber, while the replaced fluid was forced out at the wider inner end. The chamber was so designed that the rapid flow of the incoming fluid prevented cells from packing, while at the wide end the flow was too slow to carry them out with replaced fluid.

Lindbergh's success with solving a relatively complex technical problem of washing red blood cells may seem somewhat surprising, if one overlooks his persistence and attention to detail. He had no formal education to qualify him for this type of work. Until confronted with a problem on which Carrel was working, he had probably not even been near a centrifuge. But he was very quick to obtain and grasp the information needed for a given task. He did not like to accumulate technical information in advance. Some years later he wrote to Bud Gurney: "As to education and accumulation of knowledge, my advice is not to spend too much time on it. I agree with Lao-tse in this respect: 'The wise men are not learned, the learned are not wise.' "

From washing red blood cells, Lindbergh went on to tissue-culture flasks. The need for flasks through which media could be circulated continuously dated back to 1913, when Carrel first began cultivating tissues in test tubes. Lindbergh designed a continuous medium-circulation flask consisting of a culture chamber with upright inlet and outlet tubes, one on each side. The tubes served both as reservoirs and as conducting channels for the fluid. The fluid flowed through the chamber by gravity because of the difference in fluid pressure between the inlet and the outlet tubes. The differential pressure was provided by pressure-regulating bottles, with gas flow regulated by a capillary tube.

In testing the apparatus, Lindbergh was able to maintain a continuous cell culture in one flask for 105 days. The apparatus was subsequently used by other investigators, particularly by Parker and Nicholas of Yale University. As

with many of his inventions, Lindbergh left further develop-
mental work to others. After completing the work with
circulating flasks, his attention was directed to the previously described perfusion apparatus. However, he started
to work on the flasks again in 1935, a few weeks before
reaching a sudden decision to live in England. The move
to England was precipitated by the continuous disruption of
his life and invasion of his privacy by newspaper reporters.
He was particularly sensitized to the press after the kidnap-
ping of his first son and the subsequent trial of Bruno
Hauptmann.

Lindbergh's motivation for dealing with biomedical problems is difficult to analyze, and he himself would have been
hard pressed to tell why he continued to work in laboratories whenever the opportunity came. Perhaps it was
intuition that led him to start working with Carrel. Once
started, however, his laboratory work was not merely intui-
tive; it was carefully planned and executed.

His approach to biological work bore many resemblances
to his approach to flying. In the beginning of his career as
a pilot, when flying was much more dangerous than it is
today, he decided he was willing to risk being killed in a
crash if he could fly for ten years. To exchange an ordinary
lifespan for the great adventure of flying seemed a worthwhile bargain. Later, when his mental discipline and extraordinary skill as a pilot overcame the odds, and flying
became more mechanical, he began to look for wider
horizons. Association with Robert H. Goddard, the generally acknowledged pioneer of modern rocketry, enhanced
his interest in astronautics. Curiously, instrumental as he
was in obtaining funds for Goddard's research, he did not
personally witness a successful rocket launch by Goddard.
Nevertheless, even before World War II, he began to think
the greatest adventure man could have would be to travel
through space.

Lindbergh had an almost computerlike mind when it

came to flying, yet his pioneering aviation efforts often sprang from intuition rather than from reason. What made him unusual was his ability to determine precisely when intuition must give way to reason. He believed his flight with the *Spirit of St. Louis* would advance aviation's progress and accelerate the advent of mass air transport. He also knew the flight would enhance his prestige as a pilot, but he was totally unprepared for the burdens that his overnight fame brought him.

After his flight to Paris in 1927 he spent a year visiting various cities with his plane, attending luncheons and dinners, and giving addresses. After turning the *Spirit of St. Louis* over to the Smithsonian Institution in 1928, he planned to concentrate on aviation-related activities. But, paradoxical as it seems, his public image prevented him from working in aeronautics. He wanted most of all to have free time to think and to go about his business unobtrusively, but this proved almost impossible because of interference by the press. His problems with newspapers started shortly before his flight to Paris, when he had deeply resented being portrayed by reporters as an illiterate cowpoke. As time went on, he developed an argument of principle with the media. The "gentlemen of the press" maintained they represented democracy and the American people, and this, they argued, gave them unrestricted access to all public figures. Lindbergh disagreed strongly, for he thought the newspapermen represented nothing more than their own pecuniary interests.

Thus, having reached the zenith as a pilot, instead of exploiting his position Lindbergh took a step in another direction—experimental biology and, in a broader sense, contemplation of life. Intuition and love of adventure remained major factors in his life. Without these he would not have attempted the flight to Paris, or become involved in the study of biological phenomena.

The laboratories at the Rockefeller Institute provided

an ideal physical and intellectual environment for Lindbergh, protecting him from public exposure. The timing of his arrival there was also right; Carrel, by a different route, had come almost to the same point as Lindbergh in his intellectual inquiries. Both men were beginning to ask the same questions. How mechanical, how mystical was man? Could longevity be extended? Was death an unavoidable portion of life's cycle or could physical immortality be achieved through scientific methods? What would happen if a severed head could be maintained alive in a perfusion apparatus?

Due to his sudden decision to live abroad, Lindbergh's work at the Rockefeller Institute came to an end in 1935, but his move to England did not disrupt his relations with Carrel. On the contrary, the two men seemed to have been drawn closer together by Lindbergh's "exile." During the summers Carrel lived on his island off the coast of Brittany—a close proximity that allowed for frequent contact. In the winters, when Carrel returned to New York, they corresponded regularly. Nor did Lindbergh abandon his interest in the experiments at the Rockefeller Institute. Although distance made his participation impossible, he nevertheless was remarkably well informed as to the progress made by his colleagues. He was concerned with modifications of the apparatus and the way in which it was being used.

Lindbergh's work with Carrel on the perfusion of organs, which was frequently carried out at lower than normal body (hypothermic) temperatures, stimulated their mutual interest in hypothermia and "suspended animation." The accounts of certain Indians going into a trance, with their vital functions and body temperature reduced, intrigued them. Therefore, Lindbergh made a search of scientific literature on the subject and wrote to Carrel:

The most comprehensive paper I have located to date is by

S. W. Britton. . . . When I was at Saint-Gildas I spoke to you about the experiments carried out by Sutherland Simpson in 1920. . . . It seems that Britton has carried on the work of Sutherland Simpson, but with cats and other animals instead of monkeys. His results are interesting and I will outline them briefly. Simpson stated that the first laboratory study of the reduction of temperature in homoiothermic animals was made by Walther in 1862 (Virchows Archiv 24:414, 1862). It was interesting to note that all of the experiments I have looked up, including Simpson's and Britton's, were started by anesthetizing the animal with ether, C. E. mixture, etc.

In 1937 an opportunity arose to have a firsthand look at the problem. Lindbergh received a letter from Sir Francis Younghusband, who invited the Lindberghs to meet him in Calcutta. He was going to attend a Religious Congress of All Faiths, and said that Lindbergh would be able to meet there some of the most interesting men in India. Lindbergh felt such an opportunity would not arise again and decided to attend the Congress. He hoped he would find someone there to whom he might talk about the phenomena which interested him, but he found the proceedings disappointing. Despite this, he lost no opportunity to make inquiries about hypnosis, hibernation, levitation, fire walking, old age, control of bleeding, immunity to poisons and diseases, and control of various functions of the body. With the exception of levitation and old age there seemed to be definite material to study. There were all kinds of stories about both levitation and great age, but he found nothing concrete in regard to either.

On returning to England Lindbergh performed some simple hypothermia experiments on animals at his home, and wondered whether a few cooling experiments could be performed on humans. Since he would not do anything to anyone he would not do to himself, he was prepared to serve as the first volunteer in these experiments. He communicated his ideas to Carrel, who immediately dissuaded him from such an undertaking: "I would advise you not to make any experiments on yourself or your wife because such experiments are dangerous." However, Carrel's reaction is not to be construed as lack of interest in the subject. On the contrary, he was very interested in pursuing the studies with hypothermia, and asked Lindbergh to construct a hyperbaric chamber in which the temperature and the concentration of oxygen and carbon dioxide could be controlled. He foresaw the practical implications of hypothermia, and told Lindbergh in 1937: "If it is possible to reduce greatly the body temperature of a homoiothermic [warmblooded] animal, a new field is opened to medicine and surgery. The lowering of temperature will decrease pain. Surgical operations will be performed without anesthetics."

Lindbergh was just as intrigued with the possible impact of hypothermia on medicine and wrote to Carrel:

Since it is apparently possible to greatly reduce the body temperature of a homoiothermic animal, with an accompanying reduction of pulse pressure, metabolism, etc., are there not likely to be both medical and surgical uses for such a procedure?

For instance, might we not be able to construct an apparatus to maintain artificial circulation during operations on the heart? You may remember that I did some preliminary work on such an apparatus at the Institute two or three years ago. One of the main problems seemed to be the coagulability of blood at body temperature and the necessity of maintaining a large circulation. . . .

It seems to me there are many interesting experiments which can be performed in connection with the lowering of body temperature.

Indeed there were, but the turn of events allowed neither Lindbergh nor Carrel to carry out such experiments. The preceding exchange of ideas regarding hypothermia took place in 1937, when Lindbergh was still living abroad.

He did not return to the United States until April 1939. By July 1939 Carrel no longer had a laboratory where such experiments could be performed.

The situation with the perfusion apparatus was likewise frustrating. Lindbergh wanted to design a new pump in order to accommodate larger organs, and so that he could experiment with adapting it for whole body perfusion. This called for different materials, because the rigid glass chambers would not be suitable for the purpose. The old pumps also presented some minor problems that he would like to eliminate, but it was difficult to work on these from so far away. He could have sent sketches, but was afraid it would not be enough. To make progress it was really necessary to work on the apparatus itself and to supervise the technicians directly.

Work with the hyperbaric chamber continued, because it could be carried out away from elaborate laboratories. Lindbergh found a manufacturer in England who would build such a chamber according to his design. But the construction took time.

They are still having trouble with the top gasket blowing at high pressure. . . . The cause of the trouble is obvious and due to the stupid designing on their part. In fact, I think it is remarkable that the gasket holds at all. Fortunately, the trouble is very simple to fix. It could be remedied within a day in the United States. They ask for two weeks here. However, they are extremely nice about it and anxious to have the tank right before it leaves the factory. They may be a little slow, but they are much more interested in having the product right before it leaves their hands than most of our manufacturers are at home. They are really very satisfactory people to work with, but one must start working with a different conception of time than in the States.

The pressure tank was finally built. After testing it as best he could, Lindbergh sent it to New York. It was never used, since by the time it arrived Carrel had little time left in the laboratories of the Rockefeller Institute.

While living in England, the Lindberghs visited the Carrels at Saint-Gildas on many occasions. Lindbergh liked the island from the very start. After one of the visits he wrote to Carrel: "Anne and I miss being at Saint-Gildas very much and especially talking to you and Mme. Carrel. As I told you, I have never been in a place which combines so well all the characteristics which I like. I would rather live on Saint-Gildas than any other place I have ever seen. Its only drawback is, I believe, that with the present condition of France it is so far from a center where modern facilities are available." In April 1937 he noted: "Your invitation to visit Saint-Gildas has already caused us to look forward to next summer and one more visit to your wonderful island. I assure you that the days and nights we spent there last summer will always remain clearly outlined in my memory, among my most pleasant and interesting experiences."

After several years in England, in 1938 the Lindberghs moved to the Continent. They made their home on the island of Illiec, adjacent to Saint-Gildas. Lindbergh had learned from Mrs. Carrel that the island was for sale. Since French law prohibited aliens from owning property on the coast, the Carrels arranged for some friends to form a small company to purchase the property. The entire stock of the company was then turned over to Mrs. Lindbergh and was held for her by Mrs. Carrel.

Illiec lies to the east of Saint-Gildas; at low tide one can walk from the one island to the other. The Lindberghs lived on Illiec until they returned to the United States in 1939. Their life there constituted a pleasant interlude before the turmoil of World War II. The feeling Lindbergh had for the island and his life there can be captured from a letter that he wrote in 1957, thirteen years after Carrel's death, to Mrs. Carrel, who was then in Argentina. The letter followed a visit to the islands.

Yesterday Anne, little Anne (she is now bigger than her mother), Land and I walked out over the sea bottom to Saint-Gildas. . . .

We drove from Paris . . . in a small car and left it parked above the tide line at the start of the road that leads over the flats to Illiec. It was mid-morning with the tide just past low. . . . It might as well have been in the wonderful years before the war when you and Dr. Carrel were living in the buildings on Saint-Gildas, and we in the stone house on Illiec. In fact, I imagined us all there again. . . .

We crossed over the little islands between Illiec and Saint-Gildas and walked across . . . to Saint-Gildas. We climbed the hill beyond, then followed the path and road through the little fields, past the old well, across the stone bridge to the Bois du Coeur with the stone heart in place on the post and the monument you and Dr. Carrel erected to mark the spot where the message I dropped from my airplane landed. . . .

There was a service going on in the chapel . . . and outside the chapel, Antoinette came running and waving from the kitchen. . . . She has kept the house in a wonderful condition, just as it was when you and Dr. Carrel were living in it, or as close to "just as it was" as a house without its owners can be; the essential touches of daily love and use, of course, missing in every room and corner.

Antoinette escorted us through each room, and through the garden, and insisted on giving us something to eat, including a lettuce salad from the garden, in the dining room, on the same dishes we ate from when you and Dr. Carrel and Anne and I were there together. . . .

After the services in the chapel were over, we went into the chapel yard and to the grave of Dr. Carrel. . . . The little chapel above it is beautifully vine-covered, as it has been during all the years since we first visited Saint-Gildas, and the interior is carefully kept. It seemed to us again that you have chosen the most appropriate place in the world for the grave to be—no other would be right in comparison.

The closeness between Carrel and Lindbergh in the years before the war led to many discussions regarding the future. Since by then both knew their days at the Rockefeller Institute might come to an end, these usually dealt with work in time to come and with where it could be done.

Their mutual interest in continuing organ-perfusion experiments, and the possibility of initiating experiments with whole body perfusion and hypothermia, brought out the need for a new experimental animal. Lindbergh made an attempt to inbreed fox terriers. As could be expected, this failed, because of difficulties inherent in producing genetically similar dogs and because of the long time needed for such experiments. Their interests then focused on primates. They came to the conclusion that their future work would best be carried out on these animals. Since neither had any experience with monkeys, Lindbergh made a considerable effort to learn about the breeding and care of primates, particularly baboons and gibbons. He took a special trip to the Château de Claires, near Rouen, to see how gibbons were kept there on an artificial island surrounded by a shallow moat. He also went to Paris to talk to Vallery-Radot, to whom Carrell had introduced him when Vallery-Radot was visiting New York. The Pasteur Institute was maintaining a station in Africa where chimpanzees were kept, but Vallery-Radot did not seem to know too much about the colony. Lindbergh then made extensive inquiries about the possibility of maintaining a primate colony in the United States.

He solicited the help of a zoologist, Hayden B. Harris, of Chicago, and with him developed a plan for a "Research Laboratory Using Subhuman Primates." Harris's suggestion was to locate the laboratory in Maryland, owing to its temperate climate and its proximity to the laboratories of the United States Public Health Service which were planned for Bethesda, Maryland. Lindbergh thought the laboratory should be located in the eastern part of the country, where scientific men could live contentedly over long periods of time. However, the facility should not be accessible to mere curiosity seekers. If two stations in close proximity and offering two climates should prove necessary, Jamaica, with mountains 7,000 feet high, and the eastern end of Cuba, with mountains 9,000 feet high, would provide a suitable environment. The primates they planned to use were Doguera baboons, because these animals are native to a temperate climate, are long-lived, and have at least as even a temper as any baboon species; Cebus monkeys, because their intelligence was said to be very high, and their life in captivity averaged ten years; spider monkeys, because they have a meek disposition; squirrel monkeys, because they are the smallest; and chimpanzees, because they are the only anthropoid apes which can be procured in numbers.

Plans for the future continued to occupy Carrel and Lindbergh from mid-1936 until the start of the war. Lindbergh's desire to make some arrangement for continuing his and Carrel's experimental work on a long-term basis was genuine. In 1937 he wrote to Mrs. Carrel: "I am glad to hear that Dr. Carrel is making headway with his plans. I am very anxious to talk to him about them and to help in finding ways to make them materialize quickly. There is nothing to be gained by waiting longer."

In the fall of 1937 Lindbergh began to be alarmed by the lack of progress in organizing a new laboratory. In September he wrote to Carrel:

The experiments we have been making this summer are, of course, of secondary importance to your own plans for the future. It is essential to attempt to lay the foundations this winter for whatever organization you wish to carry on after you leave the Institute. To work on this effectively necessitates being in the United States. I am extremely anxious to be of any help that I can, either directly or indirectly, in forming an organization such as you have outlined. I also want to carry out some of the experiments we have started and talked about.

He was also concerned with the means by which Carrel's work might be financed:

I am inclined to believe that any large amount of money raised would have to be through direct or indirect contact with individuals who are interested in projects like those you have in mind, and who are able to contribute substantially to them. I am very doubtful about the advisability of a public appeal in starting an organization.

By 1938 Lindbergh realized he must return to the United States if he wished to do something for Carrel and himself. He judged the conditions in France unsuitable for carrying out the projects he and Carrel envisioned, but return to America with his family still posed a serious problem. Realizing that his reluctance to return to the United States might be difficult to understand for a man who crossed the Atlantic frequently, Lindbergh took time to explain to Carrel his reasons for not going home:

. . . under any ordinary circumstances we would spend the entire winter in New York. But under ordinary circumstances we would not have spent two years in England, especially when my own profession was passing through one of its most interesting periods.

I do not believe that the conditions in the United States have improved very much in the last two years. . . . Fanaticism and crime are probably as rife, politics as corrupt, and the press as irresponsible and lawless as when we left.

The Press is our really greatest problem, for we could protect ourselves against the fanatic and the criminal; we could maintain a home suitable for our children, and lead a reasonably normal and happy life in our own country if it were not for the attention which the newspapers concentrate on our movements and the interference in our affairs by the physical presence of their reporters. . . .

We are looking forward to the time when we can live at home, but at present we must not plan too definitely on returning in the near future. It is possible that we could take our children home for a visit without too great a difficulty. It would give my mother and Anne's mother great pleasure to see them. . . .

If we took the children with us, we could remain a longer time, but I do not like to look forward to the publicity with the worst element of the American press, the crowds, and the police waiting at the dock. It is bad enough to go through them alone, without the two children.

By 1939, however, with the possibility of a European war looming on the horizon, Lindbergh finally decided to make the move. He was vehemently opposed to American participation in a European conflict. To this end he was prepared to enter the political scene and lend the weight of his name to keeping America neutral. This brought him into open conflict with the Roosevelt administration and its supporters, who opposed Lindbergh's "isolationist" stand. He arrived in New York aboard the *Aquitania* on April 14. Carrel and James D. Newton met him aboard the ship before he disembarked. His mind was preoccupied with the impending task and with his desire to build up U.S. air power, which he thought was needed to maintain a position of strength.

By necessity, his biomedical interests were relegated to the background. Moreover, because of his active involvement in the America First movement, his biomedical endeavors were often treated unfavorably by the press for political reasons. A cartoon by Charles Martin picturing Lindbergh with an apparatus was captioned, "Lindbergh Mechanical Heart." Lindbergh was shown in the process of affixing a large sign to the apparatus with the word "Aryan" printed on it in bold letters. This made reference to the pro-Nazi sympathies which his political opposition imputed to him.

Attacks on Lindbergh in the press, which were frequently based on incorrect statements, greatly disturbed Carrel. In this connection, on January 23, 1939, he wrote to Paul Fuller, Jr., an attorney with the law firm of Coudert Brothers:

I have read the articles in the *World Telegram,* the *Reader's Digest, Liberty,* and several other newspapers and magazines. They are based on lies. They are doubtless inspired by a very subtle propaganda, the origin of which is not difficult to find. [Reference is made here to Lindbergh's prewar political opposition.]

The incident is of far broader significance than the defamation of a national hero. It shows the extreme danger of the modern techniques of propaganda, of either foreign or domestic origin. In fact, these techniques have reached a degree of perfection that makes them a menace to the freedom of thought of the average citizen.

I believe, as you do, that some action should be taken against such slanders. Unfortunately, Colonel Lindbergh wishes to remain silent. The only people who know the truth are Ambassadors Wilson, Kennedy, and Bullitt. I hope they will make it known to the public in the measure that may be possible.

For various reasons, clarification of Lindbergh's activities during this period did not take place until many years later. Although he chose not to become involved in a public controversy, he was disturbed by misrepresentation of the motives which compelled him to enter the political arena. To keep the record straight, Lindbergh's true feelings regarding Nazi Germany in the prewar period should be stated. He was invited to spend the winter of 1938 in Berlin, but decided against it. In November he wrote Carrel:

You are right about the inadvisability of going to Berlin at this time. As soon as serious frictions began to arise between our country and Germany, we decided to postpone our plans. As events developed further, it became clear that Berlin was not the best place for us to make our home this winter. To do so would be embarrassing for many people and from many standpoints. I am sorry, because I believe we would have learned a great deal from a winter in Germany, in aviation and in many other fields. Also, by actually living in the country I felt I might better understand the German viewpoint on the problems on which we disagree. I believe that Europe is heading for a devastating war unless some understanding is reached with Germany, and the more difficult it is to have contact with that country the more difficult an understanding will become. After all, contact does not mean support.

Lindbergh terminated his political activities with America's entry into the war and devoted his time and energies exclusively to military aviation. He did not resume biomedical work until the late 1960s.

In 1965 Lindbergh resigned from the ballistic-missile committee on which he had served for seven years and declined an appointment to the new agency that was to deal with space programs. Instead, he decided to survey the environment and study ways of life in various parts of the world. His concern for the environment was a long-lasting one; as far back as 1937 he had written to Carrel:

I believe it would be worthwhile for you to expand your ideas on the practicability of effecting the development of an individual by environment, as separate from heredity. The effects of heredity and environment are greatly confused in most people's minds. I believe that very few realize what great effects can be obtained through environment, especially if applied to a child. I think your examples with regard to the populations of mice are excellent, and that you cannot include too many of this kind in the final draft of your paper. It is the type of thing which creates the largest amount of interest and these examples drive home the practicability of your general objective.

As years went by, Lindbergh developed a firm belief in the wisdom of nature and natural selection. In his scheme of things the development and quality of an individual were the important factors. With time, natural selection would single out individuals with mental and physical qualities suited for life in a healthy, natural environment. He thought that exposure to nature and its beauty would bring closer together the people who could be taught to love and appreciate it.

He entered into a discussion along these lines with Robert M. Hutchins, President of the University of Chicago and noted nonconformist educator. Replying to one of Hutchins's letters, he said:

I'd a lot rather make a trip to Outer Mongolia than to Outer Los Angeles—and I'd rather stay there for awhile. But I am doubtful about putting my roots permanently in Outer Mongolia. I think I'd rather take a chance on the principle of evolution working out in Outer Los Angeles. I believe that production, selection, and competition are going to have a major effect on Southern California in the long run, and I'll cast my lot with the great-grandchildren of the kind of people I'd like to live with, even though the latter are in the minority at the moment. . . .

You see, I'm not as much worried about the results of an environmental natural selection among men as I am about the intermediate intellectual interference with that selection.

Although Lindbergh's concept of environment can be traced to Carrel, it would be a mistake to think of him as Carrel's complete philosophical disciple. In many ways he held an intellectual advantage over Carrel. He had a much broader view of man's scientific achievements. He did not share Carrel's faith in the power and potential goodness of science. In approaching the problem of man's relation to man, he considered the extent to which scientific research could be applicable and effective. His exposure to scientific laboratories made him aware of the limitations of the scientific method, and aware too of areas of human existence inaccessible to technology.

Lindbergh's analysis of the fundamental value of aeronautics and astronautics was disappointing to him. He had spent much of his life developing and promoting aviation and space flight; his early pioneering efforts in aviation had been wonderful years. But in retrospect the effect of aviation and space programs on human life in the twentieth century had turned out to be far less beneficial than he had originally anticipated. In fact, mankind might have been much better off without aviation and rockets. It seemed obvious the destructive effect of aeronautical science in war was greater than its constructive effect in peacetime. Aeronautics and astronautics had indeed diminished the distance between men, but distance may have been nature's greatest safeguard; now it was abolished by man's ability to destroy cities and countryside within minutes by the launching of rockets a hemisphere away. Also, separation by distance had produced a vast diversity of life, which may have been of greater value than the standardization of life resulting from rapid intercourse between the peoples of the earth.

Lindbergh agreed with Carrel's observation that worldwide environmental conditions have changed much more during the twentieth century than during all previous time since the beginning of civilization. Human adjustment to these changes has lagged behind. The surface ripples caused by this adjustment were obvious, but the actual trouble was probably hidden much deeper.

It was difficult to envision how family life could exist in modern society as it had in the past. Lindbergh thought that, in the basic sense of life, opportunities for young people were becoming fewer and fewer. Young people were not happy about this, nor would he be either, in their place. All of this posed a question that he had raised many times. Is the progress of civilization really progress? In his judgment, many modern technological advances have already gone beyond the point of serving human progress. Was civilization not then moving toward a breakdown? If so, could the trend be reversed? He was not too optimistic, but he thought that reversing the trend was worth a try.

This train of thought led Lindbergh into conservation efforts and at the same time rekindled his biomedical interests, interrupted some twenty years previously. Since his work with Carrel, his only excursion into biology had been some brief work during World War II with high-altitude flying. At that time he had spent several weeks in Dr. Walter Boothby's laboratory at the Mayo Clinic, where the physiology of high-altitude flight was under study. The breathing mask developed in this laboratory, referred to as the Mayo mask, offered a marked advantage over the old tubular mouthpieces.

When he was making ignition-breakdown tests on a Thunderbolt, in 1942–1943, Lindbergh regularly climbed to 40,000 and once reached 43,000 feet. Even stripped of guns and extra equipment, the Thunderbolt would not climb higher. During these tests Lindbergh made use of what he had learned from Boothby: above all, the valuable observation that, contrary to prevailing opinion, a pilot could detect lack of oxygen in time to do something about it before he passed out. In an altitude chamber he learned to recognize signs of anoxia rather quickly. This may well have saved his life. During one of the ignition-breakdown tests the gauge on the oxygen tanks read 50 pounds pressure when Lindbergh suddenly ran out of oxygen at 36,000 feet; the only warning he received was from his own physiological senses, but this allowed him time to reach lower altitude. Lindbergh suggested to the armed forces that all high-altitude flying personnel be trained to recognize early signs of anoxia, but this was thought impractical because it would involve training in altitude chambers, and his suggestion was not implemented.

In the mid-1960s an effort was made at the Naval Medical Research Institute to repeat some of Carrel's experiments with the Lindbergh organ-perfusion apparatus. A duplicate of the perfusion pump was constructed, but it was impossible to make the apparatus function as originally described by Lindbergh. Therefore Lieutenant V. P. Perry, the officer in charge of the project, wrote to

Lindbergh for help. Lindbergh came to the laboratory and with little effort made the pumps function properly. This was the first time his pumps had been used since 1940. Lindbergh developed considerable enthusiasm for renewed experiments. The operation of the pump was demonstrated at the meeting of the Tissue Culture Association in Miami in 1964. Subsequent to this, the Lindbergh-RIMR perfusion pumps (as now properly designated) were continuously used by investigators. The authenticity of the descriptions of their original performance was no longer questioned. With the work interrupted by Carrel's retirement again under way, Lindbergh informed the commanding officer of the Naval Medical Research Institute: "I thoroughly enjoyed taking up again the work I discontinued at the start of World War II, and seeing the advances in various techniques which have been made during the intervening years."

Lindbergh worked at the Naval Medical Research Institute and subsequently at my laboratory in Rockville, Maryland, and the University of Miami the same way as at the Rockefeller Institute. He concentrated on the task at hand and would not stop until it was completed. In short order he designed a new perfusion pump. The new pump was described in scientific literature but it was not used extensively because it had to be controlled manually.

To the last days of his life, Lindbergh maintained the highest respect for Carrel personally, not just for his technical knowledge and skill. Lindbergh said Carrel possessed one of the strongest characters he had ever encountered, and one of the keenest minds, and did not hesitate to say what he thought, even if it was to his disadvantage. Lindbergh liked him for it, although he knew the difficulties Carrel's outspokenness created.

The time Lindbergh spent on experimental research created its own inherent problem. It made him neglect other activities to an extent that few people knew. This he did willingly, for he felt that the broader a man's interests were, the more difficult it was to attend to each one of them in detail. In the end, the balance a man struck was the measure of his character.

Both Carrel and Lindbergh were strong-willed and stood firm in their convictions in the face of adversity. But publicly Carrel was outspoken and Lindbergh was not. Lindbergh remained correct in his behavior toward adversaries; he preferred to let the tide of opinion turn against him, rather than engage in unpleasant personal arguments. In his life he had experienced the satisfaction of achieving what was considered to be impossible and he had known what it was to be a national hero. He had also known what it was like to be discredited personally for his cause, and to experience vindictiveness. He had been deeply hurt when friends were found guilty of association with him. Unlike Carrel, Lindbergh reached the end of his life with the knowledge that the controversies surrounding his public activities had been placed in proper historical perspective. More important still, he had influenced the lives of many people. He hoped his warnings would prevent the abuse of life by technological developments.

12 ✇ The Rockefeller Institute for Medical Research

In 1928 Frederick T. Gates, on whose advice John D. Rockefeller had founded the Rockefeller Institute for Medical Research, sent Carrel a book by Charles Richet on the natural history of the savant. Carrel took pleasure in comparing the scientist described by Richet with those whom he had known at the Rockefeller Institute. He said in a letter to Gates:

I have been happier than Richet. The scientists with whom I have had the good fortune to become acquainted were of a larger caliber than his heroes. For instance, the beauty of the character of Noguchi is compared to that of the saints of the Middle Ages. I cherish the hope that someone endowed with a brilliant mind and the literary skill of Richet will some day write the life of a number of the wonderful individuals with whom I have had the privilege of associating at the Rockefeller Institute.

The early history of the Institute was typically American. The organization was founded in 1901 as a philanthropic corporation created under the laws of the State of New York. The original charter stated: "The objects of said Corporation shall be to conduct, assist, and encourage investigations in the science and arts of hygiene, medicine and surgery, and allied subjects, in the nature and causes of disease and the methods of its prevention and treatment."

The Rockefeller Institute was conceived not by physicians or scientists, but by laymen. Gates surveyed the state of medical research in the United States at the turn of the century and concluded that it had not kept pace with physical science. He set out to correct the situation by advising John D. Rockefeller to establish an institute devoted exclusively to medical research. No such institution then existed in the United States. Rockefeller accepted Gates's suggestion and provided $200,000 for the purpose. The original gift was placed in the hands of the Board of Scientific Directors, composed of William H. Welch, T. Mitchell Pruden, Theobold Smith, and Simon Flexner, all of whom were pathologists, and three other physicians, L. Emmett Holt, Christian A. Herter, and Herman M. Biggs.

The money was not to be used immediately for the purchase of buildings and equipment; rather, it was to be given to young investigators to foster their careers in medical science. It was also to be used to ascertain the presence of adequately trained men in the universities who were engaged in medical research. The original $200,000 was meant to be expended within fifteen years in grants and fellowships. In the meantime a study was to be made of the need in the United States for an independent institute devoted solely to medical research. The decision in favor of such an institute was reached sooner than anticipated, and met with Rockefeller's approval. Because of his ties with New York, Rockefeller decided to locate the Institute in that city. A building was rented at 127 East 50th Street, and the Rockefeller Institute for Medical Research came into being.

The original staff consisted of Simon Flexner, pathologist and Director, with whom were associated Hideyo Noguchi, Eugene L. Opie, and J. E. Sweet; Samuel J. Meltzer, physiologist and pharmacologist; and P. A. Levene, biological chemist. The studies by these scientists so impressed Rockefeller that he purchased a tract of land overlooking the East River at 60th Street and built a new laboratory on it. The laboratory, known as the Central Laboratory, opened in 1906, just before Carrel came to New York. The Institute grew steadily. By the mid-1930s its staff included 134 scientists, twenty-two of whom were Members of the Institute, and eleven Associate Members. There was also a research hospital; Carrel had witnessed its opening in 1910.

Rockefeller provided a suitable endowment for the Institute; money from the outside was neither sought nor needed. The Institute was administered by the Board of Trustees and the Board of Scientific Directors. The Trustees, who included representatives of the Board of Scientific Directors, were charged with maintaining the endowment and properties of the Institute. The Corporation was composed of the Board of Scientific Directors, who supervised the expenditure of funds from the endowment; the Trustees, who were custodians of the Institute's property; and the Scientific Director, who had unrestricted charge of scientific work.

The Institute owed its conception to Gates and its physical life to the generosity of the Rockefellers, but during its first thirty years of existence, its spirit was that of Flexner. Research activities of the Institute's members were guided by his humanism and practical sense. Collaboration among the scientists was freely undertaken; in keeping with Flexner's notion of the maximum freedom needed for scientific achievement, people were neither encouraged to work together nor discouraged from it. The scientists with whom Carrel collaborated most were Peyton Rous, Karl Landsteiner, and Hideyo Noguchi. With Rous he worked on growing viruses in tissue cultures and on preservation of blood; with Landsteiner, on the production of antibodies by spleens cultivated in the Lindbergh apparatus, and on the origins of serum proteins.

Noguchi deserves special mention, for Carrel not only worked with him but admired him as well, and learned a valuable lesson from him. Although Noguchi had a broad educational background, his scientific work depended on but a few techniques. Personally, Noguchi exemplified honesty, intellectual integrity, and dedication to his work. His upbringing endowed him with a broad cultural base that Carrel did not have. While a child, Noguchi was tutored in French, German, English, and Latin, and in Chinese literature. After graduating from Tokyo Medical College in 1897 and serving as an assistant in the General Hospital in Tokyo and the Government Institute for the Study of Infectious Diseases, he went to China to deal with an epidemic of bubonic plague. Thereafter he came to America, first to study and then to work with Flexner. When the latter went to the Rockefeller Institute, so did Noguchi. His early scientific interests coincided with those of Flexner. He devoted several years to the study of syphilis, and demonstrated the presence of *Treponema pallidum* (the disease's causative organism) in the brain and spinal cord of patients whose central nervous system was afflicted by syphilis. He cultivated a number of spirochetes in artificial media.

In 1916 in Ecuador, presumably from patients with yellow fever, he isolated a microorganism which he named *Leptospira icteroides*. This organism produced lesions similar to yellow fever in experimental animals. Noguchi thought *Leptospira icteroides* was related to *Leptospira icterohaemorrhagiae*, the causative agent not of yellow fever, but of infectious jaundice or the so-called Weil's disease. Noguchi also thought the infection with *Leptospira icteroides* was transmissible from man to animals, and from animals to man by a mosquito, *Aedes aegypti*, as had been shown for yellow fever by the Walter Reed Commission in Cuba. In this instance, the classical bacteriologic technique of which he was a master did not serve Noguchi well; yellow fever was later shown to be caused by a virus.

Carrel and Noguchi had begun scientific collaboration in 1913. Shortly thereafter, Noguchi thought he had succeeded in isolating Negri bodies (intracellular inclusions found in the nerve cells of animals and humans infected with rabies). However, what Noguchi thought to be Negri bodies were probably detached cells found in tissue cultures. But Noguchi was initially convinced of his findings, and wrote to Carrel: "I am now absolutely sure of my work. . . . Since you left I have made a remarkable finding in connection with rabies. I succeeded in obtaining a culture of protozoan-like organisms (nucleated and with membrane) from the rabies tissue; I am certain that the organism is identical with the Negri bodies." This conclusion, although erroneous, is not surprising. Negri himself thought the inclusions he described represented protozoa. Having by then gained some experience in tissue culture, Carrel urged caution, which Noguchi finally exercised, realizing that what he saw in tissue cultures were detached dead cells rather than Negri bodies. In 1923 Carrel and Noguchi performed tissue-culture experiments, the object of which was to cultivate the Rocky Mountain Spotted Fever organism; although they obtained some positive results, these were too fragmentary and were not published.

His earlier experience with yellow fever in Ecuador later prompted Noguchi to undertake a detailed study of the disease. This he did, paying for it with his life: he died of yellow fever in Accra, West Africa, on May 21, 1928. In Africa he found little resemblance between yellow fever and the disease he had studied in South America, and before his death he was conscientiously disproving his earlier claims relating to its cause.

Flexner was aware of Carrel's excursions into infectious diseases, a subject in which Carrel had no formal training. Since in these studies Carrel was merely providing a newly developed tool of tissue culture to microbiologists and pathologists, the studies were not ill advised. In fact, Flexner encouraged Carrel to make efforts in this direction. But even had he viewed with skepticism an attempt by one of his scientists to cross interdisciplinary boundaries, he probably would not have discouraged him from doing so. Flexner's ideas of research did not include rigid compartmentalization or regimentation. Despite the impression one may get by looking at a photograph of Flexner, with his stiff collar and air of formality, he was very liberal in his dealings with personnel working in the Institute's laboratories.

For that matter, so was Carrel. Although he issued written instructions to the laboratory technicians, outlining their duties and assignments to various scientists, he voluntarily ended his authority at this level. Carrel's Division of Experimental Surgery was run on a very relaxed basis; he left the people alone. Richard Bing, coming to work with Carrel from Albert Fischer's laboratory in Copenhagen, found a wholly unexpected freedom in his research. He noted that Carrel "had tremendous understanding of the weaknesses of others, as long as they had some areas of strength." Yet prior to his joining the staff of the Rockefeller Institute, Carrel had had no experience in managing a laboratory. In France and Chicago he had worked mostly by himself or with only one assistant. The art of knowing when to leave subordinates alone and when to offer them help he acquired from Flexner.

Although Flexner's policy was not to interfere in the day-to-day operation of individual laboratories, he knew just about everything that was going on in the Institute. He served on both the Board of Trustees and the Board of Scientific Directors, a combination now seldom enjoyed by any administrator. He was undoubtedly a great man, but he achieved greatness because the Rockefeller Institute gave him an opportunity to become so. He was responsible for formulating the scientific policy of the Institute, and was also its top administrator. He discharged the responsibility of the Institute's medical scientists toward the medical profession at large. He defined the problems on which work needed to be done, and to this end employed the resources at his disposal with much skill. Nor was he afraid of responsibilities; most decisions regarding the direction of research at the Institute were made by him alone. Flexner did not depend on advisory committees to protect him from mistakes or to cover up the blunders, and he made few of either. Neither was he forced by the Institute Directors to depend upon committees.

In addition to entrusting Flexner with running the scientific affairs of the Institute, the Corporation had placed another powerful tool at his disposal, that of the medical press. The Institute published the *Journal of Experimental Medicine,* of which Flexner was the editor. He made the *Journal* one of the most prestigious scientific-medical publications in the world.

Despite his high position in medical science, his influence, and his connections, Flexner maintained a simplicity of manner. He did not hide in an academic Ivory Tower, but participated actively in scientific affairs and was readily accessible.

When his services were required by the government, Flexner offered them unselfishly. He went to the Philippines during the Spanish American War, and to France during World War I. He shared Carrel's great faith in science, but his faith in the ability of mankind to use science properly was greater. In the fall of 1939 he wrote to Carrel: "The world could be so beautiful if only men would permit it. With all that science has brought, and with what it will, if let do it, in the next years, there is enough for each country. The most critical and the most doubtful things are the political leaders."

Flexner reflected on political changes in the world, but

at the same time he was aware of the difficulties that world events imposed on their unwitting participants. When the Germans overran France in the spring of 1940, Carrel was in New York, but Mrs. Carrel remained in France. On July 5 Flexner wrote to Carrel from Chocorua, New Hampshire:

The disaster which has so quickly overtaken France filled me with despair and deep sympathy for you and Madame Carrel. I have tried to sit down and write you, but somehow my pen would not write. I can imagine what you are feeling. I am wondering where you are and what you are doing to keep your mind off the tragedy in France and the rest of Europe.

Here at Chocorua the world scarcely seems to move around us. The mountains, the green of the woods, the small village, friends separated but accessible, it is like an oasis of peace. From them I feel we learn little. Only this we know, that the world of your life and my life is past, and somehow we must adjust to the new order.

Before coming to the Rockefeller Institute, Flexner had already established himself as a medical scientist, and did this against considerable odds. In 1889, he had received his M.D. degree from the University of Louisville, then an obscure school. He obtained postgraduate training at Johns Hopkins University, where he came to William H. Welch's attention. Subsequently, he journeyed to Europe to do graduate work at several European universities, then returned to Johns Hopkins in 1895.

In 1899 Flexner became Chairman of the Department of Pathology at the University of Pennsylvania. At the same time he served as Director of the Ayer Clinical Laboratory and as Pathologist of the University of Pennsylvania Hospital and the Philadelphia Hospital. Thus before assuming the Directorship of Laboratories at the Rockefeller Institute in 1901, he had gained wide experience not only in academic medicine but also in the administration of hospital laboratories. He was the author of many papers and monographs on pathological anatomy, experimental pathology, and microbiology.

Flexner's success as an administrator was in large measure due to his ability to choose the people who could best do the job. During his administration he attracted to the Rockefeller Institute many highly successful scientists, but few of these gained wide public attention. Other than Carrel, only Lindbergh was well known to the man in the street. Karl Landsteiner did not get into the lay press until blood typing was admitted as evidence into courts in paternity suits.

Between Carrel and Flexner there seems to have existed a special relationship. Each respected the other, but there was never any doubt that Flexner was the senior of the two. Nothing was ever said about it, nor did it have to be. Although Flexner and Carrel worked in the same building, the exchange between them was largely by notes. Flexner did not use the telephone frequently because telephone calls interrupt work. For the same reason, he did not come too often to Carrel's laboratory. The notes sent by Flexner ranged from social invitations to acknowledgments of reports or similar matters. The social notes, like this one sent on October 25, 1922, were simple: "If you are free next Friday evening, Oct. 27, I shall be glad if you will come to dinner at my house, 815 Madison Avenue, at 7:30 o'clock. There will be no ladies present, and I am asking only a few Institute members; please do not trouble to dress." When Flexner needed to confer with Carrel he would again summon him by note, as on May 6, 1935: "Would you mind coming over any time before next Friday and talking with me about the men who should be invited to the luncheon for Dr. Vallery-Radot next Friday? I shall not be here tomorrow, Tuesday, at all, but shall be in on Wednesday. Perhaps we can arrange the list at that time."

Luncheon with Vallery-Radot could not be considered a trivial affair, for he personified the French scientific establishment, with which Carrel was constantly at odds. As neither side had yielded ground, this contest became stalemated. In other words, the French medical and scientific establishment remained as it was—conservative and aloof, ignoring the attacks of a belligerent compatriot who lived and worked abroad. On the other hand, the irascible compatriot continued to console himself with a steady barrage of criticism directed against the impregnable walls of institutional science. In essence, Carrel was defeated from the start by being excluded from the scientific affairs of his native country. Nevertheless, outward appearances of cordiality were maintained.

In 1931, however, Carrel finally succeeded in having Flexner elected to the corresponding membership of the French Academy of Science. This was a big event—all the more so, if one recalls the difficulties he experienced with Flexner's candidacy for election to the Academy during World War I. On May 26, 1931, Carrel wrote Flexner: "I have just received a letter from Captain d'Aubarède of the French Navy, who asks me to transmit to you his congratulations on your election to the French Academy of Science. You may remember that Captain d'Aubarède was the ensign of the French Navy who showed Mrs. Flexner, you, and me over the French battleship anchored in the Hudson about twenty-two or twenty-three years ago." Flexner replied: "A thousand thanks for your nice note of the 12th. I am of course very much gratified at the great compliment which has been paid me by the election to the French Academy. It was so entirely unexpected that it came like a shock, but a pleasant shock."

In 1933 Flexner received a letter from Vallery-Radot regarding the proposed reorganization of the Pasteur Institute. Flexner transmitted it to Carrel, saying it might interest him. Clearly, he now saw a chance to patch things up between Carrel and those Carrel had criticized. Flexner went out of his way to provide a forum for reconciliations.

If he succeeded in his attempts, the success was only a temporary one. Vallery-Radot and Carrel remained antagonistic toward each other, and when given a chance, Vallery-Radot would finally "discredit" Carrel, using a political guise for the purpose.

Flexner himself was foremost in giving public recognition to Carrel's achievements. When because of illness Carrel was unable to attend a dinner at which an award was given him by New York University, Flexner went in his place. He wrote Carrel the next day: "The dinner was a large one. I think you would have been gratified by the response of the audience which greeted the announcement of your name. I am very sorry that you could not have been present in person." And when Carrel was awarded a prize for cancer research, Flexner wrote him: "I am so very happy about the Nordhoff-Jung prize and the dignified way in which it is to be bestowed upon you. Dr. Nordhoff-Jung asked me to be present, but I shall probably be away on March 28 and I have had to decline. Should I be in New York on that date, I would surely try to be present."

When Carrel received the Nobel Prize, both Flexner and his wife were overjoyed. Mrs. Flexner wrote:

I wanted to have the pleasure of writing myself to tell you how delighted I am at the great honor which has come to you, so I did not join Dr. Flexner's congratulations yesterday—but only for that reason! I do congratulate you most warmly on having received so high and so merited a tribute to your disinterested devotion to scientific ends and to the splendid results which you have accomplished. All day I have been hearing the most appreciative things said of you and echoing them too—and I hope it mayn't be long before I have the pleasure of telling you in person how proud we all are of you!

Mrs. Flexner's interest in Carrel's work was longstanding. She came to the Institute to see some of his early operations. The record of such a visit is found in one of Flexner's notes to Carrel: "I have told Mrs. Flexner about your new operation upon the heart. Will you let me know some time when it would be convenient for her to be present at the operation. Of course you should not arrange it especially, as she can come over in all probability any time that you are operating."

Flexner had kept his promise to do what he could to advance Carrel's scientific work and his standing among his peers. In 1912 he secured for him an appointment as a Member of the Institute. Preparatory arrangements for this were made by Flexner a year earlier, which indicates that Carrel's promotion was not related to the Nobel Prize. Flexner informed Carrel of the appointment in a letter of June 25, 1912:

I am writing you briefly to express my great pleasure at the advance in salary to accompany your promotion to full membership in the Institute, of which the secretary will inform you. When I left in February, only the one could be undertaken, but now owing to Mr. Rockefeller's recent generosity the other can also be accomplished. As you know, I have a very high regard for your scientific work and am made very happy by the mark of appreciation on the part of all members of the Scientific Directors and Trustees of the Institute.

Flexner saw in Carrel an unusual scientist—one who was not afraid to try new things, even if they were not within his field of specialization. Tissue culture was a case in point: Flexner gave Carrel his support in this endeavor and it paid off. Flexner was quick to acknowledge the progress in virology made possible by tissue culture. In 1931, almost at the end of his career, he wrote Carrel: "I am sorry you had to miss Rivers' talk on Friday. You would have seen two things: (1) How fundamental your tissue culture has become, not only for the physiological study of cells but for study of viruses; (2) how little progress has been made in the effort to determine what it is that happens in the tissue cultures when the viruses multiply. But you know this already."

Flexner was interested in infectious diseases, as were most pathologists of his generation. Therefore his enthusiasm for the unexpected aid provided by tissue culture in the study of viruses is easy to understand. He probably reasoned that, since Carrel had developed the tissue-culture technique which aided in the study of viruses, he could equally well come up with something if he were to study the viruses themselves. To Flexner, Carrel was just the man who could produce something unexpected. However, being aware that Carrel had no training in microbiology, Flexner kept an eye on him in order to keep him "out of trouble." In 1912 Carrel mentioned ultramicroscopic organisms in the first version of his paper "Artificial Activation of the Growth *in Vitro* of Connective Tissue," but Flexner advised him to delete mention of them.

In 1933 Carrel sent Flexner a manuscript, "The Cultivation of Viruses in Unfertilized Egg-Yolk." On reading it, Flexner commented: "I am so much impressed with the great significance of your observations of the increase of certain viruses in egg yolk, that I am inclined to suggest to you that you delay publication until you run through a new series of tests in the Autumn." The additional experiments did not support the initial observations, making Flexner's warning timely, but nothing ventured, nothing gained. This incident demonstrates how Flexner created the atmosphere in which scientists could pursue whatever studies they wished. Neither mistakes nor negative results were feared, for Flexner did not hold failure to produce positive results against the investigator.

Not all Flexner's comments urged caution. If Flexner liked something, he did not hesitate to say so, be it privately or in public, as can be seen from a letter to Carrel of April 21, 1931: "Your article in *Science* of March 20 on 'The New Cytology' is a masterpiece. I do congratulate you on it, and the Institute on the comprehensive and fundamental program, there so clearly and convincingly stated, on which you are working."

In his dealings with the scientific staff of the Institute, Flexner was always a gentleman. He made it a point not only to acknowledge all communications, but to add some personal touch even to routine correspondence. More-over, he extended his friendship not just to Carrel but to the entire staff. Thus Jacques Loeb's death genuinely grieved him. He wrote to Carrel: "The Institute and all of us personally have suffered a very severe loss in Loeb's death. We can never replace him. His example will live among us as long as we can work, and I hope his memory and his writings may serve to animate another generation of workers."

After Lindbergh achieved some measure of success with the organ-culture apparatus, Carrel submitted a detailed report on the work to the Board of Scientific Directors. Having received this, Flexner responded on March 28, 1933: "Your report to the Board of Scientific Directors is most remarkable. You have brought together a most un-usual and very numerous series of observations of the great-est biological interest. I wonder could you show the new Lindbergh apparatus and explain it to the Scientific Di-rectors at the meeting on April 22, if you are to be in New York? They would, I know, be deeply interested." Carrel re-plied: "Concerning the Lindbergh apparatus, it would be in-teresting for the Board if a demonstration were given by Colonel Lindbergh, and also if physiological results could be shown at the same time as the technique. I believe that Colonel Lindbergh is to be away at the time of the meet-ing. Would it not be better to postpone such a demonstra-tion until next fall?" To this Flexner readily agreed.

Carrel had asked Flexner to postpone the demonstra-tion for two reasons. First, it is always reassuring to ac-cumulate more data before presenting the results of one's experiments. Second, compared to Lindbergh, Carrel knew relatively little about the mechanics of the perfusion apparatus; if the apparatus malfunctioned or if some technical questions were asked, Lindbergh was the only one who could deal with the situation.

Lindbergh's presence at the Institute of course created problems with the press. Carrel did all that was possible to protect his privacy and allow him to work unimpeded. Officially, Lindbergh was a volunteer worker in Carrel's laboratory, and Flexner tactfully communicated with him only through Carrel. Dealings with the press were also left to Carrel, whose letter of September 22, 1931, to W. M. Weishaar of the *New York Herald Tribune* shows how he handled such matters:

This morning I received your message about the rumor that Colonel Lindbergh has been interested in some work in my laboratories. You will, without doubt, fully understand that I cannot make any statement on this subject. Publicity about political, economic, and scientific events is one thing. But publicity about the men who are expected to make discoveries is another thing. It is useful in the first case; in the second it is harmful. An indispensable condition for intellectual creation is the uninterrupted concentration of the mind on one subject. Such concentration absolutely requires solitude and silence. Men of science should not attract the curiosity of the public. . . .

. . . I have no doubt that your friends of the *Herald Tribune,* which always has a broad understanding of such matters, will agree completely with this opinion.

Because of the Institute's concern for his privacy, Lindbergh felt quite free to move about the buildings, to work with other people, and to lunch with the Institute's scientists. The luncheons in the Institute's dining rooms provided a forum for exchanging ideas. The time for these was usually prearranged, and occasionally outsiders would be invited. If Lindbergh was to be present, he was told about the guests in advance. Before one luncheon, Flexner wrote to Carrel on January 30, 1934: "It is very kind of Colonel Lindbergh to be willing to lunch with us and to talk of his wonderful trip. I suggest Friday of this week, or even better, Tuesday of next week, according to your and Colonel Lindbergh's convenience. Do you think it agreeable to Colonel Lindbergh to have my wife and Jimmie at the luncheon? That would make five persons altogether. A sixth would balance the table. Have you a suggestion?"

Thus Flexner went out of his way to make the Rockefeller Institute a pleasant place to work. In so doing, he protected the scientists of the Institute from being exposed to unnecessary stresses and pressures which might interfere with their work. However, Flexner's gentlemanly behavior and his easy-going manner should not be mistaken for weakness of character. Nor should it be assumed that his personal friendships with many members of the Institute's staff influenced his scientific and administrative decisions. When necessary, he was firm and decisive. He also had considerable insight into the behavior of many of his subordinates.

When the established rules were broken, Flexner took immediate action. In Carrel's absence he once fired his secretary on the spot, and told Carrel about it subsequently: "Have you been informed we let Mrs. D—— go? She has not conducted herself with propriety and discretion, but has given out material, without my knowledge or consent, for newspapers and magazines, which is quite indefensible. She must not come back here, and I hope can be cut off entirely from communication with and about the Institute." And when circumstances warranted the refusal of a request, even a reasonable one, Flexner did this without apologizing. At one point Carrel requested an additional associate and a technician. Through the Institute's manager, Flexner informed him it would not be possible to hire more personnel; further discussion of the subject was not called for.

Flexner also acted against a proposal by his early pro-tégé, Harvey Cushing, for the establishment of the National Institute of Neurology. After encountering difficulties with government agencies, Cushing turned to the Rockefeller Foundation for support. When Flexner opposed the project, Cushing suggested he did so because he was afraid it would compete with the Rockefeller Institute. However, this accusation is probably unfounded. Flexner simply thought neurological surgery could best be developed in existing hospitals, not in a special institute. After all, it was not solely a research endeavor, but rather a practical matter of developing a new surgical specialty.

Flexner aided Carrel in solving problems faced by his associates and let Carrel know he was kept up to date on their progress. In 1930 he wrote Carrel:

I think he [Ebeling] has done quite well. Even though he has been run down in the last period, I am inclined to believe that he was kept from falling into what might have been a long period, if not a permanent one, of invalidism and hypochondria, by being brought back to work. I shall not be surprised if it takes two or three years to get him completely on his feet again. In the meantime, it is important to put him to work and not to humor him. . . .

I am very happy to have your good report of de Kock and of Parker. If the latter is really good and suited to your work, we will try to place him in a situation in which he can live contentedly. Let us talk this over in the autumn. I judge that de Kock did things to help you as well as himself. I wonder, did he write up his studies before he left?

In 1935 Carrel became concerned about Ebeling, who had lost ten pounds without any apparent cause, in a very short time. On June 7 he wrote to Flexner to propose that Dr. Ebeling be sent on his vacation at once. Flexner replied on June 24:

I am writing first to tell you of the talk I had with Dr. Ebeling. He is evidently much better, and by eating whether he feels like it or not he seems to have regained about all that he had lost, and even more. He assures me that he is very well and that he is going away early. He did not look as though he were concerned about himself.

Of course Carrel too contributed to the development of the Institute. P. A. Levene, one of the original members of the Institute, expressed his feelings on Carrel's work there as follows: "Your remarks meant so much to me, not only for the thought contained in them but particularly for the fact that they came from you to whom we all in the Institute owe so much. In the early trying and struggling years of the Institute your success was of general help to all of us and we of the early group will never forget it."

Now the "early group" was leaving the stage, and a new group was making an entrance. The new group brought to the Institute not only new people, but also different ideas. Narrow specialization made inroads into science, and with it came new ways of doing things. Noguchi was gone, as was Meltzer. Flexner retired in 1935. Welch no longer provided direction to the Board. Flexner was not exaggerating when he wrote to Carrel in 1939: "The world of your life and my life is past, and somehow we must adjust to the new order."

In 1935 the new order appeared in the person of the new Institute Director, Herbert Spencer Gasser, previously Professor of Physiology and Director of the Physiological Laboratories of the Cornell University Medical College in New York City, just across the street from the Rockefeller Institute. Considered by his contemporaries to be one of the country's leading physiologists, Gasser was forty-seven years old and unmarried. Like Flexner, he was a product of the Johns Hopkins University School of Medicine. His research dealt with coagulation of blood, traumatic shock, and the physiology of nerve impulse transmission. With Joseph Erlanger he combined the amplifier with a cathode-ray oscillograph (a tube similar to a television tube), which enabled them to study the highly differential function of individual nerve fibers. For this work Erlanger and Gasser would share the Nobel Prize in Medicine and Physiology in 1944.

Gasser had gone to Cornell in 1931 from Washington University in St. Louis, where Guthrie had worked; undoubtedly he knew of Guthrie's discontent over the amount of credit given him for the work with Carrel on blood-vessel suturing. At the Institute, from the very start a personality conflict developed between Gasser and Carrel. Much younger than Carrel, Gasser did not command Carrel's respect, as Flexner had. In retrospect, Richard Bing felt the difficulties between them were "primarily the fault of the Director, who had very little respect for vision and breadth of spirit, but was more impressed by compartmentalized wisdom." Administrative details, which Flexner had kept to the minimum, were accentuated by Gasser. The free spirit of Flexner had become a thing of the past.

Since at the Rockefeller Institute the budget was controlled entirely by the Director, it was easy for Gasser to "put the squeeze" on Carrel. As is usual in such cases, the pressure was applied first to Carrel's associates. Carrel's request for salary increases for Drs. Ebeling and Parker was denied in a terse note from the Director: "The possibility of increasing the salaries of Dr. Ebeling and Dr. Parker has been considered, and it is deemed inadvisable to do so at the present time." The laboratory budget was also curtailed. Indirectly, Carrel transmitted his feelings about inadequate finances to Gasser on March 28, 1938. Gasser had asked him to loan a film on growth of cells in tissue culture for demonstration at a scientific gathering. Carrel replied that the film showing the growth of tissue cells had not been out of the vault in several years because it was so brittle that it broke easily when being shown. Therefore, to avoid irreparable damage, Carrel had to refuse requests to run it through the projection apparatus. He said he had the negatives of the film, but no money to pay for a new copy.

Suddenly the preparation of the annual scientific reports began to present problems. The type of scientific reports Flexner found satisfactory apparently did not meet with Gasser's full approval, as evidenced by a letter from him to Carrel of February 17, 1937:

The report should cover the period from April 1936 up to the present time and should include a bibliography alphabetically arranged. In making the report, I think it is better in the matter of clarity to select a few of the subjects that are being investigated for a more detailed presentation, rather than to attempt to cover everything which is going on over a course of several years. The individual subjects will then receive better treatment than they would in brief descriptions every year.

In order to keep the total report from the Laboratory within a reasonable compass, it is necessary to limit the number of pages. The number of pages in your reports for the years 1935 and 1936 including the publications were 13 and 14 respectively. I would suggest that you do not exceed this limit.

Carrel complied with the request and on March 19, 1937, submitted the required report accompanied by the following letter:

I am enclosing my report, which is limited, in accordance with your desires, to a few of the subjects that are being investigated in my laboratories. The work of Drs. Landsteiner and Parker and Bergman and Ebeling is but mentioned. The work of Dr. Dubuisson on the effect *in vitro* of thelin and corpus luteum on the Fallopian tube and uterus, by Dr. Bing on the cultivation of the pancreas, by Dr. Thygeson on cultivation of the human conjunctiva in relation to his work on virus, is not mentioned. If you find this report too long, I shall be glad to suppress one or two pages of it.

In other instances Gasser made an even more direct request for a report. He wrote Carrel on September 11, 1936: "I am preparing a report on the work of the Institute for the Corporation, and am planning to include selected topics of special interest. One of these is the perfusion of isolated organs. No mention of this subject has been made to the Corporation since the preliminary note written three years ago. So the subject may be treated as a whole. As the total report is to be very short, I cannot allow more than 5 typed pages to this subject."

Gasser's insistence on detailed description of a few individual subjects, rather than description of the overall activity of a group of scientists, represented a shift from Flexner's broad view of research to project-oriented science. For a scientist accustomed to the freedom under Flexner, the transition to intellectual regimentation was difficult. Furthermore, the presentation of only selected topics to the Board might invite misinterpretations regarding the amount of work generated by the laboratory, in proportion to the funds expended.

Carrel's "American dream" suddenly became a nightmare. The environment in which he had worked unperturbed for so many years had turned hostile. Official disapproval of Carrel's activities was voiced by Gasser, who took exception to Carrel's free public expression of opinions on various subjects. On February 6, 1936, Gasser warned Carrel in a confidential memorandum:

The exactions which the world places on science makes me hold a most conservative attitude about the making of statements. When the latter are made on no matter what subject without the rigorous precaution which is exerted in one's own experimental field, they create in the rebound the possibility of raising doubt with respect to the correctness of conclusions about which the expected scientific care is exerted. The importance of this fact outweighs in my mind any interest in science which may be aroused in the mind of the public by more popular treatment of material, and is the real reason for my writing of this letter.

Carrel paid no attention to the warning and continued to

present his views in lectures, the lay press, and commencement addresses. The conflict between him and Gasser increased in intensity until it became common knowledge. Members of the Institute began to take sides. Some used Carrel as an excuse to express their own dissatisfaction with the new administration. Members who had joined the Institute early in its inception were particularly sensitive to the changes. By 1938 Gasser decided the time had come to put them in their place.

13 ☢ Retirement

Carrel was much perturbed by the prospect of retirement. He was unprepared for it, thinking that it simply could not happen to him. When he finally realized what was taking place, he saw it as a final triumph for the Director. His feeling of annoyance was reinforced by the premature announcement of the retirement in *Science*—an announcement that someone at the Institute sent in without his knowledge. He wrote to the editor: "The announcement of my retirement, made in the June 17th [1938] issue of *Science*, on page 549, has been brought to my attention. Although I will be sixty-five years old this month, my retirement from this Institute will not take place until July 1st, 1939. As the notice reads now, it indicates that I retire the first of the coming month. Would you be so kind as to have a corrected notice inserted, at your convenience?"

What bothered Carrel was not his retirement per se, but the closing of all his laboratories and the dissolution of the Division of Experimental Surgery. The decision to close the Division produced a great deal of bitterness in Carrel. He wrote to William O'Neil Sherman, Chief Surgeon of the Carnegie Steel Company, with whom Carrel co-operated on the treatment of wounds sustained in industrial accidents: ". . . my department and myself are being suppressed just at the time when we are developing, with great success, methods that apply to the whole field of biology, from anatomy, embryology, physiology, and especially to endocrinology, to biological chemistry, pharmacology, and pathology. I hope to continue my work with Lindbergh in some other institution."

The closing of the laboratories continued to concern him, as evidenced by another letter to Sherman:

Should war occur, there would be a repetition of the surgical errors of 1914. From the point of view of treatment of infected wounds, modern surgeons are as ignorant as were their predecessors twenty-five years ago. It is a great pity. For such ignorance is bound to cause the loss of innumerable lives and limbs. There will be no possibility of me to be of any help, because I am being forced out of scientific work at the Rockefeller Institute.

As yet I have not made any definite plans. I shall probably have to take up some kind of commercial work. It is the first time that a recipient of the Nobel Prize has been compelled to give up science and start another career. Such action has never been taken, even in Germany. The work of Lindbergh is also being stopped. This means that the very important and promising experiments which we were making on the cultivation of viruses, especially poliomyelitis virus, and the cultivation of organs, have come to an end.

Carrel's strong feelings with regard to his retirement were not entirely unjustified. Until he reached sixty-five, the Institute did not have a mandatory retirement age. Flexner had retired at seventy, and William Welch at eighty-three. Landsteiner and Levene were still working at seventy, but they too would have to retire if Carrel did. So would Florence Sabin, who had just turned sixty-seven, and Winthrop J. V. Osterhout, sixty-eight. With the advent of the new retirement policy, Gasser would remove from the Institute's active rolls the most significant remnants of Flexner's "old guard." This would serve a dual purpose: it would eliminate the disciples of the old regime, and give him the added resources to appoint his own protégés to the staff. Gasser did not have much sympathy for experimental surgery, and his plans did not include continuing this type of work.

Gasser exerted all the pressure he could on the Board of Scientific Directors and the Board of Trustees to pass the mandatory retirement resolution. The timing of his efforts leaves little doubt that he wanted the policy adopted in time to retire Carrel at the first opportunity. The mandatory retirement rule was adopted, but it contained a provision "that, at the discretion of the Board, members, upon retirement, may be given annual support for continuation of their personal research from year to year." The key words were "personal research," for what constituted "personal research" was to be determined by the Director. Gasser had formally offered Carrel permission to continue a laboratory on a "personal basis." However, the offer did not include technical personnel to continue organ-perfusion and tissue-culture experiments, nor would it provide space for Lindbergh to work in. After much delay Carrel declined the offer. The laboratories were to be closed in their entirety. He instructed his secretary to answer all inquiries about his retirement with the following statement: "Doctor Carrel's division will be closed and his staff disbanded on July 1, 1939, because he has reached the age of sixty-five. On account of this administrative rule, the work of Doctor Carrel and Colonel Lindbergh will not be continued at the Rockefeller Institute for Medical Research." He asked that no more and no less be said on the subject.

The *History of the Rockefeller Institute, 1901–1953*, written by George Corner, describes Carrel's retirement as follows:

In 1939 and 1940, as already stated, six Members of The Rockefeller Institute's Department of Laboratories reached retirement age. Florence Sabin returned to her native Colorado to begin the notable new career sketched out in Chapter 9. Landsteiner, Levene, Michaelis, and Osterhout all continued to work at the Institute, which provided laboratory facilities and secretarial and technical assistance adequate for their individual needs. Carrel did not request similar provision. He had become more a philosopher and mystic than a productive scientist. Flexner had been troubled by Carrel's failure to publish a report of the cancer research in the large mouse colony [memorandum Simon Flexner's hand, dated June, 1938, made available by James T. Flexner] and, in view of the growing demands upon a strained budget, the new Director [Gasser] and the Board were doubtless relieved by his outright retirement. The situation distressed Carrel's friends, but as things turned out it was of little moment, for Carrel in his eagerness to make a bold stroke for his native country soon returned to France, ending his days there amid the confusion of World War II and its aftermath.

This excerpt from the official history of the Institute reflects little accuracy other than Gasser's relief at being rid of a difficult customer, and Corner's own view of what constitutes a productive scientist. First of all, the initial statement is misleading. As mentioned earlier, five of the six members of the Institute referred to by Corner were several years beyond the newly established mandatory retirement age; Carrel alone was forced to terminate an active scientific career at sixty-five. Second, Corner does not mention the fact that Carrel's ill feelings were precipitated not so much by his own retirement as by the abolition of the entire Division of Experimental Surgery.

If one reads between the lines, the Division's dissolution may have been directed at Lindbergh rather than Carrel. By this time Lindbergh had emerged on the scene of national politics. For obvious reasons the administration of the Rockefeller Institute did not wish to be associated with any political stands. As long as Lindbergh worked at the Institute, such an association could be made by inference.

The statement about Carrel becoming unproductive simply does not stand up to close scrutiny. In the last two years of the laboratories' operation, scores of papers were published by Carrel and his co-workers. To label Parker, Ebeling, Baker, and Bing unproductive was equally incorrect. These investigators have published extensively and left their mark on tissue culture. Nor was Carrel's own reputation as a scientist tarnished in the late 1930s, as suggested by Corner. When a prestigious new journal, *Surgery*, was first published in 1937, William F. Rienhoff, Jr., asked Carrel to contribute one or more editorials for an early issue. Busy writing *The Culture of Organs*, Carrel replied: "I wish indeed that I might have the pleasure of acceding to your suggestion. But the nature of my work this winter makes it materially out of the question for me to secure the leisure to write anything of so important a nature as the contribution you mention."

To give Carrel full recognition for his work, the Board of Scientific Directors of the Rockefeller Institute for Medical Research, at a meeting on June 10, 1939, passed the following resolution:

In consideration of the service which Doctor Alexis Carrel has rendered to the Rockefeller Institute for Medical Research during the thirty-three years he has been on its staff, through his development of the technique of blood vessel suture, his studies on the healing of wounds, his work on tissue culture which has not only brought forth new knowledge, but also has demonstrated the constancy of cell strains and provided a valuable means for the growing of viruses and preparation of vaccines, and through the opening of the new field of organ culture and

In appreciation of his deep-felt interest in the broad problems that mankind must face and solve if it is to improve its lot, it was

RESOLVED that a minute be spread upon the records of the Board of Scientific Directors and that a copy of this minute be made and conveyed to Doctor Carrel as a token of the high esteem in which his work is held by its members.

The statement regarding Flexner's alleged concern about the 1938 scientific report is puzzling. Having retired in 1935, Flexner was not actively involved thereafter in the administrative affairs of the Institute. Since in compiling the official history of the Institute, Corner presumably had access to the Institute's records, it is difficult to understand why he had to rely on fragmentary information passed on to him by Flexner's son. In going over Flexner's letters and memoranda to Carrel, this writer has found no expression of sentiment regarding Carrel's cancer research such as was ascribed to him by Corner. Furthermore, since 1935 all reports prepared for the Board of Scientific Directors had been compiled in accordance with Gasser's directions. Since the reports were limited in length, it is not surprising that Carrel chose to elaborate on the subjects with clear-cut results, such as organ culture, rather than devote the entire report to voluminous mouse studies, the results of which were open to different interpretations.

Carrel's retirement caused considerable stir in the press. The *New York Times* devoted a special article to the subject. Waldemar Kaempffert, Science Editor of the *Times*, wrote Carrel on April 8, 1938:

You will be celebrating an important birthday on June 28th. The *New York Times* would like to commemorate the occasion by publishing in its Magazine Issue of the 26th, the preceding Sunday, an interview with you which I am to write. Following my usual practice, this will be submitted to you for correction and approval before publication. Since I know so much about you and your work, I shall probably not have to take up much of your time.

I know you don't like interviews, but I think that the occasion is such that an exception can be legitimately made. When do I come to see you?

This Week, in an article entitled "The Amazing Doctor Carrel," described him as a man whose work was underlined by a deep meaning. Frederick Sondern, Jr., the author of the article, noted: "It is not science for the sake of science alone that interests him, but the conviction that a fuller knowledge of the construction and function of man as a whole will make a better and happier man." The *New York Herald* and many other newspapers carried news of Carrel's retirement, with comment. Throughout, Carrel himself maintained remarkable composure and would not belittle the Institute or its Directors to the press, although he had ample opportunities for doing so. The *New York Times* observed, "Doctor Carrel, who had been pictured in published reports as being forced out, declined to discuss the matter."

In all due fairness to the Board of Directors of the Institute and to John D. Rockefeller, Jr., it must be pointed out that placing Carrel on the retirement list was not done with the object of leaving him entirely "out in the cold." The Board members thought he still could be accommodated in a laboratory. This Gasser promised to do and the matter was left in his hands. In view of the personality conflict between him and Carrel, Carrel chose not to seek a compromise and ask Gasser for favors.

The alleged financial strain on the Institute's budget, given as the reason for closing the laboratories, probably did not enter into the picture at all. When Coudert wrote John D. Rockefeller, Jr., and offered to furnish funds for the laboratories' continuation, the offer was not even given serious consideration. Instead, Rockefeller replied to Coudert in a very thoughtful manner, outlining his feelings on statutory retirement. Rockefeller's sincerity in adhering to the established policy, in the belief that it served a common good, cannot be doubted. He reasoned that people went on working as long as they were able to, largely because no provision had been made for their later years, but the trend of the time was clearly toward the making of such provision and toward a definite retirement at a fixed age.

But Rockefeller was under the impression that Carrel

would be able to continue his work. He probably did not realize that tissue and organ-culture experiments could not be continued without adequate technical support. He said, "Fortunately for men of the caliber of those now retiring, there is a provision which makes possible the supplying, at the request of the individual, laboratory facilities available to these four scientists. While they are necessarily on a reduced scale, nevertheless the opportunity is afforded to each of these gentlemen for the continuation of his research work, if he so desires."

However, whether out of obstinacy or because of machinations by the Institute Director, Carrel did not ask for even token financial support from the Institute. After over thirty years' existence, the laboratories of the Division of Experimental Surgery were closed and Carrel's associates dispersed throughout the country.

In January 1940 the *World Telegram* carried a curious news item: "Obituary: That Chicken Heart of Doctor Carrel's is Dead at 28. . . . News of the death was discovered when the *World Telegram* made its routine annual checkup on the heart's 28th birthday." At the Institute the manager, who would not give his name to the newspapers and who, according to the same report, wasn't the slightest bit interested in the vital statistics of a chicken heart anyhow, explained that all Carrel's work had been suspended until the scientist returned from Paris, if and when he did return. In fact, Carrel's laboratory staff had been disbanded when he left the country in July 1939, presumably in retirement status, although the manager said he was as much in doubt as to the biologist's status as anyone else. "Listen," he said, "the Institute didn't encourage this business about the birthday of the chicken heart. All the experiments were discontinued, however, and presumably the chicken heart, which actually is the fragment of an embryonic chicken heart, was allowed to die a natural death."

The newspaper report was accurate enough, but this

kind of publicity did not suit the Institute Director. Shortly after the appearance of the story he let the *World Telegram* know that "when Doctor Carrel left last July, he arranged to have a private laboratory continue the chicken heart tissue experiments. The Institute's failure to disclose the fact yesterday arose from the Institute's obligation to keep the name of the laboratory confidential, and was in accord with the Institute's policy of confining any statements strictly to work that goes on within its own laboratories."

Why Gasser did not want to tell anyone that a few cultures of the chicken heart fibroblasts were taken to the Lederle Laboratories by Carrel's former associate, Ebeling, is anyone's guess. However, the possibility exists that he did not want Ebeling commenting to the newspaper reporters on the wisdom of disbanding the first, and one of a very few, tissue-culture laboratories in the United States.

14 🕮 The Coming of the War

Retirement from the Rockefeller Institute had caught Carrel literally off guard. He was left with an office and a secretary, but without laboratories. The Division of Experimental Surgery, with all of its technical and scientific staff, had been disbanded. Since he felt he had been unfairly dealt with, his natural inclination was to pack up his equipment and move elsewhere to resume the work of his laboratories. He explored several possibilities. At first he proposed to establish "Highfield Laboratories," near Hopewell, New Jersey, where he could continue work with Lindbergh and Dr. R. W. G. Wyckoff. Detailed plans for the operation of his laboratory were drawn up by Carrel, and Lindbergh offered to donate four hundred acres of land on which the laboratory could be built. However, Carrel was unable to raise the necessary funds for the laboratory, and the project died a natural death. He then began discussions with Dr. John H. Kellogg, who wanted to build a laboratory at the Battle Creek Sanitarium in Miami Springs, Florida, but this project likewise did not materialize. Attempts by Raymond C. Parker and others to place Carrel in several universities were also unsuccessful.

Meanwhile, with the closing of the laboratories imminent, Carrel occupied himself mainly by writing. He said he was continuing his career as a "man of letters." His literary and journalistic endeavors proved successful. For a first article on breast feeding, the *Reader's Digest* paid $500 more than the price stipulated in the contract, because the publisher considered the article "outstanding." For a second article, the publisher sent Carrel's agent a telegram of congratulations. Carrel was enchanted to be with people who were young and active, and to be associated with a magazine which had a wide circulation. But then he realized that the shorter the article was, the more difficult it was to write. He wrote a third article, entitled "Health," which brought enormous publicity. Proposals had been made to him by several newspapers to write daily or weekly columns. To have an audience of several million people, to whom he could convey his ideas on a regular basis, had a certain appeal to Carrel. However, his wife opposed the plan, so he decided to study the question. Mrs. Carrel thought her husband should pursue his scientific studies. She did not care for the majority of Carrel's colleagues at the Rockefeller Institute in the first place and very strongly supported Carrel's feelings regarding the bad treatment he received at the hands of the Institute's administration. If Carrel were to devote himself entirely to writing, this would preclude taking up the studies discontinued in New York. This would also keep him from returning to France, an alternative of which Mrs. Carrel was much in favor.

When World War II suddenly broke out in September 1939, Carrel was in France. Though too old to enter military service, he nevertheless tried to do something useful, in the belief that the events of World War I would be repeated. His impressions of the early weeks of the war are recorded in a letter to Coudert, dated October 10, 1939:

What you write is profoundly true. This cataclysm is the final expression of a state that has established itself little by little in the democracies as in the totalitarian countries.

The first thing for me to do was to see in what measure I

could contribute to the progress of the treatment of the wounded and also to the solution of the very grave problems that the presence of the refugees creates in many regions of France. These unfortunates not only find themselves in very bad conditions, but they make life difficult for those who lodge them. For the moment, I am at the Ministry of Public Health. I shall see in two or three weeks whether it is possible to work effectively with the Military Health Service. I should easily be able to aid them in the question of hemorrhages, shock, infections. But it is necessary to know whether the little organization materially indispensable for this work can be realized, whether the necessary men can be obtained. If I am not able to work under conditions suitable to obtain positive results rapidly, I shall return to New York.

Carrel stated to friends that, after the war had begun, there was only one thing for him to do—to try to be of some use in the sphere of his technical knowledge. A Senator whom he knew requested the Minister of Public Health to attach Carrel to his Cabinet. This was done, and Carrel got the impression that this appointment would allow him to do what he thought most urgent: organizing the military blood transfusion service.

Of course it did not take a great scientific mind to realize that blood transfusions would be essential in the treatment of hemorrhages. Some of the doctors in the Health Department came to precisely the same conclusion and proceeded to get things organized in a great hurry, but with equally great carelessness. Carrel noted in a private letter that "the Health Department and the doctors of Paris have moved with an unbelievable swiftness. 'French swiftness' is not an exaggeration. It is true. It will cause the death of many people."

The declaration of war and the general mobilization brought back memories of World War I. But being well informed on technological developments, Carrel was sure this war would be different from the last one, and the loss of life greater. He said repeatedly that people did not understand the immensity of what was going to happen.

In the summer of 1939 Carrel became somewhat detached from his personal affairs in New York. He began to realize war was on the horizon and no one could do anything to prevent it. Once things became inevitable, his calm gave way to despair. Carrel remembered the other war, and said again and again that it had produced nothing but immense human suffering.

At the end of July Carrel went to Paris. The extreme danger of the international situation was obvious to him, but he noticed no nervousness, nor any undue concern on the part of the government. It seemed as if those in power thought the possibility of an armed conflict remote. Life was going on as usual. Carrel went back to Saint-Gildas.

In August mobilization became imminent. On Saint-Gildas the Carrels were straining to hear the bells in the villages on the coast: the sinister tocsin which announced invasions and other calamities in the past, and now the general mobilization. All Carrel could do was to sit and wait, brooding over the future. An old man at the end of the road—old, but with a clear vision as to what was to come. For he remembered only too well the mangled bodies, and the blood and stench of infected wounds. He knew that nothing was ready to alleviate the suffering, that no preparations had been made to avoid unnecessary loss of life. The lessons of the previous war had been forgotten.

When the bells rang, more than thirty men were called to the Army from a village in Brittany of about three hundred. Carrel thought how strange was the simplicity of great human tragedies. The sun was still shining, the birds were singing, and people went about as usual. But tomorrow these young men working in the fields would be shot to pieces, asphyxiated by gases, and everything would be changed.

At this stage of life Carrel could have stepped to the sidelines, and done so gracefully. He was too old for military service, and was known to believe that while millions were preparing the work of destruction, a few must be concerned with building the future. Though he preferred to be in New York, he felt compelled to remain in France to do what he could for the war effort, and so went off to Paris.

He had expected the armies to go into action quickly after the declaration of war. When nothing happened, he tried to analyze why. Deep inside, he knew the war machine would start rolling sooner or later.

Again in Paris during this second war of his lifetime, he walked in solitude and silence. The street lights were wrapped in black curtains and lit only the trunks of a few trees. The dome of the Invalides was visible in the moonlight. The lights of the passing cars were dim blue, as were the store windows. Carrel did not understand what was happening to him and admitted it was total darkness. With anguish he wondered what the attitude of the United States would be. The international atmosphere was very different from that of the last war. No one could guess the future. Carrel experienced profound sadness, although without depression. He wrote to his nephew that that night, on the deserted streets of Paris, he seemed to have heard the voice of Dante rising from the depths of ages and repeating:

Through me ye enter into town of woe,
Through me ye pass into eternal sorrow,
Through me ye join the nation of the lost.

For the past year Carrel had lived in anticipation of events to come. He held that the outbreak of the major war in Europe, with its wholesale destruction, would spell the end of Western civilization as he knew it, for he felt that only the totalitarian states could profit from the conflict. He expressed this sentiment repeatedly, and maintained this position openly until the collapse of France. In the spring of 1940 in a letter to Coudert he wrote:

". . . our immediate concern should be the war, and the possible destruction of Western civilization. . . . It is of capital importance to articulate democratic ideals that France and England are fighting to preserve. But every civilized man should realize that life would not be worth living in a world dominated by Hitler and Stalin."

Carrel's feelings on the prospect of a European war were clearly and publicly stated. He predicted that the European war would develop into a global conflict.

After the publication of *Man, the Unknown,* Carrel had become a public figure. He spoke out on many issues. He thought it was his duty to warn the American public about the possibility of war. In an unpublished manuscript found among his personal papers, he said, in 1939:

We must think about war. Technology has narrowed the Atlantic and Pacific oceans to a dangerous degree. Isolation is impossible. Domestic and foreign propaganda is attempting to confuse our minds on vital issues.

The presence of the totalitarian states profoundly disturbs Europe and Asia. Germany and Italy are openly preparing for attack. Democratic nations have been compelled to arm.

War menaces civilization in its entirety. We have to realize its significance. For we, our children, and our children's children will bear its consequences.

Carrel envisioned the conflict as one which would cause great destruction, and maintained that the meaning of the war had changed. Because of the increase in the magnitude of destruction, the future war would result in the loss of the "best stock of people." He was certain it would be different from the last one, due to the transformation in armaments brought about by science and inventions, aerial bombers, submarines, long-range guns, new explosives, tanks, poisonous gases. Women and children would not be respected. Aviation might bring immediately to the heart of the enemy country explosives, gases, incendiary bombs. War would become totalitarian.

He continually stressed the futility of World War I, with its enormous destruction of life and subsequent lowering of the level of intellectual existence. He commented on it thus in an unpublished manuscript he was preparing for the *Reader's Digest*:

The victors suffered as cruelly as the vanquished. Natural selection ceased to operate. For the fittest were given the more dangerous duties. The flower of youth was killed. There is today a striking scarcity of great men in France and England. Could European nations stand such a loss again? The future of the white races is at stake. . . .

Carrel held modern war to be not only a disastrous enterprise but an absurdity, because it would not lead to the solution of vital problems.

World War II had started suddenly and, as predicted by Carrel, at a time set by a European dictator. As much as Carrel disliked French officialdom, he could not imagine France other than allied with America in a common cause. Unlike his friend Lindbergh, he did not believe America should remain neutral in a European conflict. But in deference to Lindbergh's opinions, he had not been vociferous in expressing contrary views of his own. Lindbergh knew of their differences, and while these were academic before the war, they assumed a more personal character after war broke out. Lindbergh's activities before Pearl Harbor were based largely on his conviction that the European war could be brought to an abrupt end at a conference table, and that America's involvement would be detrimental to a peace settlement. He explained his position in a letter to Mrs. Carrel written in October 1939:

It is difficult to write to someone in Europe today, for the outlook and values of life have changed so greatly since the war began. I know it is impossible for us, here in America, to fully realize how one feels in the midst of the situation in Europe today. . . .

Many of us in America have been hoping for peace before the winter is over—I say hoping because one does not feel confident in the outcome. I have taken a stand that this country should not enter the war, and that peace in the near future is the only way of preserving the quality, the prestige, and the influence of our modern civilization.

I shall write no more in this letter, for I realize that people in France, being a part of the war, must disagree with this stand I have taken—which I believe is best for all of us, and the only hope for the preservation of the things we value most. But whether or not we agree in regard to national policies, I want you and Dr. Carrel to know that regardless of what may take place, my respect and admiration for you and for him will not be changed. And neither will my love for France be affected by the bitterness and intolerance which is bound to increase as time passes if the war goes on.

I intend to continue my stand against America becoming involved in the war, and to support an early peace in Europe whenever I have an opportunity of doing so. This is bound to alienate many of my friends in Europe and I can only say that it is the policy which I am convinced is best for everyone concerned, and that therefore I must support it.

The war on land was slow in starting. Therefore Carrel, if things had turned out differently, would have had ample time to organize the research effort to which he wished to devote himself. But, hard as he may have tried, and notwithstanding his official appointment to the Ministry of Health, his efforts were of no avail. Carrel's only firsthand experience in protracted dealings with the French government had been during World War I, so it was natural for him to assume that his success in that war might be repeated. But in World War I he had been in the Army and dealt with the Army, and he had had the strong backing of the Rockefeller Institute. Now he had to deal with civilian agencies in a much different capacity, nor could he count on the support of his American friends. He was astonished by what he saw, and after three months of trying to get things organized, became discouraged. He wrote in a private letter:

I am wasting most of my time here, because the difficulties involved in doing the least little thing are excessive. If I myself didn't see what is happening, I would not have believed it. There is, in Paris, an expression which I did not know, but which is a frightening symbol. The expression is "speak French." It means slipping an envelope of bills into your questionnaires!

Carrel proposed to organize a laboratory—"less overwhelming than Compiègne"—to study hemorrhagic shock, poison gases, and surgical infections. Blood transfusion would be of course an integral part of the treatment of hemorrhagic shock. Since he lacked the financial and technical support of the Rockefeller Institute, and since the Ministry of Public Health did not show much interest in research, Carrel thought the best thing to do would be to associate himself with the Pasteur Institute, particularly with Vallery-Radot. This he tried to do, with the view that their past differences might be forgotten in the face of the present adversity. In his efforts to get something started, Carrel located one of his former Army administrative officers from the last war. However, the man was not enthusiastic enough to do again what he had done twenty-five years before. Carrel's attempts to organize a field laboratory were paralyzed by administrative inertia. Much to Carrel's amazement, the people acted as if there were no war at all. In mid-October 1939 he reflected:

It is very difficult to accomplish anything here. For a long time people have been in the habit of working little and badly. . . .

I am trying to organize some laboratories at the Pasteur Institute, in order to find a way to preserve blood for transfusion and facilitate its transport. The public thinks we have discovered procedures for preserving blood like the cherries in brandy. In reality, there is no truth in it. Blood spoils very quickly.

Paris left a bad taste in Carrel's mouth. Since the last war, it too had changed. Except for the presence of men in uniform, life in the city continued as in peacetime. There seemed to be no urgency about anything, and the officials of various government departments continued to bicker among themselves. Carrel again noted: "What I see is extraordinary. Instead of making war against the Germans, there is fighting among the French. Like the atmosphere of a lunatic asylum. No one wants to serve. A rush for money. Schemes everywhere." What concerned Carrel most was the incredible loss of valuable time. In war, time lost could not be regained. Everywhere Carrel saw negligence. He became more and more pessimistic.

Things had not improved by December. The efforts to establish a field laboratory and perhaps a hospital modeled after Compiègne had met with little success. Carrel's thoughts were turning more and more to America. On December 20 he wrote to an acquaintance in New York:

It was most kind of you to have discussed with the Colonel [Lindbergh] the matters concerning the laboratory. Since the cost of the laboratory and the whole work is small—hardly the cost of one torpedo—I believe that the French government should support it. If they are not interested enough to do it, it is not worth while to go on with the enterprise, and I will go back to New York. This war is very strange. The danger is greater inside than outside. If there was co-operation instead of antagonism, everything would be easy. It is literally impossible to work on account of the obstacles created by the ill will of almost everybody. It seems that every administration wants to fight every other administration rather than the Germans.

The change in the national spirit, the lack of purpose combined with total nonsupport of the government, which were undoubtedly responsible for the quick defeat suffered by the French after the German invasion, were observed by Carrel from the outset. He found the situation difficult to grasp and made up his mind to return to New York, but in March 1940 he was still in Paris. On March 11 he noted: "I have not left Paris. I must remain in this bad dream, in this crowd of idiots, imbeciles, and brigands. I have very much wanted to leave and to leave for good. However, it is difficult to decide because of Anne, and because of the things that one ought to be able to do."

Carrel's wife showed no interest in accompanying her husband to New York. She was busy organizing "soldiers' homes" at the front. Convinced she had a mission to perform, she was not hesitant in emphasizing the importance of her work. She went about accomplishing her mission "in style," wearing pretty uniforms and surrounded by people whom Carrel mostly did not care for. At one point Carrel, exasperated by her entourage, remarked in a letter to a relative: "Couldn't Anne seize the pretext of R.'s health to go to the Mediterranean coast and thus break away for a while from the miserable creatures who surround her?" Finally realizing that his time was being wasted, Carrel made definite plans to return to New York, and booked passage on a steamer sailing from Genoa on May 18. His wife chose to remain in France.

Ironically, once Carrel's plans to leave for New York became known, the laboratory for which he had waited seven months was suddenly constructed at Garches without a hitch in a few weeks. On May 15 Carrel wrote to a nephew: ". . . What is comical is the necessity for my departure at the very moment when I could begin my work seriously. What a strange country!" Strangely enough, Carrel never grasped how things worked in France. True to his own words, he came to live in a world which appeared to him as strange as the world of the Greeks or the Syrians. He simply could not understand why, at this time of national emergency, Frenchmen chose to sabotage one another's efforts.

On the eve of sailing, Carrel wrote to Dr. Ralph E. Scovel, a friend from San Francisco: "I have learned a good deal during the last eight months. The need for a profound change is acute, far more acute, than in the United States."

15 ❦ The Last Years

Carrel arrived in New York on May 28, 1940, aboard the steamship *Champlain*. During the crossing France had been invaded by Hitler and collapsed. The weeks after his arrival were full of anxiety. Paris fell on June 14, and on June 22, outside Compiègne, the German-French Armistice was signed under humiliating circumstances. There was no communication connection with France during the cataclysm. Carrel did not know what had happened to his wife nor even where she was.

The new government of France, headed by Marshal Pétain, was duly recognized by the United States. Carrel attempted to learn of his wife's whereabouts through the State Department, but had no luck until he solicited help from his friend James D. Newton, who asked Charles Edison, the Secretary of the Navy, to intercede on Carrel's behalf. Edison telegraphed Undersecretary of State Sumner Welles and asked him to do something about it. On Welles's instructions the American Embassy in France located Mrs. Carrel, and sent a telegram informing Carrel of her whereabouts, stating that she was well.

Thus reassured, Carrel went to Nantucket Island for a rest. The stay at Nantucket provided him with tranquillity and isolation. All of a sudden his character mellowed. Richard Bing, also vacationing on Nantucket, observed that

Carrel became more sociable and entered freely into conversations not related to work—a change also noted subsequently by his friends in New York. Carrel liked the old village constructed by the fishermen and whalers, for it had kept its charm and reminded him of the coast of Brittany. Carrel needed such an environment in order to write again. He said that all he had written the previous winter in Paris was "worth absolutely nothing."

But the tranquillity so essential for creative work was difficult to find, because Carrel was concerned about France. Everything published about the French was cast in an unfavorable light. Communications were so completely interrupted between the United States and the occupied zones that he had absolutely no information about what was happening.

The silence from Paris, Brussels, Amsterdam, and Copenhagen promised nothing good. It occurred to Carrel that the war might last a long time, and that the food situation in France could become acute. The specter of a general famine in occupied Europe had begun to haunt Carrel. Therefore he thought it essential to convince the American public of the need to prevent it.

In October he returned to New York, believing America would remain neutral. The majority of the American people were opposed to war. Carrel noted acidly that enthusiasm for war was found mainly among the old people, and among those who would themselves not fight. He had difficulty in assessing American public opinion, and was concerned about the lack of national unity which existed prior to Pearl Harbor. He observed that he had the same impression now in America as abroad the previous winter—almost like prewar France. However, he also noted that underneath the country was strong. It would only be necessary for truly strong elements to unite it and to get away from party politics.

Carrel attempted to busy himself in New York by trying

to organize relief for French civilians. By now he had completely abandoned his plans to work on hemorrhage, blood transfusions, and wound infection. If America remained neutral—and Carrel thought it would—there would be no interest in such work. If it were carried out in France it might benefit the German Army, which Carrel had no intention of doing. He could have gone to England with some volunteer group, but he did not wish to do this either. Like many Frenchmen, he was embittered by the British destruction of the French Mediterranean Fleet and by the blockade, which he construed to be directed against the civilian population. The latter was particularly distressing to him because it prevented food and medical supplies from being sent to Unoccupied France.

Carrel was not in sympathy with anti-Pétain sentiment, for his respect for the hero of Verdun was overwhelming. Marshal Pétain's government was the lawful government of France, and the Marshal was defending the country's interests under the most trying of circumstances. France did not capitulate but had signed an armistice, and was Pétain not trying to live up to its terms?

He would do what he could to protect the French population from the effects of the lost war and German occupation. Half of France was still free and could serve as a base for this endeavor. The United States was not at war with any of the European belligerents, and would most likely remain neutral for the duration of the conflict. He began planning an American Field Hospital to be sent to France, and became its Medical and Surgical Director.

However, like so many projects Carrel had recently undertaken, this one did not materialize either. In the end, the directors of the American Field Hospital decided to send it to England rather than France. Carrel was bitterly disappointed by this decision, and immediately resigned his membership in the American Field Hospital Corps. In this connection, on October 7, 1940, Carrel wrote to the Vice-

President (the President of the organization had also resigned) of the Corps:

I am surprised that the Board of Directors of the American Field
Hospital Corps has decided to send your field hospital to
England instead of France, where it is badly needed. The British
had no moral right to refuse a stricken population the assistance
of a few physicians, vaccines, and serums. We, as civilized human
beings, should not accept submissively the inhumane decision
of the English authorities. To help a race to survive is different
from helping a government or a nation. Epidemic diseases are
more devastating than battle, especially in a starved population.
By causing the death of multitudes next winter, they may considerably weaken the wonderful human strain that inhabits
France. The life of the French race is as important for the whole
world as it is for France. In spite of the decay of its government
and its institutions, France . . . could again produce new
Lavoisiers, Claude Bernards, Pasteurs, Curies. I profoundly
deplore that you have given up the idea of helping this great people in its hour of need. The public health organizations in
England are still intact. They need neither your assistance nor
mine. I beg you, therefore, to allow me to sever my connection
with the American Field Hospital Corps.

As the war dragged on, newspapers began to predict
famine in France. Carrel could no longer remain idle; he
had to show the American people how serious its consequences would be and so perhaps sway public opinion
in favor of organizing relief programs for the French civilian
population. An excellent opportunity to study and document the effects of war and starvation presented itself in
Spain. The Civil War there had ended but recently; its
effect on the civilian population had been devastating. If
Carrel could bring this home to the American people, then
perhaps the American government could be persuaded to
initiate relief programs to prevent a similar occurrence in
France. He could make himself heard by writing in the

Reader's Digest and the newspapers. Thus by the end of 1940 Carrel had begun to think seriously about going to Spain and then to France. He again tried to organize a mobile hospital to take to France, but authorization for the hospital to cross the British blockade could not be obtained. Therefore he abandoned the idea completely. Meanwhile he harbored no illusions about conditions in France under the Occupation. According to his friends, he was almost pathologic in his anti-German feelings, being convinced Germany's ambition was to reduce France to what it had been before the Treaty of Westphalia.

His wife had written him, telling him not to return to France, but the letters never reached him. She knew that, if he were to go to Saint-Gildas, he would be a virtual prisoner there, of use to no one. But Carrel himself felt that, if ever his people needed him, it was now. Also, he had not seen his wife for over eight months; if she needed him, he would rejoin her without hesitation. But if he could not return to America and the war proved long, the consequences of his isolation in France would be serious for him personally.

Carrel finally made up his mind to go to Spain, and then on to France and Mrs. Carrel. On this trip he was accompanied by James Wood Johnson, a well-known American philanthropist. They left for Lisbon on February 1, 1941, aboard the steamer *Siboney*. In his application for a re-entry permit to the United States, Carrel stated he would return in two months. His secretary at the Rockefeller Institute and his friends were expecting him back in May. Both Carrel and Johnson purchased return tickets from Lisbon to New York from Pan American Airways. The price of each ticket was $525.00, a considerable sum for those days. Carrel also paid his American income tax for 1940 in the amount of $879.11 and asked for a formal receipt, so that on re-entry he could produce evidence that his tax was paid —something required of all resident aliens.

Carrel and Johnson reached Lisbon safely, but they were delayed there by a storm. When at last they reached Madrid, Carrel found things in Spain much worse than he had imagined. He noted privately, "The Spanish are very resistant. They continue to live under conditions I thought fatal for human beings." The results of their observations and the chronicle of their travels in Spain were soon published by Johnson in two articles in the *Saturday Evening Post*: "We Saw Spain Starving," and "Ah, Madrid, Rumors, Suspicion, Fear." The accounts of the plight of children in Spain were eloquent, factual, and horrifying. Some of the children in the orphanages had lost their parents at the hands of the Reds, the others at the hands of the Whites. Pellagra in children was almost epidemic, and malnutrition and anemia were rampant. Yet what Carrel saw in Spain was only a prelude to what was to come. Soon the front pages of newspapers would carry pictures of French children searching for food among the garbage cans in Paris. In less than a year, pictures of dead children littering the ground of Europe would not even be newsworthy.

Carrel and Johnson's expedition to Spain ended when enough material for the two articles had been collected. They then went on to Unoccupied France, to survey conditions there.

In April 1941 Carrel's secretary, Miss Crutcher, received a letter from him from Vichy. He said that traveling was very difficult and slow, but that he and Johnson had bought a car in Vichy and visited the cities of Roanne, Lyons, Valence, Avignon, Aix, and Marseilles, seeing many people. He said the food situation in Unoccupied France did not seem quite as bad as in Spain: "Now I am going to Occupied France. Mr. Johnson is still in Marseilles. . . . Tonight I will take the train for Paris. I hope to see Madame Carrel very soon. I still hope to sail for America or take the clipper during the first days of May. . . . The catastrophe in France is greater than can be dreamed. Fortunately, the people do not realize the extent of the disaster."

Johnson returned to New York from Marseilles. Before parting, he asked Carrel how best to write the story for the *Saturday Evening Post*. Carrel replied: "Note what actually happened and let the matter take care of itself." However, they decided to confine the story to Spain, for the description of deteriorating conditions in France, by bringing unwanted publicity, might jeopardize the relief work which Carrel still hoped to organize.

The letter to Miss Crutcher made its way into the newspapers via Henry Creange, a friend of Carrel's, to whom Miss Crutcher sent a copy of it. A news item under the headline "French Don't Realize Plight, Dr. Carrel writes Cape Man," appeared in the *Boston Herald*. Miss Crutcher was very disturbed by this development, for she feared if Carrel's description of actual conditions in France were reported to Paris by agents in America, his return to New York would be made very difficult. Carrel was traveling with a French passport, and the mere denial of an exit permit would prevent him from leaving France.

As feared, the newspaper story had repercussions. Nothing was heard from Carrel for some time. In his second *Saturday Evening Post* article, which appeared in July 1941, Johnson said: "There is still no news of Doctor Carrel. Everyone says, 'Don't worry. He will find a way to get out when he wants to.' But I am not so sure." Few people in the United States knew what conditions were like in Europe under Nazi occupation.

Shortly after the appearance of the "French Don't Realize Plight" story, a wire was sent by one of the American news services via Berlin. The dispatch stated: "Carrel finds conditions in Vichy, France, very satisfactory." The same news service also reported that Carrel would take the post of Minister of Health in the Pétain government. The latter was incorrect, while the reference to "satisfactory" conditions was obviously intended to counteract the publication of Carrel's letter to Miss Crutcher. What was Carrel to do when interviewed by German reporters in Occupied France —tell them things were rotten? He knew the press reports controlled by Goebbels's Propaganda Ministry would be altered to suit the purpose of the censors.

Incredible as it seems, news reports transmitted via Germany were still taken at face value in the United States. All of a sudden, Carrel was called a Nazi supporter, a villain. The *New York Times* reported in July 1941: "Dr. Alexis Carrel has been commissioned by Marshal Henri Philippe Pétain's government to organize in France an institute for scientific and medical research, modeled after the Rockefeller Foundation. The Institute would be in the Occupied Zone, where Dr. Carrel is sojourning at present. Funds for its operation would be granted through subventions by the State." This news was taken as proof of allegations against Carrel, and some of his former colleagues at the Rockefeller Institute were quick to condemn him. The administration of the Institute did not discourage the sentiment.

Anti-Carrel sentiment reached its height on February 24, 1944, with an attack by a New York radio commentator, Fulton Oursler. Responding to a listener's question as to whether Carrel was collaborating with the Nazi government, Oursler replied:

Unbelievable as it sounds, officials of the French Press and Information Service have assured me that Doctor Carrel, winner of the Nobel Prize and great scientist, has become an ardent pro-Nazi. When last heard of, he was in beautiful Brittany province of northern France, at work on a scientific project. This news is very hard for me to understand. It was only a few years ago that Doctor Carrel and I spent an entire afternoon together after a long luncheon. We talked that day of the future of mankind, of goodness and beauty, of the scientific interpretation of prayer. He talked like a saint. Now he has gone into partnership with the Devil. You will recall that he wrote a book called

Man, the Unknown. Perhaps he wanted to show us that the title of his book was true.

The information given in Oursler's broadcast was obviously incorrect. Carrel was not engaged in any scientific projects in Brittany. In fact, he was in Paris. Information received from the French press, controlled by the German Propaganda Ministry, could hardly be considered reliable. To term Carrel pro-Nazi was simply irresponsible.

For one thing, Carrel's philosophical outlook precluded such a possibility. As late as October 1940 he wrote in a manuscript of a book he intended to publish as a sequel to *Man, the Unknown*: "The purpose of human life is personalized, not absorption by society as preached by totalitarian doctrine. 'Society does not exist for the individual,' says Mussolini, 'but the individual for society.' There is a radical difference between the objective of life and that which we have learned from the observation of nature. The biological concept of life is more closely related to those of Plato, the Catholic Church, and eighteenth century philosophers than to those of Hitler or Mussolini."

Nor were the conditions under which Carrel lived those of the privileged persons looked after by the Occupation authorities. For lack of funds, in 1942 he lost the Château La Batie, which his mother had bought in 1901. He infinitely regretted the loss of the old house. La Batie was the only place in France where he felt at home. On May 5, 1943, he wrote to a relative in Lyons: ". . . for 15 days I have eaten almost nothing. To eat vegetables, one needs a large stomach. I have never eaten vegetables and my stomach cannot absorb them."

Carrel had written Miss Crutcher on January 19, 1942. The letter reached her on February 25. It was mailed from Lyons, and Carrel said this was the first time he had been able to come to the Unoccupied Zone since the summer before. He asked that a message be transmitted to Dr. Alan

Gregg, Director of the Rockefeller Foundation, to the effect
that he had taken under his name all the rooms and equipment of the Rockefeller Foundation in France, so as to preserve the property for the duration of the war.

In July 1942 Carrel wrote to his friend Coudert from
Vichy:

It is naively unbelievable that our life has been overthrown to
such an extent. I knew that our civilization was not likely to live.
But I did not believe that chaos would come so quickly. I believe that it is necessary to construct at the same time that everything is collapsing. It is strange that we have been able to realize,
at this moment, the institution of which we have talked so often.
This "Institute of Man," which is a sort of apparatus for finding
the solution of the fundamental human problems, was founded by
a law in November 1941, signed by Marshal Pétain. And we
have been functioning since January 1, 1942. The institute is
composed of physicians, engineers, economists, statisticians,
architects, chemists, industrialists, historians, anthropologists,
geneticists, etc. There have been incredible difficulties to sur-
mount. But the organism that we have created is very tenacious
of life, because it is composed solely of men of 28 to 35 years,
on an average. A few only from 38 to 42 years. Life is laborious.
The cold, last winter, was very disagreeable. In our apartment
the temperature was never higher than 43–44°. Often it was
only 39 or 40°. At certain times food was insufficient. Anne
lost about 45 pounds. She has regained a little at present and is
well. She works with us with great activity. In the capacity of
farmer, she has permission to go into the prohibited zone of the
coast of Brittany, because life must continue. The fields must be
cultivated and the cows cared for, for it is necessary for the
population to live.

On September 11 he again wrote Miss Crutcher from
Vichy: "I am very much pleased to receive your letter. It
was the first one in many months. I am again in Vichy for a
few hours. My work is very hard. I had to stay in Paris the
whole summer. Food is not good and in too small quantity.
We hope to go to Saint-Gildas at the end of September or

in October. Traveling is extremely difficult. It seems that practically none of the letters I sent to New York during my last stay in Vichy have reached their destination. Please ask Dr. Flexner and Dr. Gasser whether they have received any letters from me."

However, it was immaterial whether or not Carrel's letters were received at the Rockefeller Institute, for the Institute Director had determined they were not to be answered. On February 22, 1942, he called Carrel's secretary to his office and instructed her not to send anything to Carrel. This included the reprints of published papers. He said any information received by Carrel would be of use to the Germans. Shortly thereafter, Carrel's office—the only thing he had left at the Institute—was turned over to someone else and Carrel's papers were put in boxes and placed in the basement.

The last letter to Miss Crutcher was written by Carrel on August 30, 1944—five days after the liberation of Paris:

This is the first opportunity to send a letter to New York. Unfortunately, I am only given a short time to write it. I hope that you are well and that all my friends at the Institute and elsewhere are well. Please remember me to all of them and tell them I hope to see them soon after the nightmare is over. We have suffered a great deal. Mme. Carrel fortunately is in good health. I have been severely ill for a year. I am not yet well. We are suffering mostly from bad food and excess of work. Our work has succeeded quite well. I have organized an institute as described in the "construction of civilized man" read in 1937 at Dartmouth College. The situation here is terrible.

On August 31 the *Washington Post* and the *New York Herald Tribune* carried an Associated Press dispatch from Paris stating Carrel had been arrested by the French Forces of the Interior. The report was incorrect, apparently based on a rumor. However, accusations against Carrel had indeed been made. Vallery-Radot, the newly appointed head of the Public Health Ministry in the de Gaulle government, removed Carrel as the Head of the Foundation for the Study of Human Relations, and shortly thereafter closed the entire Foundation. Vallery-Radot was also quoted by the press as saying that the Ministry "had discovered important new evidence conclusively showing him [Carrel] to have been a collaborationist." No charges were ever formally brought against Carrel. The "new evidence" was not sufficient even for post-Occupation prosecutors to bring anyone before the French courts. However, the new Minister's accusations were not publicly withdrawn. Later he allegedly admitted in private he had made an error and should not have been so hasty in judging Carrel. Carrel categorically denied any wrongdoing, but the accusations and charges leveled against him took their toll. Already in poor health, he fell ill and remained so for two months. On November 6, 1944, the *New York Times* and the *New York Herald Tribune* reported of the man whose name had appeared often on their pages: "Doctor Alexis Carrel died in Paris on November 5th." In Paris the last irony was exacted by the French radio. In a newscast it stated that Carrel had fled his apartment to avoid standing trial. Carrel had been dead, of heart failure and pneumonia, for almost a day at the time the news was broadcast.

Brigadier General T. Bentley Mott, a former U.S. military attaché to France, was in Paris at the time. He conveyed his impressions of post-Liberation France and of circumstances surrounding Carrel's death in a letter to Coudert:

I find a perfectly delightful sentiment here for America and for our soldiers, excepting only in the Government pronouncements and Assembly speeches, where never a word of gratitude is heard. The French always deserve a better government than they get. I was deeply affected by the details of Carrel's death. He died really of a broken heart; he could not stand the accusations made against him. . . .

Alas, these purifiers have done to him what some others did to Einstein and to Mann. But he saved for us the home of the

Rockefeller and Carnegie Institutes here and his work *must* go on.

Lindbergh was just as direct in his appraisal of the situation. He wrote in a letter to Dr. Roy O. McClure:

Undoubtedly you have by now read the press accounts of Dr. Carrel's death together with some of the inaccurate and badly garbled details of his life, philosophy, and accomplishments. The news came to us as a great shock, even though we had reports of his illness. It is distressing that a man who cared so deeply for his country and who was as much concerned about the welfare of mankind as Carrel should die under such a cloud of accusations. I suppose that it is to be expected in revolutionary times, and I feel sure that in the more objective future his actual accomplishments and character will show these accusations in their true light. Personally, I regard Carrel as one of the great men of his time. Regardless of whether his philosophy was right or wrong in instances, it was carefully thought out and courageously stated. Many of the men who now accuse him are those whose short-sightedness and political indifference, if not actual dishonesty, brought about the conditions in which France now finds herself.

After a third of a century, hindsight allows one to look at Carrel's activities in France during World War II without emotion. The allegations leveled at him seem insignificant when viewed from the vantage point of history. But the question of the day—whether one should have gone along with Pétain or opposed him—is still a complex one.

Finding himself in France in 1941, Carrel, unlike many Frenchmen, was faced with a real choice. Probably he could have extricated his wife from the Occupied Zone and returned to the United States via Spain. Instead he chose to remain, because he felt his place was in France. While wholesale destruction was going on, he would plan for rebuilding the future. He accepted the offer of the existing government to head the "Fondation Française pour

L'Étude des Problèms Humains," as his Institute for the Study of Man was officially known. In the public eye, this made him an ally of Pétain. But accepting the job as regent of a scientific institution in Vichy France is one thing; being a Nazi sympathizer and a collaborator is another. Carrel shunned appointments to high offices in the Vichy government. He was allegedly offered the Directorship of the Ministry of Public Health and the Presidency of the French Red Cross, but declined both.

During the last years of his life, the work of the Foundation occupied all his energies. Although the Foundation existed but a short time, having become inactive in 1944 and officially closed in 1945, the concept of its operation was very broad. For the first time a scientific organization became concerned with man and his environment. But even in those trying days Carrel continued to criticize French politicians and scientific institutions. In forming his Foundation, he departed radically from the tradition of the French scientific establishment. He had only young "upstarts" working with him. Carrel's World War I colleague Pierre Lecomte Du Nouy, who in 1943 succeeded in leaving France via Portugal, said that in general French scientists were antagonistic toward Carrel and his endeavors. Among other things, Carrel was accused by his Paris colleagues of undermining the structure of French universities with his Foundation.

The representatives of the Establishment who came to power through the Resistance movement labeled Carrel's activity "collaborationist," which was tantamount to dishonor. Carrel's removal as regent of the Foundation constituted one of the first orders issued by Vallery-Radot, the new Minister of Health. This may have served a dual purpose: the shadow cast on Carrel's character would also negate his criticism of French science.

The harsh assessment of Carrel's wartime activities was not shared by many Frenchmen. André Gros, who worked with Carrel at the Foundation in Paris during the Occupation, wrote thirty years later:

It is my firm conviction that not a single serious mistake was made by Carrel during that terrible period of 1940–1944. He thought only of France, the West, and the world. He thought only of the destiny of man. Nor has it ever been proven nor can it be proven that he pursued with respect to the occupying power a relationship that in any way could be condemned, either then or now. Indeed, in the face of the agony of the Occupation, a large majority of the members of the Institute adopted an attitude of courage and honor, as did Carrel himself. Some, with Carrel's full knowledge, worked for the Institute by day, and by night for the Resistance.

Carrel's efforts at the Foundation have not received the recognition they deserve. The Foundation was original in its organization and operation. Its achievements, attained under the most difficult circumstances, were not unimpressive. The Foundation was a first attempt at the method of collective "synthetic thinking" described by Carrel in his Dartmouth College address in 1937: "Man considered by the specialists according to their particular concepts is not complete man. . . . To amalgamate the findings of biology and sociology, there is . . . need of a center of collective thought, an institution consecrated to the integration of knowledge, to the elaboration of a true science of man."

One of the primary tasks of the Foundation was to study the relationship between the individual and his environment. At the same time, members of the Foundation attempted to examine various factors affecting the individual considered as an organic and spiritual whole. The Foundation tried to co-ordinate the efforts of institutions devoted to the analysis and improvement of human activities. If successful, it would have produced information indispensable for safeguarding the future after the war.

The programs formulated by the Foundation's staff were

214

applicable on a national scale. The few previous attempts at collective thinking of the kind envisioned by Carrel were limited to areas of special interest. Never before had the technique been applied to multiple fields of human activity. The Foundation not only was original in its concept, but also pioneered certain projects. In the late 1930s qualitative studies of population were practically unknown, and research in nutrition was neglected. Such investigations were first on the list of the Foundation's endeavors.

The foundation investigated problems related to general human welfare. Special knowledge in many fields was integrated, so that it would serve the total human interest. The Foundation offered advice with regard to the construction of housing for moderate-income workers. An architect was assigned the task of making these recommendations. He called to his aid a team of experts in fields different from his own. A public-health specialist contributed information on the relation of the structure of a house to the health of its occupants, showing how windows could be placed so as to ensure proper ventilation; how stairways should be constructed to minimize accidents; and how the shape of a kitchen contributed to the hygienic preparation of food. A psychologist chose the colors of walls and ceilings. A sociologist dealt with the relationship between the size of living rooms and the accessibility of a family to its neighbors. An economist offered his views on how elaborate a house workers with various incomes could safely afford.

Another main preoccupation of the Foundation was child care and welfare. Researchers visited various sections of France to document what was being done for children by local health authorities. Since nutritional studies were in their infancy in France, the Foundation compiled a handbook recommending a diet for children of all ages. The formulation of norms for children's height and weight was undertaken. Of particular interest was the creation of a new continuous health-report form for children. This resulted from co-operation between teachers, school physicians, physical education instructors, and psychologists. The form gave an integrated picture of the child, if kept current.

A method of measuring work fatigue was the subject of another study. A new specialist—the so-called "work engineer"—was suggested for furthering both the welfare and productivity of the factory worker. The work engineer, or efficiency expert, was to be a specialist in a given industry who would work closely with the plant physician, psychologist, and other experts, so as to develop operational procedures that would benefit both manufacturers and workers.

Carrel believed that most studies were limited by rigid intellectual concepts. He suggested reversing the usual scientific process: why not experiment *first,* and *then* evolve a theory from the results? He was still looking at scientific method as a means of emerging from chaos and barbarism. He retained his faith in the ability of man to determine his own future.

16 🕮 Views on the Conduct of Scientific Research

Carrel held very definite opinions on the way scientific research should be conducted. In an effort to carry out his experiments, Carrel had to swim repeatedly against strong currents of contemporary scientific opinion. With luck, and the help of a few fellow scientists with vision, he overcame the obstacles and repeatedly saw himself proven correct. However, the final outcome could well have been different, and Carrel knew it. Many scientists had neither the perseverance nor the strength of conviction to carry on in the face of strong opposition. They either gave up their endeavors or took the path of least resistance.

Carrel felt that proponents of new ideas and new technical advances should not face an uphill fight before they could earnestly begin their work. In the address he delivered at the dedication of the Medical Building at Ball Memorial Hospital in Muncie, Indiana, on April 24, 1937, Carrel expressed disapproval of the tendency—just then emerging—for administrators to "manage" scientists. Were he alive today, he would unquestionably oppose the current system of short-term support of scientific research, based on peer review. After all, most of Carrel's scientific undertakings were initially viewed unfavorably by his peers. Carrel thought scientific investigation could be made more productive than in the past. But to achieve this, researchers

217

must be freed from existing conditions which render concentration, devotion of unlimited time to a given problem, and intellectual contemplation impossible.

Carrel maintained that ideal conditions for the intellectual and technical endeavors of scientists could be created easily and cheaply. The initial success of the Rockefeller Institute was due primarily to Simon Flexner, who devoted his time and energy to creating just such conditions for his scientists. Carrel asserted that neither Lavoisier, Pasteur, nor Einstein would have made any discoveries had they been subjected to the hardships which are the common lot of most American, let alone French, men of science. Money is wasted when research is conducted under the direction of people who, although themselves not capable of performing scientific investigation, act as intermediaries between their advisors and the men who are hired to perform a particular task within given time limitations. Most successful scientific discoverers were endowed with a great power of concentration; Pasteur could not work unless he was free to devote himself for weeks without interruption to the same subject. To Carrel, it was an open question whether Pasteur could have accomplished much if placed in a modern institution of learning with his work dependent on grants, deadlines, and inefficient institutional administration.

Carrel tried to apply the principle of concentration to his own work, particularly when writing. In a passage from a letter of 1933 to John Dewey, Chairman of the Nobel Centennial Committee, Carrel declined an invitation to attend a banquet celebrating the occasion:

It is not possible to carry on scientific investigations in the turmoil of modern life. Thus, I decided to remain in isolation and silence. Today I am in the midst of intricate problems. I must devote myself exclusively to them. I have to stay in solitude for some time to come. Public addresses, banquets, large scientific meetings, and publicity are not compatible with such a life. Besides, I have a sufficiently accurate appreciation of my own importance to feel sure that the impressiveness of the celebration of the Nobel anniversary will not suffer in the least from my absence. Believe that I am extremely grateful to you personally for having asked me again to take part in this celebration.

However, desire for solitude was not the main reason for Carrel's not wanting to attend the Nobel Centennial. True, at the time Carrel was writing *Man, the Unknown,* and he needed to work alone. But the need for solitude and concentration did not prevent him from meeting friends at the Century Club, or visiting and dining with Flexner, or spending time in long conversations with Lindbergh and others. The real reason may have been Carrel's firm belief that the Nobel Prize should be awarded only to investigators actively engaged in research. This was Nobel's intent, but the Committee awarding the prize for medicine and physiology disregarded it. In many instances, the prize was given for past achievements to scientists no longer active in research. Carrel clearly expressed his sentiments on the matter in the continuation of the letter to Dewey:

You will easily understand the reasons that have compelled me to refrain from taking part in any public meetings or general banquets, and in this one especially. The scientific Prizes are not given primarily as a reward for discoveries already made, but as an encouragement for future work. Nobel intended that they should promote new developments in science. Since I had the honor of receiving the Prize for Physiology and Medicine, I have always remembered this thought.

Carrel tried to adhere to this principle in making nominations for the Prize. He nominated Hideyo Noguchi three times and Jacques Loeb four times. In 1928 he nominated George Minot, who shared the Prize with Murphy and Whipple in 1934. But the classical case was that of Peyton Rous, whom Carrel nominated in 1935, 1936, and 1937.

In 1966, at the age of eighty-seven, Rous was awarded the Prize for the same work.

Carrel believed the pursuit of intellectual work called for a special environment. He pondered the ideal conditions for carrying out scientific work, stating that these were not only ill defined but not even studied. He also noted the difficulty of carrying out scientific work in a modern metropolis, and related this to conditions within the institutions, to inadequate living quarters, time spent commuting to and from work, and lack of privacy. Carrel recognized that privacy had become a great luxury no longer accorded American scientists. The construction of houses and apartments was such that intellectual life was very difficult to achieve for scientists with families. There was no room for books, let alone a library, and usually very limited space for a study. Privacy was also invaded by the continuous administrative surveillance of work performed in laboratories.

Carrel felt a way could be found to maintain scientists in cities in the mental and physical states conducive to their work. In a letter to the President of the American Philosophical Society, he noted: "There is no place in this country which can be devoted exclusively to the progress of thought. The universities are primarily organized for the teaching of large numbers of students. They fulfill a social need of great importance. It is not possible, nor desirable, to modify them radically. Therefore, a new institution must be evolved which would be entirely devoted to pure scientific culture."

He was keenly aware of the dire consequences of too much organization and direction of scientific work. He also accurately predicted that the quantitative increase of scientific research would bring disproportionate administrative regimentation. For Carrel, administrative restraint was fatal to originality. He made this point repeatedly at the meetings of the Board of Directors of the Institute for

Advanced Study at Princeton University. He said that the fundamental principles underlying the operation of the Institute should be informality, absence of rules, and autonomy of divisions. These conditions were necessary to prevent a growing and viable institution from becoming old and rigid. In Carrel's judgment, most scientific institutions had grown senile by forfeiting originality through bureaucratic control and an incessant accumulation of rules and regulations. Carrel thought that if the individual institute directors were allowed to retain autonomy, they in turn would allow the members of their institutions flexibility, and would not hamper them with rigid rules and regulations.

In response to an article in the *New York Times* calling for an organization of the efforts on cancer research, Carrel wrote to Waldemar Kaempffert, the *Times* Scientific Editor: "It may be that a genius for organization will not succeed in giving originality and imagination to those who congenitally do not possess it. . . . Has not scientific research, unfortunately, become a regular profession, whose members are honorable, but tame men. . . . How many of these men are endowed with creative imagination? And is not creative imagination indispensable for discovery?"

Although Carrel was a champion of individualism, he felt that investigators in one field should remain in contact with those in other fields of specialization. But he was not advocating the formation of committees; indeed, he was quoted as saying that no important discovery can be made by a committee of scientists. He felt that, if given an opportunity, free association would develop between scientists of their own volition, in what he termed an "organic manner."

Carrel maintained that, after an initial burst of activity, most organizations devoted to scientific research decline in originality and productivity. He suggested a study and precise definition of the factors responsible for this decline, but he also felt that some of these were fairly obvious and could be remedied easily. If the cause of decline lay with the investigator himself, he could be made to retire. In the long run, it would be less expensive to pay a pension than to maintain an unproductive man in a laboratory. If the loss of an investigator's productivity was due to natural senescence, nothing could be done to prevent it. The heads of scientific institutions must be aware of this phenomenon, and appoint men of different ages as heads of departments or laboratories. However, in the final analysis, what was most responsible for the decline of scientific institutions was not people growing old, but the bureaucratic spirit, self-satisfaction, and administrative apathy.

Carrel's opinions on medical and biological research were based on observations made in two countries with widely divergent systems of research administration—France and the United States. Carrel's observations, supported by those of many of his countrymen, emphasized the extreme bureaucracy and unwarranted conservatism of French scientific and medical establishments. Scientific work in France was controlled by a small group of government-selected scientists turned administrators. To receive an academic appointment, one had to remain for a long time in the subservient position of eternal candidate. Advancement in an academic environment was almost impossible without the help of an influential "protector." The candidate, once placed in a desired position, was expected to be eternally grateful to his sponsor. Under these conditions, little room was left for the evolution and development of original talent.

In French academic life, medical and scientific faculties were dominated by the University of Paris. This virtually eliminated competition, since no novice could enter the scientific arena unless approved of by some group at that university. Carrel thought the situation in France so bad that the only solution would be to send a large group of young Frenchmen to study in the United States, Scandinavia, and Germany. The artificially controlled lack of academic vacancies and therefore, in many instances, lack of free choice forced scientists to specialize within narrow disciplines, thus destroying the concept of scientific humanism. Science became so interwoven with politics as to become nothing more than a means of acquiring positions of prestige within the governmental structure.

Disappointed as Carrel was with the regimentation of science in France, he had not lost sight of scientific achievement in general. The success of medical research was proven by vital statistics: in 1900, the average life expectancy in the United States was forty-nine years; in 1937, it was almost sixty. Yellow fever, plague, cholera, smallpox, typhus, and typhoid no longer invaded Western countries in epidemic proportions. Tuberculosis was being controlled. Prevention of tetanus was successful. Prospects were good for continuing success in the treatment of infectious diseases. Ehrlich's specific therapy for syphilis had proven effective. Sulfa drugs had been discovered.

However, in Carrel's opinion the most spectacular advances in therapeutics made in his lifetime were in surgery. Surgery had been reborn after Lister and it remained highly individualistic. A new era began as soon as it was learned how effectively to protect wounds against bacteria. Billroth, Kocher, and others had opened the field of gastrointestinal and glandular surgery. Halsted had shown how to handle tissues so that the healing process would not be impaired. Cushing had brought the nervous system under surgical jurisdiction. Bone surgery had emerged in the hands of Dr. Leopold L. Ollier. With Carrel's help, blood vessels could be repaired. Anesthesia was vastly improved. By the time Carrel was reaching the end of his career, virtually every part of the body except the heart could be opened and repaired with minimal risk to the patient. Since the advent of blood transfusion, made possible by the discovery of blood groups by Carrel's colleague Landsteiner, surgical hemorrhage could be dealt with. Thus in a relatively short span of time surgery made great strides.

To Carrel, these practical advances demonstrated the amazing success of medical research. The broadness of vision of those who made this possible had been rewarded beyond all expectations. But the work of medical scientists was far from completed, and Carrel wondered along what road it would progress in the future. Could the conditions that stifled scientists in France occur in the United States? Was it certain that in the future, as in the past, physicians would attempt only to cure and prevent disease, or would their role be extended into other spheres of life?

In modern society human suffering may be caused by less tangible forces than recognizable organic lesions. The task of medical research may become more complicated than in the past. Diseases will continue to be fought, but their nature may change. The price paid for the suppression of smallpox, poliomyelitis, tuberculosis, cholera, plague, pneumonia, and rheumatic fever may be cancer, renal disease, arteriosclerosis, and a host of other ailments. Overcoming one of the scourges of mankind may simply make room for another. Therefore medical researchers must be prepared to deal with a host of unanticipated situations. To be available for the task, research laboratories and institutions must continue their operation without interruption, and scientists must be ready to switch their areas of endeavor.

For Carrel, the most urgent current need was to unravel the nature of viral diseases and come up with the means for their treatment and prevention. Malignant tumors may be caused by viruses, but then again they may not. To train scientists to search for the association of tumors and viruses, and to insist that they conduct their research along these lines, is a mistake. What needs to be done instead is to train young scientists to be good virologists. They will follow their own course, and perform the work simply because they like to do it. Whether any practical results will emerge from the efforts is difficult to predict. In the past, many therapeutic discoveries were made by scientists who were not looking for them, while those who looked for them frequently were unsuccessful.

Carrel was deeply concerned with mental health in Western countries. He remarked, in the Muncie, Indiana, speech: "We have neglected the fact that human beings are composed not only of cells, organs, and humors, but also of mind. The body cannot be separated from the mind. However, our great research institutions have long ignored the existence of the mind. In fact mental activities, as well as physiological activities, fall within the province of medical research." Carrel fully shared Raymond Fosdick's feeling about the need for a rational basis for psychobiology. His peripheral interest in psychic phenomena and clairvoyance, mentioned in *Man, the Unknown*, should be interpreted only as an attempt to encourage the study of mental activity in the laboratory.

This broad view of medical research led Carrel to speculate on the ultimate goal of medical science. This, he decided, should be the study of man. "The characteristics of man as a whole are responsible for the strength or the weakness, the happiness or the misery of each one of us. Mind cannot be considered as independent of the body, and the body as independent of its environment." Carrel's feelings on psychobiology are not farfetched, if viewed in the light of present-day concepts. In 1976, the biologist Julian M. Davidson wrote: "If the proper study of mankind is man, it is a paradox worth pondering that consciousness, the receptacle of all that is truly human, has not yet found a place in the life sciences." He was not implying that neuroscientists were not interested in the mechanisms of sleep and wakefulness. Rather he was commenting on the fact that experimenters felt compelled to limit themselves to

225

---

physical and behavioral variables, so as to stay within the realm of scientific respectability.

Carrel's attitude toward scientists themselves was a very simple one. He tabulated a set of conditions under which scientific discoveries were made in the past. These above all included individual freedom, administrative noninterference, and suitable physical and psychological environments. If these principles were violated and scientists were subjected to undue regimentation, the conditions for research would become similar to those Carrel so vigorously opposed in France. Scientific despotism, regardless of what form it takes or whether it stems from individuals, committees, institutions, or government agencies, is not compatible with scientific productivity.

Strong echoes of Carrel's sentiments can be found currently among some American scientists. In fact, one may ask whether Carrel's fears of institutional senescence have not been realized in the United States. In science it does not take long to establish traditions, or for traditions to become doctrines. And, by definition, doctrines and dogmas encourage punitive measures against those who do not subscribe to them. Everyone agrees that research is a noble endeavor, but somehow both the legislative and executive branches of the government, the philanthropic agencies and research institutions, are afraid to give researchers a free rein. Regulatory efforts are based on what appears important to legislators. By allocating funds for selected fields of endeavor, generally on the urging of experts who themselves work in these fields, they make scientists shift their interests in accordance with economic necessity.

Project-oriented research has become a way of life for American scientists. Whether it has any advantages over the laissez-faire system advocated by Carrel is questionable. Albert Szent-Gyorgyi, a Nobel Prize winner, feels that it does not, and believes that no one can adequately judge the value of another man's project. He insists that none of the great discoveries were ever made by projects; they were all made by intuition. Michael Reilly, in *World Medicine* (1976), has pointed to the "galloping fossilization" that our research attitudes are undergoing—precisely the point Carrel had warned about. With rare exceptions, administrators appointed to foster research have succumbed to institutional rigidity. Having become project-oriented, the system discourages ideas not consistent with the current trends. Today any idea that seems worth pursuing must be formulated as an elaborately described project; the investigator must state in detail not only why he wants to do the work, but also the exact amount of time to be devoted to it.

Thus young investigators wishing to explore new ground must cope with views firmly entrenched in the minds of well-established colleagues. New ideas are killed by elaborately constructed and seemingly well-founded criticism, and approved approaches to research prevail. In short, the system which Carrel condemned may have been duplicated in the United States, but on a much larger scale than in France and with more finesse. The French may have prevented physicians from becoming scientists or excluded them from laboratories; also, they had too few laboratories. Carrel objected to this and pointed to the United States, where there existed both the laboratories and the freedom. Now we have even bigger and better laboratories, but for many scientists the curtailment of freedom makes it difficult to work in them.

Scientific endeavors are in a way related to artistic ones. If one wants good music, one looks for good composers to write it. It would be inconceivable for a committee to direct a composer to write a concerto for harp, piano, and orchestra in four movements in F minor, with a strong participation of the brass section. When writers have been told what and how to write, the results—even in the best of hands—have been mediocre. The same is true for science. A most brilliantly designed experiment will fail in the

hands of a competent but half-interested individual; once
a scientist sells himself on a project because "that's where
the money is," it is natural for him to become only half-
interested.

Szent-Gyorgyi's experience with review of his work by
his peers has been similar to that of Carrel. Of the four
major discoveries he made, two were rejected by leading
scientists in the field. This is not unnatural, and certainly
not unusual. Most discoveries would not be discoveries, if
they were not at variance with accepted concepts. The ad-
herents of concepts guard them against deviations. In science this has always been so. Kocher complained to Carrel
that his operation on the thyroid gland was unjustly criticized by his French colleagues. "I wish you had been there
to hear what they said. Simply denying the effect of the
operation because they cannot do it, that was the result of
the meeting."

Carrel, being a strong advocate of scientific freedom,
was of course also a firm believer in scientific honesty.
While scientific data are open to interpretation, "stretching"
the truth is inadmissible. However, the current system of research support in the United States encourages scientists to
act deviously. Frequently, to obtain funds, only part of the
story is told. Since, according to Szent-Gyorgyi, the ability
to predict results is valued as much as in the days of the
Delphic Oracle, it enhances one's reputation to perform
the experiments, withhold the results, propose a new project,
predict the outcome, and then verify the prediction.

What would Carrel have suggested as a solution to this
state of affairs? He would agree with Szent-Gyorgyi and
probably suggest something very simple: train young physicians to be scientists, and to have open minds, then place
them in a proper environment. The good and interested
ones will continue doing research, the indifferent ones will
eventually abandon science, unless it is unduly financially
rewarding; the process of separation will not be difficult.

To obtain adequate scientific results, one has to work very hard and put in long hours. There is no other way. One has to be intensely interested in one's work to be willing to do this. A scientist who is not devoted to his work will not spend his leisure time in a laboratory. Therefore the formula for success seems simple: find the ones who are devoted, support them, and leave them alone. They will do the rest.

The second major issue of concern to Carrel was the lag of science. He noted a large lapse of time between scientific discovery and its practical application. He felt this time should be shortened as much as possible, since industrial and technical capacities depend on the rapid practical application of scientific discoveries. However, he did not suggest an effective way of accomplishing this. In his own case, the lag between the development of experimental surgical techniques and their adoption in daily practice had been considerable. The techniques for experimental vascular operations had been worked out by 1912, but clinical vascular surgery developed spectacularly only after World War II. Intrathoracic operations were made possible by the discovery of the endotracheal tube in 1909; the first pneumonectomy was not performed until 1933. Work with tissue culture suffered the same fate; although Carrel had worked with several collaborators on growing viruses in cultured cells, cell cultures began to be used for vaccine production on a large scale only in the 1960s.

Carrel postulated that a scientist must be a realist. He had no formula for salvation, but he stood firmly by his conviction that once the process of institutional or individual degradation begins to take place it is difficult to stop. He did not think of himself as a reformer, but rather as a man of vision. His vision encompassed a new type of institution and an environment where scientists would have maximum freedom. As far as he was concerned, the history of science had shown that all great departures from erroneous tradi-

tion followed someone's abstract thoughts. Carrel had no
intention of imposing anything on anyone, certainly not in
science. He was convinced of the goodness and the powers
of the scientific method, and wanted to see it exploited to
its fullest capacity.

Carrel saw no virtue in conducting scientific research
without a purpose. Commenting on Hutchins's book in a
letter to Agnes Myer, he noted that the impression of the
President of the University of Chicago seemed to be that
a host of modern laboratory workers gather facts just in
order to gather facts. Carrel suggested that perhaps the
mediocrity of the average scientist was responsible for
Hutchins's admiration of metaphysics. He himself believed
the world needed, not metaphysics, but a better understanding of the scientific method, a more thorough appreciation
of concrete reality, and organization of knowledge. To
accomplish this he called for a set of institutions in which
scientists could work unimpeded on long-term studies without having to justify their short-term activities.

Selected References

Bainbridge, W. S. "Report on medical and surgical developments of the war." *U.S. Naval Medical Bulletin.* Washington, D.C.: Government Printing Office, 1919.

Baker, L. E., and Carrel, A. "Effect of liver and pituitary digest on the proliferation of sarcomatous fibroblasts of the rat." *The Journal of Experimental Medicine,* vol. 47, 1928, p. 371.

Carrel, A. Aneurisme artérioso-veineux du creux poplite." *Lyon Médicine,* vol. 89, 1898, p. 413.

Carrel, A. "Cancer du pylore; gastro-entero-anastomose postérieure." *Lyon Médicine,* vol. 92, 1899, p. 20.

Carrel, A. "La technique opératoire des anastomoses vasculaires et la transplantation des viscères." *Lyon Médicine,* vol. 98, 1902, p. 859.

Carrel, A. "Anastomose bout à bout de la jugulaire et de la carotide primitive." *Lyon Médicine,* vol. 99, 1902, p. 114.

Carrel, A. "Les anastomoses vasculaires, leurs techniques opératoires et leurs indications." *Revue Médical du Canada,* vol. 8, 1904, p. 29.

Carrel, A. "Anastomosis and transplantation of blood-vessels." *American Medicine,* vol. 10, 1905, p. 284.

Carrel, A. "The transplantation of organs. A preliminary communication." *The Journal of the American Medical Association,* vol. 45, 1905, p. 1645.

Carrel, A., and Guthrie, C. C. "Transplantation of veins and organs." *American Medicine,* vol. 10, 1905, p. 110.

Carrel, A., and Guthrie, C. C. "De la transplantation uniterminale des veines sur les artères." *Comptes Rendus des Séances de la Société de Biologie,* vol. 49, 1905, p. 596.

Selected References

Carrel, A., and Guthrie, C. C. "Functions of a transplanted kidney." *Science*, vol. 22, 1905, p. 473.

Carrel, A., and Guthrie, C. C. "Extirpation and replantation of the thyroid gland with reversal of the circulation." *Science*, vol. 22, 1905, p. 535.

Carrel, A., and Guthrie, C. C. "Complete amputation of the thigh, with replantation." *American Journal of Medical Science*, vol. 131, 1906, p. 297.

Carrel, A., and Guthrie, C. C. "Anastomosis of blood-vessels by the patching method and transplantation of the kidney." *The Journal of the American Medical Association*, vol. 47, 1906, p. 1648.

Carrel, A. "Heterotransplantation of blood vessels." *Science*, vol. 25, 1907, p. 740.

Carrel, A. "Surgery of blood-vessels and its application to the changes of circulation and transplantation of organs." *Johns Hopkins Hospital Bulletin*, vol. 18, 1907, p. 18.

Carrel, A. "Hetero-transplantation of blood-vessels preserved in cold storage." *The Journal of Experimental Medicine*, vol. 9, 1907, p. 226.

Carrel, A. "Calcification of the arterial system in a cat with transplanted kidneys." *The Journal of Experimental Medicine*, vol. 10, 1908, p. 276.

Carrel, A. "Further studies on transplantation of vessels and organs." *Proceedings of the American Philosophical Society*, vol. 47, 1908, p. 677.

Carrel, A. "La transfusion directe du sang." *Lyon Chirurgical*, November 8, 1908, p. 13.

Carrel, A. "Thyroid gland and vascular surgery." *Surgery, Gynecology and Obstetrics*, vol. 8, 1909, p. 606.

Carrel, A. "On the experimental surgery of the thoracic aorta and the heart." *Annals of Surgery*, vol. 52, 1910, p. 83.

Carrel, A. "Graft of the vena cava on the abdominal aorta." *Annals of Surgery*, vol. 52, 1910, p. 462.

Carrel, A. "The treatment of wounds." *The Journal of the American Medical Association*, vol. 55, 1910, p. 2148.

Carrel, A., and Burrows, M. T. "Cultivation of adult tissues outside of the body." *The Journal of the American Medical Association*, vol. 55, 1910, p. 1554.

Carrel, A., and Burrows, M. T. "Cultivation of tissues in vitro and its techniques." *The Journal of Experimental Medicine*, vol. 13, 1911, p. 387.

Selected References

Carrel, A. "The ultimate result of a double nephrectomy and the replantation of one kidney." *The Journal of Experimental Medicine*, vol. 14, 1911, p. 124.

Carrel, A. "Ultimate results of aortic transplantation." *The Journal of Experimental Medicine*, vol. 15, 1912, p. 393.

Carrel, A. "Technique and remote result of vascular anastomoses." *Surgery, Gynecology and Obstetrics*, vol. 14, 1912, p. 245.

Carrel, A. "The preservation of tissue and its application in surgery." *The Journal of the American Medical Association*, vol. 59, 1912, p. 523.

Carrel, A. "Artificial activation of the growth in vitro of connective tissue." *The Journal of Experimental Medicine*, vol. 17, 1913, p. 14.

Carrel, A. "Neue Untersuchungen über das selbstandige Leben der Gewebe und Organe." *Berliner Klinische Wochenschrift,* vol. 51, 1913, p. 509.

Carrel, A. "Experimental operations on the orifices of the heart." *Annals of Surgery*, vol. 60, 1913, p. 1.

Carrel, A. "Science has perfected the art of killing. Why not saving?" *Surgery, Gynecology and Obstetrics*, vol. 20, 1915, p. 710.

Carrel, A.; Dakin, H.; Daufresne, M.; Dehelly, G.; and Dumas, J. "Traitement abortif de l'infection des plaies." *Presse Médical,* vol. 23, 1915, p. 397.

Carrel, A. "Les principes de la technique de la sterilisation des plaies." *Archives de Médecine et de Pharmacie Militaires*, vol. 65, 1916, p. 489.

Carrel, A., and Hartman, A. "Principles of the treatment of wounds." *Medical Record*, vol. 92, 1916, p. 789.

Carrel, A., and Dehelly, G. *The Treatment of Infected Wounds.* New York: Paul B. Hoeber, 1917.

Carrel, A., and Ebeling, A. H. "The multiplication of fibroblasts in vitro." *The Journal of Experimental Medicine*, vol. 34, 1921, p. 317.

Carrel, A., and Ebeling, A. H. "Heat and growth-inhibiting action of serum." *The Journal of Experimental Medicine*, vol. 36, 1922, p. 645.

Carrel, A. "Leukocyte secretions." *Proceedings of the National Academy of Sciences*, vol. 9, 1923, p. 54.

Carrel, A., and Ebeling, A. H. "Survival and growth of fibroblasts in vitro." *The Journal of Experimental Medicine*, vol. 38, 1923, p. 487.

Selected References

Carrel, A. "The mechanism of the formation of sarcoma." *The Journal of the American Medical Association*, vol. 84, 1925, p. 1795.

Carrel, A. "Mechanism of the formation and growth of malignant tumors." *Annals of Surgery*, vol. 82, 1925, p. 1.

Carrel, A. "Some conditions of the reproduction in vitro of the Rous sarcoma virus." *The Journal of Experimental Medicine*, vol. 43, 1926, p. 647.

Carrel, A., and Ebeling, A. H. "The transformation of monocytes into fibroblasts through the action of Rous virus." *The Journal of Experimental Medicine*, vol. 43, 1926, p. 461.

Carrel, A. "Things that doctors do not know." *Cancer*, vol. 4, 1927, p. 110.

Carrel, A., and Rivers, T. M. "La fabrication du vaccin in vitro." *Comptes Rendus des Séances de la Société de Biologie*, vol. 98, 1927, p. 848.

Carrel, A.; Olitsky, P. K.; and Long, P. H. "Multiplication du virus de la stomatite vésiculaire du cheval dans des cultures." *Comptes Rendus des Séances de la Société de Biologie*, vol. 98, 1928, p. 827.

Carrel, A., and Ebeling, A. H. "The fundamental properties of the fibroblast and the macrophage. IV. The malignant fibroblast of Jensen sarcoma." *The Journal of Experimental Medicine*, vol. 48, 1928, p. 285.

Carrel, A. "The nutritional properties of malignant cells." *Proceedings of the American Philosophical Society*, vol. 63, 1929, p. 129.

Carrel, A. "The new cytology." *Science*, vol. 73, 1931, p. 297.

Carrel, A. "Physiological time." *Science*, vol. 74, 1931, p. 618.

Carrel, A. "The physiological substratum of malignancy." *Emmanuel Libman Anniversary Volumes*, October 1932, p. 289.

Carrel, A. "Monocytes as indicators of certain states of blood serum." *Science*, vol. 80, 1934, p. 565.

Carrel, A. *Man, the Unknown*. New York: Harper and Brothers, 1935.

Carrel, A., and Lindbergh, C. A. "The culture of whole organs." *Science*, vol. 81, 1935, p. 2112.

Carrel, A. "The function of science in our civilization," Charter Day Address. University of California, San Francisco, 1936.

Carrel, A. "Culture of whole organs; technique of culture of the thyroid gland." *The Journal of Experimental Medicine*, vol. 65, 1937, p. 515.

Carrel, A. "The making of civilized man." *Dartmouth Alumni Magazine*, vol. 30, 1937, p. 3.

Carrel, A. "The past and future of medical research." Address at dedication of new Laboratory and Memorial Building, Ball Memorial Hospital, Muncie, Indiana, April 24, 1937.

Carrel, A., and Lindbergh, C. A. *The Culture of Organs*. New York: Paul B. Hoeber, 1938.

Carrel, A. Personal papers, reports, correspondence, etc. Carrel Collection, Georgetown University School of Medicine, Washington, D.C.

Corner, George, *A History of the Rockefeller Institute (1901–1933)*. New York: The Rockefeller University Press, 1964.

Dehelly, G. "Surgical closure of wounds." *Transactions of the American Surgical Association*, vol. 33, 1918, p. 122.

Durkin, J. T. *Hope for Our Time*. New York: Harper & Row, 1965.

Ebeling, A. H. "Dr. Carrel's Immortal Chicken Heart." *Scientific American*, January 1942, p. 22.

Fisher, A. *Alexis Carrel—As I Knew Him*. Kobenhavn: Saetryk Af Bibliotek for Laeger, 1953.

Flexner, S. "Obituary for Dr. Alexis Carrel." *Year Book of the American Philosophical Society*, 1944.

Foot, N. C.; Baker, L. E.; and Carrel, A. "The behavior of abnormal thyroid tissue cultivated in the Lindbergh apparatus." *The Journal of Experimental Medicine*, vol. 70, 1939, p. 39.

Gibson, C. L. "The Carrel method of treating wounds." *Annals of Surgery*, vol. 66, 1917, p. 262.

Guillot, M., and Woimant, H. "Application de la méthode de Carrel aux formations de l'arrière." *Revue de Chirurgie*, vol. 36, 1917, p. 1.

Hughes, B., and Banks, S. *War Surgery, from Firing-Line-to-Base*. New York: Wm. Wood & Co., 1919.

Johnson, J. W. "Ah, Madrid! Rumors, Suspicion, Fear." *The Saturday Evening Post*, July 5, 1941.

Lindbergh, C. A. "A method for washing corpuscles in suspension." *Science*, vol. 75, 1932, p. 415.

Lindbergh, C. A. "An apparatus for the culture of whole organs." *The Journal of Experimental Medicine*, vol. 62, 1935, p. 409.

Lindbergh, C. A. *Autobiography of Values*. New York: Harcourt Brace Jovanovich, 1978.

Selected References

Lindbergh, C. A. Personal papers at Yale University Library, New Haven, Conn.

Lyle, H. H. M. "Disinfection of war wounds by the Carrel method." *The Journal of the American Medical Association*, vol. 68, 1917, p. 107.

McDonnell, W. N. "The preparation of Dakin's solution and the Carrel technique in the treatment of infected wounds." *Medical Bulletin*, vol. 12, 1918, p. 1.

Malinin, T. I., and Lindbergh, C. A. "Organ culture and perfusion by the Carrel method." Papers of the Alexis Carrel Centennial Conference, Georgetown University, Washington, D.C., 1973.

Mottier, G. *L'Ambulance du Docteur Alexis Carrel.* Lausanne: Editions La Source, 1977.

Parker, R. C. *Methods of Tissue Culture.* New York: Paul B. Hoeber, 1938.

Sherman, W. O. "The Carrel method of wound sterilization." *Surgery, Gynecology and Obstetrics*, vol. 24, 1917, p. 255.

Soupault, R. *Alexis Carrel 1873–1944.* Paris: Plon, 1952.

Szent-Gyorgyi, A. "Research grants." *Perspectives in Biology and Medicine*, vol. 18, 1974, p. 41.

Tuffier, T., and Carrel, A. "Patching and section of the pulmonary orifice of the heart." *The Journal of Experimental Medicine*, vol. 20, 1914, p. 3.

"War Work of the Rockefeller Institute for Medical Research." *Military Surgeon*, vol. 42, 1920, p. 491.

Index

237

Index

Cardozo, Benjamin, 41
Carnegie Institute, 212
Carnot, Sadi, 4
Carrel, Alexis
    blood-vessel suturing technique
        of, 3, 4, 5–7, 9–11, 24–28, 37,
        42, 95, 176
    cancer research and, 99–101,
        168, 183, 185
    cardiac surgery and, 44–45
    childhood and education of, 3–4
    Dakin method of treating
        wounds and, 66–73, 75–90, 95
    death of, 211–12
    Flexner and, 8, 30, 69, 73, 82–
        83, 101–2, 163, 164–67,
        168–76, 183, 185, 210
    Gasser and, 176–79, 180–88, 210
    hemorrhaging, treatment of, and,
        91–92
    hypothermia and, 141–43, 147
    limb transplantations by, 46–48
    Lindbergh and, 63, 125–34,
        135–38, 141–57, 171–73, 181,
        189, 198, 212
    Man, the Unknown and, 31,
        109–23, 194, 208, 225
    marriage of, 32, 41–42, 97–99
    mousery experiments of, 102–3,
        183, 185
    as Nobel Prize winner, 52–53,
        57, 168, 169, 181
    organ cultivation and perfusion
        and, 103–4, 124–34, 135, 141,
        145, 147, 171–73
    organ transplants by, 43–53, 126
    orthopedic surgery and, 92–93
    retirement of from Rockefeller
        Institute, 180–89
    shock, dealing with, and, 90–91
    social life of, 32–36, 40–42, 201,
        219
    tissue culture and, 54–65, 96,
        99–102, 126, 162, 163, 169–
        70, 229
    views of on conduct of scientific
        research, 217–30
    during World War I, 66–93,
        95–96
    during World War II, 190–216
Carrel, Anne (wife), 32, 41–42,
    97–99, 145, 147, 148, 165,
    190, 192
    during World War II, 195, 200,
        204, 205, 209
Carrel-Billiard, Alexis (father), 4
Century Club, 32, 33, 40, 41, 109,
    112, 137

Chambers, Dr., 58
Chartier, Dr., 16
Château de Claires, France, 147
Chevrier, Dr., 16
Chiari, Hans, 22
Chicago, Illinois. See University of
    Chicago
China, 161
Churchill, Sir Winston, 80–81, 88
Clairmont, Dr. Paul, 39
Clarke, T. Wood, 53
Clifford, Father Cornelius, 41
Compiègne, France, 68, 73–74, 75,
    78, 79, 81, 86–87, 90–91, 97
Congress of Experimental
    Cytology, 62
Cornell University Medical
    College, 133, 175
Corner, George W., 99–101, 182–
    83, 184, 185
Coudert, Frederick R., 32, 41, 186,
    190, 193, 209, 211
Coudert brothers, 151
Creange, Henry, 206
Crile, George, 7, 26, 27, 68
Crippled Hand and Arm, The
    (Beck), 22–23
Crutcher, Miss, 205, 206, 207, 208,
    209, 210
"Cultivation of Viruses in
    Unfertilized Egg-Yolk, The"
    (Carrel), 170
Culture of Organs, The (Carrel
    and Lindbergh), 125, 184
Curie, Madame, 105–6
Cushing, Harvey, 7, 8, 10, 26, 27,
    51, 67–68, 120, 174, 223

Dakin, Henry, 69, 73, 75, 81
Dalbey, Robert, 96–97
Dante, 118–19, 193
Dartmouth College, 112, 214
d'Aubarède, Captain, 167
Daufresne, Maurice, 75
Davidson, Julian M., 225
de Gaulle, Charles, 210
Dehelly, Georges, 75, 80, 84, 87,
    90
de la Mairie, Mrs. See Carrel,
    Anne
de Martigny, Adelstan, 16, 17, 18,
    90
de Martigny, François, 16–17
Depage, Antoine, 78, 79
Depew, Mrs. Chauncey, 78
Deutsche Medizinische
    Wochenschrift, 85–86
Dewey, John, 218, 219

Index

Index